Unaccompanied Children in European Migration and Asylum Practices

Unaccompanied minor migrants are underage migrants who leave their country and are separated from their parents or legal/customary guardians. The concept of the best interests of a child is widely applied in international and national legal documents and several guidelines, and often pertains to unaccompanied minor migrants given that they are separated from parents, who are not able to exercise their basic parental responsibilities. This book takes an in-depth look at the issues surrounding the best interests of the child in relation to unaccompanied minor migrants, drawing on social, legal and political sciences in order to understand children's rights not only as a matter of positive law but mainly as a social practice depending on personal biographies, community histories and social relations of power.

In its first part, the book considers theoretical aspects of children's rights and the best interests of the child in relation to unaccompanied minor migrants. Adopting a critical approach to the implementation of the Convention on the Rights of the Child, authors nevertheless confirm its relevance for protecting minor migrants' rights in practice.

The second part of the book goes on to examine the actual legal framework related to unaccompanied minor migrants and the implementation of children's rights and their best interests in the reception, protection, asylum and return procedures. The case studies are based on empirical research, from interviews with key experts and unaccompanied minor migrants in Austria, France, Slovenia and the United Kingdom. The contributors point to the discrepancy between the states' obligations to take the best interests of the child into account when dealing with unaccompanied minor migrants and the lack of formal procedures of best interests determination in practice. The chapters expose weaknesses and failures of institutionalised systems in selected European countries in dealing with unaccompanied children and young people on the move.

Mateja Sedmak is a Research Councillor at the Science and Research Centre Koper, Slovenia.

Birgit Sauer is a Professor of Political Science at the University of Vienna, Austria.

Barbara Gornik is a Research Assistant at the Science and Research Centre Koper, Slovenia.

Routledge Research in Asylum, Migration and Refugee Law

Available titles in this series include:

Refugee Protection and the Role of Law
Conflicting Identities
Edited by Susan Kneebone, Dallal Stevens, Loretta Baldassar

Gender in Refugee Law
From the Margins to the Centre
Efrat Arbel, Catherine Dauvergne, Jenni Millbank

Asylum-Seeker and Refugee Protection in Sub-Saharan Africa
The Peregrination of a Persecuted Human Being in Search of a Safe Haven
Cristiano D'Orsi

Migrant Rights at Work
Law's Precariousness at the Intersection of Immigration and Labour
Laurie Berg

Unaccompanied Children in European Migration and Asylum Practices
In Whose Best Interests?
Edited by Mateja Sedmak, Birgit Sauer and Barbara Gornik

Forthcoming titles in this series include:

European Asylum Law and the Rights of the Child
Ciara Smyth

Asylum Law in the European Union
Francesco Cherubini

The Socio-Economic Rights of Asylum Seekers
Liam Thornton

Unaccompanied Children in European Migration and Asylum Practices

In Whose Best Interests?

Edited by Mateja Sedmak, Birgit Sauer and Barbara Gornik

Routledge
Taylor & Francis Group
LONDON AND NEW YORK

First published 2018 by Routledge

2 Park Square, Milton Park, Abingdon, Oxfordshire OX14 4RN
52 Vanderbilt Avenue, New York, NY 10017

Routledge is an imprint of the Taylor & Francis Group, an informa business

First issued in paperback 2019

British Library Cataloguing in Publication Data
A catalogue record for this book is available from the British Library

Library of Congress Cataloging in Publication Data
Names: Sedmak, Mateja, editor. | Sauer, Birgit, editor. | Gornik, Barbara, editor.
Title: Unaccompanied children in European migration and asylum practices : in whose best interests? / Edited by Mateja Sedmak, Birgit Sauer & Barbara Gornik.
Description: New York : Routledge, 2017. | Series: Routledge research in asylum, migration and refugee law | Includes bibliographical references and index.
Identifiers: LCCN 2017012349| ISBN 9781138192560 (hbk) | ISBN 9781315639888 (ebk)
Subjects: LCSH: Unaccompanied immigrant children—Legal status, laws, etc.—Europe. | Unaccompanied immigrant children—Government policy—Europe. | Emigration and immigration law—Europe. | Immigrants—Moral and ethical aspects.
Classification: LCC KJC6057. U53 2017 | DDC 342.408/2—dc23
LC record available at https://lccn.loc.gov/2017012349

ISBN: 978-1-138-19256-0 (hbk)
ISBN: 978-0-367-26700-1 (pbk)

Typeset in Galliard
by Keystroke, Neville Lodge, Tettenhall, Wolverhampton

Contents

Author biographies

Corentin Bailleul studied Law and Political Sciences at the University of Lille 2 and completed his Master's degree in International Migration at the University of Poitiers. He has conducted research on unaccompanied minors' access to protection during the deprivation of liberty at the transit zone of Paris Charles de Gaulle airport and has also provided legal guidance to migrants detained at the French borders. Between 2014 and 2016, he was engaged as a research officer for the European project MINAS where he was in charge of conducting research on the interpretation of the best interests of the child when applied to unaccompanied children in France. His current research interests focus on age assessment procedures. He is also involved with support organisations providing legal assistance to young migrants.

Marie-Bénédicte Dembour is Professor of Law and Anthropology at the University of Brighton. Her numerous publications include the award-winning monograph *When Humans Become Migrants: Study of the European Court of Human Rights with an Inter-American Counterpoint* (Oxford University Press, 2015), *Are Human Rights for Migrants? Critical Perspectives on the Status of Irregular Migrants in Europe and the United States* (Routledge, 2011, co-edited with Tobias Kelly), 'What are human rights? Four schools of thought' (*Human Rights Quarterly*, 2010), *Culture and Rights: Anthropological Perspectives* (Cambridge University Press, 2001, co-edited with Jane Cowan and Richard Wilson). She has been invited to give talks throughout the world and has held visiting positions in various institutions.

Ayşe Dursun studied Political Science and English Studies at Goethe University in Frankfurt am Main. Currently, she is a doctoral student at the Department of Political Science at the University of Vienna. Previously, she worked as a junior researcher in the same department. Her research areas include women's movements, intersectionality, gender policies and migration. She was granted the Marietta Blau Grant by the Austrian Federal Ministry of Science and Research in 2016. In autumn 2016, she attended the Centre for Gender Studies at the School of Oriental and African Studies (SOAS), University of London, for research purposes.

Barbara Gornik, PhD, is a Research Assistant at the Science and Research Centre of Koper. She studied Anthropology and Cultural Studies at the Faculty of Humanities, University of Primorska. In her work she deals with human rights, adopting standpoints of the anthropology of human rights and discourse theory. She is particularly interested in examining the impact of nationalism on the interpretation and implementation of human and children's rights. At the Science and Research Centre of Koper, she also works within the Public Opinion Centre.

Margrite Kalverboer is a Professor by special appointment of Child, Pedagogy and Migration Law at the University of Groningen. She graduated in Law as well as Orthopedagogy at the University of Groningen and researches the development of children and their legal position in migration law, civil law and criminal law. Margrite is the Children's Ombudsperson in the Netherlands.

Jyothi Kanics is an expert on children's rights and child protection. Since 1995 she has been active in non-governmental and international organisations including UNICEF and Save the Children, advocating for the rights of vulnerable migrants such as unaccompanied and trafficked children. She completed Master's degrees in International Relations at Yale University and in International Human Rights Law at the University of Oxford. She is currently working on her PhD in Law at the University of Lucerne within the National Centre of Competence in Research, NCCR – on the move, supported by the Swiss National Science Foundation.

Erik J. Knorth, PhD, is Professor of Child and Youth Care at the Department of Special Needs Education and Youth Care, University of Groningen, the Netherlands. His research is on child and family welfare, with a special interest in children and adolescents with emotional and behavioural problems who are (at risk of being) placed in family foster or residential care.

Blaž Lenarčič, PhD, is Research Fellow at the Science and Research Centre of Koper. Until 2016 he was Assistant Professor at the Faculty of Humanities and the Faculty of Kinesiology at the University of Primorska. From 2011 to 2015 he was a member of the Government's Commission for GMO management. He is a member of the editorial board of the scientific journal *Družboslovne razprave* and a member of the board of the Slovene Sociological Association. His research interests are the effects of ICT on broader society, analysis of social networks, social capital, the sociology of sport and migration.

Zorana Medarić is a sociologist and a researcher at the Science and Research Centre Koper and lecturer at the Faculty of Tourism Studies of the University of Primorska. She graduated in Sociology at the Faculty of Social Sciences of the University of Ljubljana and received her Master's degree in Sociology and Social Politics at the same faculty. Since 2006 she has been employed at the Institute for Social Studies of the Science and Research Centre of Koper. She is involved in several national and international projects in the fields of sociology of everyday life, interculturality, migration and tourism.

Carla van Os graduated in both Law and Orthopedagogy. She is working at the Study Centre for Children, Migration and Law on a PhD concerning the best interests of the child determination in the asylum procedure for recently arrived refugee children. At the request of lawyers and guardians, the Study Centre writes diagnostic behavioural scientific reports about which decision is in the best interests of the child.

Wendy Post is Associate Professor of Methodology and Statistics at the Centre for Special Needs Education and Youth Care, University of Groningen, the Netherlands. Her research focuses on validity issues (statistical conclusion, internal, construct and external validity). Her special interests are advanced statistical modelling, measurement theory and scientific integrity (ethics).

Birgit Sauer is Professor of Political Science at the University of Vienna. Since 2014 she has been speaker of the Research Network 'Gender and Agency' at the University of Vienna. She was member of several EU research projects. Her research fields include comparative gender equality policies, gender, religion and democracy, right-wing populism and racism, theories of state and democracy and the politics of emotions. Recent publications include: 'Gendering "the people": heteronormativity and "ethno-masochism" in populist imaginery' (with Stefanie Mayer und Iztok Sori), in: Maria Raniera (ed.) *Populism, Media and Education: Challenging Discrimination in Contemporary Digital Societies* (Routledge, 2016).

Mateja Sedmak, PhD, is a Research Councillor and since 2007 the Head of the Institute for Social Studies at the Science and Research Centre of Koper, Slovenia. She has lectured at the Faculty of Humanities, Faculty of Tourism Studies and Faculty of Kinesiology at the University of Primorska. She is the editor of the *Annales, Series Historia et Sociologia* review and a member of the editorial board of *Družboslovne razprave* and *Italian Sociological Review*. She is a member of the board of the Slovenian Sociological Association. She leads several national and international projects. Her research interests are ethnic studies, intercultural studies, transculturality, sociology of the family and sociology of everyday life.

Tjaša Žakelj is a sociologist. She defended her doctoral thesis in 2011 at the Faculty of Social Sciences, University of Ljubljana, Slovenia. During the MINAS project she worked as a research associate at the Science and Research Centre, University of Primorska. Her research interests include sociology of everyday life, sociology of the family, internet dating, gender inequalities, interethnic relations and currently employment forecasts. She has explored her areas of research in a number of original scientific articles, has co-authored several scientific monographs and is the author of a scientific monograph on building contemporary romantic partnership on the basis of internet dating.

Elianne Zijlstra, PhD, is a behavioural scientist at the multidisciplinary Study Centre for Children, Migration and Law of the University of Groningen. She conducts behavioural scientific research on children in legal decision-making in migration law, more specifically concerning the assessment and determination of the best interests of the child. She has a special interest in trauma, vulnerability and resilience of refugee children.

1 Introduction

Unaccompanied minor migrants in Europe: between compassion and repression

Barbara Gornik, Mateja Sedmak and Birgit Sauer

Introduction

This book is the result of research started three years ago, at that time not knowing that the issue of the migration of refugees to Europe would escalate to such an extent as it did in 2015, when more than one million refugees arrived in the European Union (EU). Among these refugees, nearly 90,000 asylum seekers applying for international protection were considered unaccompanied minors (Eurostat 2016). The situation has not changed much since then in that many refugees are still waiting to start a new life in a safer place than their countries of origin. This book comes just in time to address and remind readers about the obligations resulting from the peremptory norms of international law that EU member states are obliged to respect when dealing with refugees. The contributions in this volume give primary consideration to the rights and best interests of unaccompanied minor migrants and present their normative, methodological, procedural and practical aspects; the chapters closely examine the implementation of the rights of unaccompanied minor migrants in relation to particular asylum and migration procedures after arriving in Europe and analyse their best interests according to different views and interpretations.

The best interests principle is one of the most vital concepts and criteria for decisions made regarding unaccompanied minor migrants and it is referenced in practically all asylum and migration policies, strategies and recommendations produced by the European Commission, European Council and European Parliament. European and consequently also national legislation recognises the importance of the Convention on the Rights of the Child (CRC) and formally places the standards of the Convention at the heart of all actions concerning unaccompanied minors. Specific reception measures, higher standards of protection and childcare guarantees are to be applied from the moment a minor enters EU territory until a durable solution is found.

All these key standards of international law which function well on paper have been put under scrutiny in theory and practice by the contributors of this volume. The objective of this book is to tackle the interpretation of the rights of the child and the best interests principle in the case of unaccompanied minor migrants in Europe at political, legal and practical levels. The contributions point to the discrepancy between states' obligations to take the best interests of the child into account when dealing with unaccompanied minor migrants and the lack of a formal process of best interests determination in practice. The contributions herein examine the conceptual aspects of the best interests of the child including an analysis of the legal, political, NGOs' and unaccompanied minors' points of view, demonstrating that these interpretations can differ, contradict or overlap. The authors deconstruct the power relations residing within the discourses of children's rights and best interests, indicating that these rights are constructed and decided upon by those in power who make decisions on behalf of those who do not possess authority (e.g. minors). Moreover, focusing on procedures related to reception, asylum procedures, protection measures and the return of unaccompanied minor migrants, the contributions highlight the practical dimensions of the application of the best interests principle or its lack.

The case studies presented in the second part of the book build upon biographical stories, narratives and auto-perceptions of unaccompanied minors, and thus address the experiences of the children themselves. To analyse the views and experiences of unaccompanied minors themselves is of particular importance as there is an omnipresent lack of research on unaccompanied minors exploring their own perspectives (Wernesjö 2011). The empirical data used in the case studies presented here was mainly collected within the international project 'In Whose Best Interest? Exploring Unaccompanied Minors' Rights through the Lens of Migration and Asylum Processes', carried out in Slovenia, Austria, the United Kingdom and France in 2014 and 2015. This insight into the national context reveals that the principle of the best interests of the child is often severely compromised. Even when a more concrete definition of the principle can actually be found in theory, practical application does not always follow (Sedmak *et al.* 2015). Moreover, many European countries have not adopted formal procedures for best interests determination, which is one of the reasons why the policies and treatment of unaccompanied minor migrants is subjected to discourses of neoliberalism, nationalism, xenophobia, racism and the like. Formally assessing and determining their best interests in all decisions affecting the lives of unaccompanied minor migrants would mean a further step towards measures for higher standards of protection in ensuring additional procedural safeguards.

Who are unaccompanied minor migrants?

Unaccompanied minor migrants are individuals under the age of majority, who for various reasons leave their home countries and live without their parents or legal or customary guardians. This group includes minors in a variety of circumstances: for example, minor migrants who have left their countries alone, children who have been separated from their families along the migration journey, and first- or second-generation migrants whose parents have been deported (Bhabha 2009). They may be separated from both parents or from their previous legal or customary primary caregiver, but not necessarily from other relatives or adults who are not *de jure* responsible for taking care of the minor. The term 'unaccompanied minor migrant' thus highlights the fact that these minors are not being cared for by an adult who, by law or custom, is responsible for doing so. Additionally, the term recognises that separation from their parents puts minor migrants in a particularly vulnerable and uneasy position.

Unaccompanied minor migrants arriving in Europe are generally boys aged between 14 and 17,[1] and frequently come from economically less developed countries where their educational opportunities are limited or where there are ongoing armed conflicts or other forms of violence, such as Afghanistan, Syria, Eritrea, Somalia, Gambia and Morocco. While their numbers in the EU member states ranged between 11,000 and 13,000 over the period from 2008 to 2013, this almost doubled in 2014 to reach slightly more than 23,000 individuals, and nearly quadrupled in 2015, when 88,300 asylum seekers applying for international protection in the member states of the EU were considered to be unaccompanied minors. They arrive in Europe on foot, by plane or ship, or hidden in trucks and trains via smuggling networks without proper documentation for a legal stay.[2] The European Migration Network (EMN 2015) reports that unaccompanied minors often flee their country for economic and aspirational reasons, poverty or a lack of opportunities for education and employment, whereas others migrate for safety reasons, fear of persecution or serious harm, violation of human rights, armed conflicts and religious or political unrest. Some leave because of domestic violence, recruitment as child soldiers and forced marriages (Hopkins and Hill 2008).

The United Nations High Commissioner for Refugees (UNCHR) highlights that the motives for fleeing one's country of origin are not always known. Some minors are too young to fully grasp their reasons for migration; some are not able to share their experiences with the authorities due to trauma or other issues; others are reluctant to reveal the real reasons for fear of being deported or because they wish to protect their families. The act of departure should be considered an attempt to resolve the (critical) situation they are in with one decisive action. From this perspective, their departure should be seen as a desperate act of (self) protection (Kirkpatrick 1992). Moreover, some authors point to a feeling of guilt on the part of children on the move because in leaving a dangerous situation, and being privileged to do so, they have left their families behind (ibid.). As explained in a UNCHR study, the decision for minors to travel unaccompanied is often approved by family members as the minors themselves usually do not have sufficient resources to cover the cost of the journey. Despite many of the families knowing the risks of irregular migration, they choose to send their children either because they see the potential benefits as outweighing the risks or because they feel they have no choice but to send them (UNHCR 2014). The paradox of this situation is articulated by Christiansen and Foighel (1990, cited in Kohli 2014): parents send their children away into the unknown because they love them even though they know they may permanently lose contact with them as a result.

The unaccompanied minor migrants arriving in Europe are usually allowed to enter state territories regardless of whether they meet the entry requirements. In contrast to adult migrants, they can only be returned to their country of origin or to a third country to a member of his or her family, a nominated guardian or an adequate reception facility in the state of return (Return Directive 2008: Article 10). Non-asylum-seeking minors who do not fulfil the entry conditions may thus be refused entry at the border and returned to their own country later on in the migration process through assisted return. If unaccompanied minors apply for asylum, they live in migrant reception facilities and gain access to certain rights while awaiting a decision on their application. In the event that their claim is refused, they will not normally be granted a residence permit and are expected to return to their home country. As previously mentioned, due to their minority they cannot be returned unless they are sent to a member of their family, a nominated guardian or an adequate reception facility. As a result, only a few unaccompanied minors return voluntarily, while most continue to live in reception centres until they are close to 18 years old (UNICEF 2015). At the European level, there is no accurate aggregated data regarding how many unaccompanied minor migrants receive permanent residency. Due to existing conflicts and war zones, the recognition rates for international protection have increased. For example, in Germany it rose from 36 per cent in 2010 to 84 per cent in the first three months of 2015 (SCEP 2015), while in Belgium it reached 69 per cent in 2015 (SCEP 2016).

The vulnerability of unaccompanied minor migrants

From the Western perspective, childhood is generally thought to be one of the most vulnerable periods of an individual's life as this is a time of intense formation of self-understanding, self-identity and worldviews. Children are viewed as vulnerable because of their inexperience, naiveté, fragility and general physical and psychological weakness. It is during this period, as they are becoming adults, that they receive formal or informal education and learn how to adapt to everyday life challenges. Along with primary socialisation, children also develop within the formal education system. In the European context (and also reflected strongly in the CRC), formal education is seen as an instrument which offers support for the development of a child's identity, personality, talents and physical and psychological skills. These are all perceived as vital in order for children to progress and enjoy equal opportunities in present-day society. Equally important is enjoyment of leisure activities, engaging in play and recreational activities, and participating freely in the arts and cultural life. Social support and medical care are likewise decisive factors for accomplishing optimal growth in children.

Unaccompanied minor migrants are often deprived of some of what is typically perceived to be a 'normal' childhood. In this respect, they are recognised as being vulnerable and exposed to risk. Vulnerability, as defined by Enenajor (2008), refers to the presence of factors that increase the chance of exposure to harms such as physical and mental abuse, whereas risk is described as a condition that increases the likelihood of negative developmental outcomes. The vulnerability of children is reflected in national and international legislation which applies to individuals who fall within a specific age range from birth up to the age of majority.

For example, the CRC recognises children as a vulnerable group of people in need of additional protection: 'the child, by reason of his physical and mental immaturity, needs special safeguards and care, including appropriate legal protection, before as well as after birth' (preamble). Due to their dependency, children are vulnerable when living in settled family conditions and even more so when they lack sufficient means for a decent and proper existence. The UNHCR (1994) additionally identifies refugee children as vulnerable because they are susceptible to disease, malnutrition and physical injury.

Many countries have policies concerning groups of children who are seen as more vulnerable due to their challenging circumstances. Sadako Ogata, former United Nations High Commissioner for Refugees, reasonably asserts that refugee children face far greater dangers in regard to their safety and well-being than the average child (UNCHR 1994). He draws attention to the sudden and violent onset of emergencies, the disruption of families and community structures, and the acute shortage of resources which deeply affect the physical and psychological conditions of refugee children. In the midst of emergencies and in the search for solutions, the separation of families continues to affect refugee children of all ages. As Spinder (cited in Enenajor 2008) believes, it is separated children in particular who are one of the most vulnerable groups among refugees and asylum seekers.

Unaccompanied minor migrants travelling without their parents are additionally vulnerable owing to the demanding travelling conditions; they need the support of adults not only for physical survival, particularly in the early years of childhood, but also for their psychological and social well-being (UNHCR 1994). Moreover, they are at risk of being manipulated and are particularly susceptible to the influence of adults. They are often exposed to unpredictable dangers at the hands of smugglers or to rights violations in the custody of police when apprehended at transit points or destinations. Undocumented minors who live in host societies outside institutional care are additionally vulnerable as they are considered to be particularly exposed to the risk of trafficking, sexual or economic exploitation and violence.

There are other consequences of separation from parents. Unaccompanied minors are deprived not only of their normal social, economic and cultural environment but also of their emotional development. Unaccompanied minor migrants lose their role models by leaving their families. Parents normally act as role models for their children, contributing significantly to the development of their identities and to their acquisition of skills and values (UNHCR 1994). Their development is further hampered by the loss of their normal livelihood and pattern of daily life, which results in a critical change as minors become solely responsible for taking care of themselves at a very early stage. As vividly expressed by Kohli: 'in becoming forced migrants and refugees, they experience the death of everyday life' (2014: 84). Some are not up to the task without the support of a social network and are consequently further at risk of neglecting their developmental and emotional needs because of separation from their parents. A range of possible emotional, developmental and behavioural issues has been noted with unaccompanied minor migrants, including problems sleeping, concentration disorders, nightmares, depression, withdrawal, anxiety, post-traumatic stress symptoms, somatic symptoms, severe grief reactions and sadness, aggression, diminished interest, hyper-arousal, low self-esteem, severe feelings of guilt, a fatalistic view of the future, substance abuse, violent behaviour, suicidal acts, psychosis and delinquent behaviour (Derluyn and Broekaert 2008).

The continuity of experience required for normal development may be further undermined for refugee children when they come into contact with different cultures. In many cases, the language and customs of the local population in the country of asylum, as well as that of officials and aid workers, may be quite different from those of the refugee community (UNHCR 1994). The first years are the most stressful for newly arrived minor migrants and some of them regret leaving their homes; only after being separated from their family members and social network do they realise how difficult it is to be on their own without the protection and support of family. Unaccompanied minor migrants are constantly moving between the past and hopes for the future (Kohli 2014), and their life circumstances, specific life trajectories and the constant struggle to establish an ordinary everyday life contribute to their early maturation. An important aspect of the vulnerability of the unaccompanied minor migrant is that, in comparison with adults, minors generally have less capacity to independently achieve a good quality of life. They can be handicapped in this aspect due to their inexperience and naiveté. Last but not least, according to Mai (2010: 78), once they arrive in Europe, unaccompanied minors 'fall into places marked by a specific set of opportunities and possibilities, which are already established places of marginality and irregular/illegal livelihoods in the country of destination'. Consequently, they have *a priori* limited possibilities to achieve a 'normal' everyday life.

The legal obligations of international law

The rights of unaccompanied minor migrants are defined by two main international legal domains – United Nations human rights and humanitarian law and EU law. For this reason it is important to clarify the actual legal context that affects the lives of unaccompanied minor migrants after they arrive in Europe as well as to explain which legal acts form a political and legal basis for claiming protection. The *UN Convention relating to the Status of Refugees* (UN 1951) is vital for recognising the needs of minor migrants fleeing war and persecution. This document offers permanent protection (refugee status) to persons who face a well-founded fear of being persecuted for reasons of race, religion, nationality, membership of a particular social group or political opinion (Article 1). Unaccompanied minor migrants who cannot prove the existence of a well-founded fear of persecution may be granted subsidiary protection under EU law, namely the *Qualification Directive* (2011),[3] if substantial grounds have been shown to believe that they would face the real risk of suffering serious harm if returned to their country of origin, such as the death penalty or execution, torture or inhumane or degrading treatment or punishment, or serious and individual threat to a civilian's life or person by reason of indiscriminate violence in situations of international or internal armed conflict (Qualification Directive 2011: Article 2).

Additionally, irregular unaccompanied minor migrants may be granted 'authorisation to stay for humanitarian reasons', which is in line with Article 6 of the EU *Return Directive* (2008) stipulating that 'Member States may at any moment decide to grant an autonomous residence permit or other authorisation offering the right to stay for compassionate, humanitarian or other reasons to a third-country national staying illegally on their territory'. This article is applied when dealing with minors who are not eligible for international protection – that is, refugee status or subsidiary protection status – as defined by law, but who should nonetheless protected against removal under the obligations imposed by international human rights instruments such as the CRC and the principles that derive from it. In this respect, in many cases the CRC forms the fundamental basis for the rights claims of unaccompanied minor migrants. In contrast to the procedures related to adult migrants, European states rarely implement return policies when dealing with unaccompanied minor migrants who do not have permission to enter their territories (see ECRE 2011). Unaccompanied minor migrants are, in this sense, recognised as children in need of additional protection – a decisive fact which constitutes the recognition of their claims related to the protection of their rights.

Legal obligations deriving from the CRC deal with concepts and principles which apply to children only, such as the best interests of the child, durable solutions, the development of the child's personality and the right to a standard of living adequate for the child's physical, mental, spiritual, moral and social development and general well-being. These are the rights to which all children are entitled as individuals without any distinction and which serve as a political basis for claiming entrance, residence and protection, as well as additional support for unaccompanied minor migrants in host countries.

The principle of the best interests of the child is probably one of the most widely used in international and national (domestic) legal documents and several guidelines regarding unaccompanied minors. It is used as a concept that describes the well-being of the child depending on his or her age, maturity, family and living environment. Due to its relativity, there is no standard definition of the best interests of the child in a conclusive sense. The UNHCR *Guidelines on Determining the Best Interests of the Child* (2006) allow for specific safeguards and documentation requirements within which the decision-maker should consider the various factors of each particular case, taking into account rights and obligations as set out in the human rights instruments, so that the final decision protects the minor in the best possible manner. In regard to unaccompanied minors, the primary concern of determining his or her best interests should be the factors relating to the parents' circumstances, safety and physical and psychological well-being. In another report, the UNHCR (1994) explains that when making a long-term plan for an unaccompanied minor in line with the child's best interest, one should consider many factors including 'the desirability of continuity' of culture and language (CRC: Article 20), the preservation of family and nationality (CRC: Article 8), and the child's own desires, which must be considered according to the child's 'age and maturity' (CRC: Article 12). The best interests assessment is especially important when concerning unaccompanied minors as they are separated from parents who are not able to fulfil their basic parental responsibilities.

The practice in many European countries, however, shows that the concept of the child's best interests is not taken as seriously as recommended by UN bodies. For instance, the UN Committee on the Rights of the Child has clarified, in *General Comment No. 6 on the treatment of unaccompanied and separated children outside their country of origin,* that in order to fulfil the obligations set out by the CRC, the best interests determination must be '*documented* in preparation of any decision fundamentally impacting on the child's life' (UNCRC 2005: para 19, emphasis added). Further on, in the *General Comment No. 14 on the right of the child to have his or her best interests taken as a primary consideration*, the Committee points out that the obligation of particular countries is to ensure a rights-based approach, engaging all actors to secure the holistic physical, psychological, moral and spiritual integrity of the child and promote his or her human dignity. In this regard, all decisions concerning the unaccompanied minor migrant should be made through *assessing* and *determining* the best interests as well as the *evaluation* of the possible positive and negative impact (UNCRC 2013: para 6). The recommendations and obligations clearly stipulate that national agencies must explain how the rights of unaccompanied minors have been respected in the decision and what has been considered to be in the child's best interests and on which criteria, as well as how the child's best interests were weighed against other considerations.

The moral economy of European asylum and migration policies

The current state of affairs and the rights of unaccompanied minor migrants arriving in the EU are not only defined by the rules of international law, but are in our view even more profoundly shaped by asylum and migration policies which overwhelmingly impact their life stories. Despite the fact that EU asylum and migration legislation is designed in line with the general provisions of international human rights law, in practice many aspects of European policies demonstrate an attempt to circumvent the obligations set out in the CRC and child protection policies. Although the EU member states, in accordance with the CRC, have consistently introduced special provisions related to unaccompanied minor migrants, national governments and local authorities still frequently avoid their legal responsibilities – for instance, when providing adequate reception conditions, recognising their special needs and offering additional legal, social and psychological support. The EU migration and asylum policies can be seen as Janus-like when manifesting humanitarian aims through a restrictive and repressive approach.

The treatment of unaccompanied minor migrants in the EU is no exception; it likewise reflects the paradigmatic tensions between the discourses and practices of compassion and repression, between the sentiments of sympathy and concern for order, and between the politics of pity and policies of control as observed by Fassin (2005). Each of these discourses creates a different legitimacy for unaccompanied minor migrants regarding their future and their rights and obligations. According to Fassin (2005: 369), the overall attitude exemplified in migration and asylum policies has changed from relative tolerance to general mistrust, while the expression 'false refugees', used to refer to economic migrants under the pretence of seeking political asylum and taking advantage of the European welfare system, has become a central figure of bureaucratic thinking.

The oscillation of EU migration and asylum policies between humanitarianism and national security and border control becomes especially evident when governing the lives of those who need help but at the same time may disturb the economic development and the organisation of modern nation-states, such as in the case of irregular minor migrants and asylum seekers. It is wrong to assume that the states' policies are against migration as such; however, the current situation shows that their prime concern is to exercise their sovereign right to decide who is allowed to enter their territories, for which reasons and for how long. In line with the contemporary neoliberal mantra, it is those carefully selected migrants with specific skills and knowledge who become the desirable part of migration, which is thought to bring long-term economic development. In contrast, the uncontrolled arrival of irregular migrants and asylum seekers represents the 'uninvited' ones as resulting in economic, social and political cost and a burden to society. According to this mantra, it is these kinds of migrants who must be reduced in numbers to a level that has as low an impact as possible on the public expenditure.

Unaccompanied minors mainly arrive in Europe in the form of uncontrolled migration, making them more or less separated from the political sphere as they lack citizenship or permission to stay and are in need of humanitarian assistance justified by their vulnerability as children. As one can see in these cases, the lives of unaccompanied minor migrants become dependent on charity and lose political importance; in relation to this, Gündoğdu (2015: 113) highlights that when states, courts and rights advocates turn to compassion to make decisions about migrants' suffering, they risk unmaking the equal personhood of those migrants and rendering their rights dependent on a capricious moral sentiment. Or, as stated by Fassin (2005: 368), what they are not able to get as a right may be given to them from the standpoint of compassion; recognition of refugee status thus appears as an act of sympathy rather than the fulfilment of political debt towards citizens of humanity (ibid.: 376).

A humanitarian approach to children's rights is thus problematic not only because unaccompanied minor migrants are left to the goodwill of national authorities but also because it turns them into 'unspeaking subjects'. In other words, they lack political legitimacy to claim full membership in society as rightful subjects; instead, membership may be generously granted to them on the basis of their vulnerability. Unaccompanied minors are thus not understood on a political level but mainly on the level of humanitarianism, where compassion serves as a basis upon which to decide their rights and decreases the political cause of their claims. Under a humanitarian principle, it is their vulnerability in relation to their age that is recognised as the most effective legal basis for defending their interests. For this reason, much concern on the part of national authorities is dedicated to establishing the age of migrants, where the disputed cases often result in the conclusion that they are not young enough and thus are no longer vulnerable enough to claim their rights. Age assessment in general seems to be one of the most significant and at the same time most controversial points in the process of applying for international protection (as seen later in the book).

Bhabha (2009) explains in relation to unaccompanied minor migrants that they are *de facto* or functionally stateless by virtue of migrant status and consequently face restricted access to some of the basic children's rights. The contributions of this book in many ways demonstrate that, once they arrive in Europe, unaccompanied minor migrants are treated differently to children with resident status in that they are not automatically granted the right to stay, enrol in school, and find suitable accommodation or work. Despite the principle of non-discrimination enshrined in the CRC, the discrimination stemming from the (ir)regularity of resident status is one of the most commonsensical, established and far-reaching differentiations in the contemporary world (Brubaker 1999: 64) and unaccompanied minor migrants are no exception in this regard. The power of the discourse of civic exclusion is seen in the fact that few effectively question the resulting practices of the exclusion of irregular residents which affects children as much as adults. In addition, this exclusion is presented as legal and commonsensical so that it is not seen as a violation of children's rights. If the CRC principle of 'non-discrimination' were taken seriously by the governments of modern nation-states, none of the minor migrants (either refugees or economic migrants) would be subjected to the scrutiny of asylum and migration procedures. As opposed to children holding regular residence or citizenship status, unaccompanied minor migrants first need to prove their 'right to be here' to be entitled to the full range of rights. In other words, they have to attain their 'right to have rights' (Arendt, 1962), either through recognition of refugee status or through age assessment and recognition of their vulnerability. The described differentiation between one group of children and the other can be, in our view, explained as discrimination on the basis of resident status – for example, citizenship, immigration status or statelessness.

The CRC may establish the vulnerability argument, which in most cases formulates the legal basis for claiming the right of unaccompanied minor migrants to stay; however, as it turns out in many cases, this only postpones the execution of the sovereign right of nation-states to exclude the undesired category of immigrants – in this case, irregular unaccompanied minors who formally become adults. As soon as minors staying in the host country reach the age of majority, they are no longer entitled to the benefits they receive as a result of their vulnerability. After reaching 18, the argument of compassion ceases to exist and so too do governments' obligations towards young adult migrants. Many are returned to their home countries. This casts reflection upon how 'durable solutions' are understood in cases of unaccompanied minor migrants lacking a permanent residence permit and moreover points to the ineffectiveness of this principle; despite the fact that best interests determination assumes various solutions for unaccompanied minor migrants – integration in the host country, a third-country solution or return to the country of origin – it often seems that eventually only one durable solution is available for irregular unaccompanied minor migrants – namely, return.

Overview of the chapters

The chapters of this book are based on the previously described basic standpoints. This introduction is followed by three 'theoretical' chapters dealing with ideological, normative and methodological aspects of the unaccompanied minors problematic; these are followed by the presentation of four case studies – namely, the situation of unaccompanied minors in Austria, Slovenia, France and the United Kingdom. Each of the chapters focuses on selected aspects which appear especially intriguing in a concrete national context.

Barbara Gornik, in Chapter 2, 'At the crossroads of power relations: the Convention on the Rights of the Child and unaccompanied minor migrants', demonstrates that unaccompanied minor migrants represent a 'place' where two completely different subjectivities meet and are weighed against each other – that is, the subjectivity of an immigrant on one hand and that of a child on the other. In her account she provides an explanation of how the rights of unaccompanied minors are negotiated within the nexus of knowledge and power concerning the relation of child versus migrant. She begins by asking what is the ultimate criterion of the national and international legal systems that defines the rights of unaccompanied minor migrants, and what is the decisive instance in determining the interpretation and implementation of children's rights, their best interests, and principle of non-discrimination, personal development and safety. She explains the main points of a critical approach to the CRC, including some contemporary criticisms which appear in social sciences and humanities in relation to human and children's rights law. To demonstrate the power relations manifesting in the implementation of the rights of unaccompanied minor migrants, she delves into the questions of age, autonomy, best interests and the principle of non-discrimination. The overall aim of the chapter is to grasp the international children's rights discourse within the political context of contemporary migrations which profoundly shapes the implementation of unaccompanied minor migrants' rights.

In Chapter 3, 'The best interests of unaccompanied and separated children: a normative framework based on the Convention on the Rights of the Child', Jyothi Kanics presents a summary of the normative framework at the international level provided in the CRC. The role of the UN Committee on the Rights of the Child is further examined as the body responsible for monitoring the implementation of the CRC by State Parties. Also examined is its work concerning the best interests of the child as well as authoritative guidance from the Committee. It is this treaty which explains how the best interests principle should be applied in all measures affecting unaccompanied and separated migrant children who have particular needs and special rights under the CRC. Yet, as non-nationals, they often face discrimination and rights violations. It is even more important when aiming for the realisation of their rights to make the best interests of the child a primary consideration in all decisions that may affect the child in order to prevent discrimination, disappearances and exploitation. Finally, the chapter highlights the need to identify a durable solution in line with the best interests of each individual child through a best interests determination.

The last chapter in the first section, written by Carla van Os, Elianne Zijlstra, Erik J. Knorth, Wendy Post and Margrite Kalverboer, presents a new 'Methodology for the best interests of the child assessment for recently arrived unaccompanied refugee minors'. Based on thorough research at the Study Centre for Children and Law in the Netherlands, the chapter presents a methodology for assessing the best interests of the child for recently arrived unaccompanied refugee minors. The authors describe the process of evaluating best interests assessment processes in order to adapt them for early-stage interviews with unaccompanied minors. The authors argue that this group of minors require a specific methodology of diagnostic interview as they are not at all familiar with the situation and actors in the Netherlands, they do not speak the language and they are still afraid of what they might face in the asylum process. The interview therefore focuses less on the development of the child in the Netherlands and more on their situation in their country of origin and during the journey. The case of Elsa illustrates how the new methodology helps to build trust and a positive attitude and also provides agency to the child and the guardian.

Chapter 5, written by Ayşe Dursun and Birgit Sauer, gives insight into 'Asylum experiences in Austria from the perspective of unaccompanied minors'. The main aim of the chapter is to demonstrate that despite the deprived conditions of migration and discriminatory practices of the Austrian state – especially in comparison with native unaccompanied minors – minor refugees claim their agency. This is especially important as the Austrian asylum regime is characterised by a tension between institutional suspicion and restriction towards unaccompanied minor migrants on the one hand and childcare and protection on the other. Based on interviews with minor migrants, the authors demonstrate how they co-constitute the framework and conditions in which they live in Austria. While the conditions at the initial reception centre (where asylum seekers are sent) are rather poor for unaccompanied minors, the situation in provincial accommodation facilities (where minor refugees are sent after being accepted into the asylum process) provides more space to organise everyday life in a self-determined way.

Chapter 6, '"Not our children": unaccompanied minor asylum seekers in Slovenia', written by Mateja Sedmak, Blaž Lenarčič, Zorana Medarić and Tjaša Žakelj, presents the path of unaccompanied minors in search of international protection in the Republic of Slovenia and the discrepancies between children's rights that have been legally adopted and their actual implementation in daily life. From the point of view of children's rights, unaccompanied minors in Slovenia have a different status to national children. They are 'not our children' and this is the explanatory framework of the actual situation. Through the narratives of both professionals and unaccompanied and former unaccompanied children themselves, the chapter reveals that unaccompanied minors who seek protection in Slovenia are often treated not primarily as children, but rather as foreigners, immigrants and individuals who wish to exploit the Slovenian social welfare system. There is a clear discrepancy between formally declared rights and their implementation; violation of the principle of the best interests of the child is frequently observed. This can be seen from the first moment in the formal procedures as applied by the Slovene border police, followed by different rights related to accommodation, health, education, work, etc. which are often completely ignored in practice, despite having been properly introduced into law. Finally, unaccompanied minors live in a state of chronic uncertainty, without seeing a durable solution.

Chapter 7, written by Corentin Bailleul, analyses 'Coping strategies of unaccompanied minors lacking protection within the French context'. The chapter describes how French legal provisions regarding unaccompanied minors lead to a high degree of exclusion of this group from care facilities. The author then demonstrates which strategies young migrants – mainly young men – employ to regain protection, find places to live or stay and obtain food. The actions of these young migrants and also the support of NGOs are considered significant. The chapter is based on participant observations, starting from the day-to-day-experiences of young migrants coping with their situation. The author goes on to show how important it is for young migrants to politicise their cause and participate in collective action to improve their situation in France. The chapter introduces an innovative method of conducting studies with migrant minors, namely the regular presence of researchers over three months in public places where minor migrants spend their days.

In Chapter 8, 'Surely not! Procedurally lawful age assessments in the UK', Marie-Bénédicte Dembour highlights the problematic practice of age assessment in the case of unaccompanied minors in the UK. She demonstrates how age assessment is actually conducted and how easily the process can fail to respect guidance and best practice. In this regard the following points appear most problematic: age assessment interviews too often take place in inappropriate places (e.g. a police station); youngsters may be inappropriately accompanied; the interview is not always prevented from turning into an adversarial process; the proceedings are dominated by a quest to prove that which cannot be proven; and, finally, the focus on this quest has the effect of discouraging the application of the supposedly central principle of the benefit of the doubt. The author demonstrates that in the age assessment process, the age of unaccompanied minors is frequently overestimated. This is despite a legal framework that insists on giving the young person the benefit of the doubt as to their claimed age. The reason why the benefit of the doubt is not always given the upper hand is that there exists a fundamental contradiction between the ideas of children's rights and protection on one hand and migration restriction policy on the other. The final concluding remark is that the only reasonable position from a human and children's rights perspective is to recognise the obligation to treat the youngster as a person of the age they claim to be.

Notes

1 Eurostat (2016) reports that 13 per cent of unaccompanied minors were under the age of 14 in 2015.
2 For example, it is estimated that nearly all unaccompanied minors in Germany have been smuggled (EMN 2015).
3 Directive 2011/95/EU of the European Parliament and of the Council of 13 December 2011 on standards for the qualification of third-country nationals or stateless persons as beneficiaries of international protection, for a uniform status for refugees or for persons eligible for subsidiary protection, and for the content of the protection granted.

Bibliography

Arendt, H. (1962) *Origins of Totalitarianism*, Cleveland, OH, and New York, NY: Meridian Books.

Bhabha, J. (2009) 'Arendt's children: Do today's migrant children have a right to have rights?', *Human Rights Quarterly*, Vol. 31, No. 2, 410–451.

Brubaker, R. (1999) 'The Manichean Myth: Rethinking the Distinction Between "Civic" and "Ethnic" Nationalism', in H. Kriesl, K. Armingeon, H. Siegrist and A. Wimmer (eds) *Nation and National Identity: The European Experience in Perspective*, Zurich: Verlag Rüegger.

Derluyn, I. and Broekaert, E. (2008) 'Unaccompanied refugee children and adolescents: The glaring contrast between a legal and a psychological perspective', *International Journal of Law and Psychiatry*, Vol. 31, No. 4, 319–330.

ECRE (2011) *Comparative Study on Practices in the Field of Return of Minors*, Online. Available online at https://ec.europa.eu/home-affairs/sites/homeaffairs/files/e-library/documents/policies/legal-migration/pdf/general/return_of_children final.pdf (accessed 7 March 2017).

EMN (2015) *Policies, Practices and Data on Unaccompanied Minors in the EU Member States and Norway*, Available online at https://ec.europa.eu/anti-trafficking/sites/antitrafficking/files/emn_study_2014_uams_0.pdf (accessed 9 February 2017).

Enenajor, A. (2008) 'Rethinking vulnerability: European asylum policy harmonization and unaccompanied asylum seeking minors', *Childhoods Today*, Vol. 2, No. 2, 1–24.

Eurostat (2016) *Eurostat Press Release*, 2 May 2016. Available online at http://ec.europa.eu/eurostat/documents/2995521/7244677/3-02052016-AP-EN.pdf (accessed 9 February 2017).

Fassin, D. (2005) 'Compassion and repression: The moral economy of immigration policies in France', *Cultural Anthropology*, Vol. 20, No. 3, 362–387.

Gündoğdu, A. (2015) *Rightlessness in an Age of Rights: Hannah Arendt and the Contemporary Struggles of Migrants*. Oxford: Oxford University Press.

Hopkins, P. and Hill, M. (2008) 'Pre-flight departure circumstances and accounts of transnational migration: The experiences of unaccompanied asylum-seeking children and young people', *Children's Geographies*, Vol. 6, No. 3, 257–268.

Kirkpatrick, B. (1992) *Brewer's Concise Dictionary of Phrase and Fable*, Oxford: Cassell.

Kohli, R. (2014) 'Protecting asylum seeking children on the move', *Revue Européenne des Migrations Internationales*, Vol. 30, No. 1, 83–104.

Mai, N. (2010) 'Marginalized Young (Male) Migrants in the European Union: Caught between the Desire for Autonomy and the Priorities of Social Protection', in J. Kanics, D. Senovilla Hernández and K. Touzenis (eds) *Migrating Alone: Unaccompanied and Separated Children's Migration to Europe*, Paris: UNESCO.

Qualification Directive (2011) *Directive 2011/95/EU of the European Parliament and of the Council of 13 December 2011 on standards for the qualification of third-country nationals or stateless persons as beneficiaries of international protection, for a uniform status for refugees or for persons eligible for subsidiary protection, and for the content of the protection granted*. Available online at http://eur-lex.europa.eu/legal-content/EN/TXT/PDF/?uri=CELEX:32011L0095&from=en (accessed 9 February 2017).

Return Directive (2008) *Directive 2008/115/ EC of the European Parliament and of the Council on common standards and procedures in Member States for returning illegally staying third-country nationals*. Available online at http://eur-lex.europa.eu/legal-content/EN/TXT/PDF/?uri=CELEX:32008L0115&from=EN (accessed 9 February 2017).

SCEP (2015) *Newsletter No. 43 – Summer 2015*. Available online at www.scepnetwork.org/images/sceptemp.pdf (accessed 9 February 2017).

SCEP (2016) *Newsletter No. 45 – Summer 2016*. Available online at www.scepnetwork.org/images/12/296.pdf (accessed 9 February 2017).

Sedmak M., Lenarčič, B., Medarič, Z. and Žakelj, T. (eds) (2015) *A Journey to the Unknown. The Rights of Unaccompanied Migrant Children: Between Theory and Practice*, Koper: Univerzitetna založba Annales.

UNCRC (2005) *General Comment No. 6: Treatment of unaccompanied and separated children outside their country of origin*. Available online at www2.ohchr.org/english/bodies/crc/docs/GC6.pdf (accessed 9 February 2017).

UNCRC (2013) *General comment No. 14 on the right of the child to have his or her best interests taken as a primary consideration (art. 3, para. 1)*. Available online at www2.ohchr.org/English/bodies/crc/docs/GC/CRC_C_GC_14_ENG.pdf (accessed 9 February 2017).

UNHCR (1994) *Guidelines on the Protection and Care of Refugee Children*, Geneva: UNHCR.

UNHCR (2006) *Guidelines on Determining the Best Interests of the Child*. Available online at www.unhcr.org/4566b16b2.pdf (accessed 9 February 2017).

UNHCR (2014) *Why do children undertake the unaccompanied journey? Motivations for departure to Europe and other industrialised countries from the perspective of children, families and residents of sending communities in Afghanistan*. Available online at www.unhcr.org/548ea0f09.pdf (accessed 9 February 2017).

UNICEF (2015) *Children's rights in return policy and practice in Europe: A discussion paper on the return of unaccompanied and separated children to institutional reception or family*. Available online at https://ec.europa.eu/anti-trafficking/sites/antitrafficking/files/childrens_rights_in_return_policy_and_practice_in_europe.pdf (accessed 9 February 2017).

Wernesjö, U. (2011) 'Unaccompanied asylum-seeking children: Whose perspective?' *Childhood*, Vol. 19, No. 4, 495–507.

2 At the crossroads of power relations

The Convention on the Rights of the Child and unaccompanied minor migrants

Barbara Gornik

Introduction

The Convention on the Rights of the Child (CRC) is one of the most widely ratified international documents.[1] Over the past decades, children's rights have become an influential element of contemporary national policy-making as well as a powerful instrument within the international human rights regime. Children's rights form the minimal moral standards that are meant to transcend political boundaries and social and cultural differences; they are conceptualised as embodying a universal morality beyond state borders (Pupavac 2001). The concept of rights as such carries in itself a deeply rooted meaning implying protection and benefits for the right-holder. Such a view, in my opinion at least, impedes critical thinking; it narrows the view on children's rights without questioning their wider effects within society and neglects how and upon which criteria they come to be children's rights. A critical approach to rights does not make them 'bad' either, but, more importantly, it shifts the attention to the power relations which reside and reproduce through the contemporary system of children's rights.

In this chapter I do not argue for the elimination of children's rights or the related concepts, especially as I recognise the indispensable value they have in defending the interests of unaccompanied minor migrants. My analysis instead focuses on a critical understanding of the CRC but at the same time highlights the standpoints which speak in favour of international children's rights law and its significance for minor migrants. My primary aim is to expose particular rationalities, values and norms which decisively impact the implementation and argumentation of children's rights. I observe that the relationship between unaccompanied minor migrants and the international children's rights regime is deeply demarcated by the citizenship status of the minors in question and the fact that they are foreigners in a particular country. Children's rights in the CRC may be formulated as transcending the borders of states and political interests, but in reality unaccompanied minors are in many regards situated in an unequal situation in comparison with national children solely due to the fact that they are migrants.

This is especially important for understanding the limits of international law applied to unaccompanied minor migrants, whose situation more often than not demonstrates that children's rights are neither self-realising nor a straightforward phenomenon.

Unaccompanied minor migrants represent a place where two completely different subjectivities meet and are weighed against each other – that is, the subjectivity of an immigrant on one hand and that of a child on the other. The rights related to each of the subjectivities are frequently in opposition. Unaccompanied minor migrants are entitled to particular rights solely as children; according to *Directive 2008/115/ EC of the European Parliament and of the Council on common standards and procedures in Member States for returning illegally staying third-country nationals*, their best interests should be taken into account (Return Directive: Article 10); their stay in a host country may be extended when attending school (Return Directive: Article 7); they can only be detained for the shortest possible period of time and as a measure of last resort (Return Directive: Article 17); they should be provided with accommodation in institutions with personnel and facilities that take into account the needs of persons their age (ibid.), etc.

While many agree that children need to be sensibly protected, many also believe migrants have to be carefully selected and their application for residence in a country thoroughly examined. It is within this nexus of knowledge and power – child versus migrant – that the rights of unaccompanied minors are negotiated. The fundamental question in this regard is what is the ultimate criterion of the national and international legal systems that defines the rights of unaccompanied minor migrants? In other words, what is the decisive instance that determines the interpretation and implementation of children's rights, their best interests, and principle of non-discrimination, personal development and safety? What is the governmental rationale that significantly affects the rights of unaccompanied minor migrants? These obviously overreach the scope of the present chapter but nevertheless represent the main starting point of the argument presented in the following sections.

To facilitate the above argumentation, the chapter begins by briefly explaining the main points of a critical approach to the CRC, including some contemporary criticisms from the fields of social sciences and humanities in relation to human and children's rights law. Thereafter, I offer a counter argument to the presented criticisms by elaborating upon the relevance of children's rights for unaccompanied minors. In order to demonstrate the power relations which manifest in the implementation of the rights of unaccompanied minor migrants, I turn to the question of age, autonomy, best interests and migration status. In the final section I show that the CRC is characterised by the limited enforceability and flexibility of its provisions. The overall aim of the chapter is to grasp the international children's rights discourse within the European political context of contemporary migrations and the power relations which profoundly shape the implementation of the rights of unaccompanied minor migrants.

Critical understanding of the Convention on the Rights of the Child

The instruments of human and children's rights are repeatedly presented as apolitical, pre-political and even an anti-political means for achieving social justice and protection for powerless individuals against an excess of state power. In the same vein, childhood is often separated from politics, especially when scientifically examining and dealing with 'natural' child development and 'biological' children's needs. However, in relation to international documents such as the CRC, the political element must be recognised. In this section I focus on three main aspects which I think we must bear in mind when considering the CRC: (1) the element of Western values and the Westernisation of the world; (2) the element of moral imperialism and interventionism; and (3) the element of professionalism and limiting autonomy of children.

A critical understanding of children's rights manifests in their denaturalisation and demythologisation by bringing them to a tangible context within societies and by scrutinising their implementation from the point of view of power relations. Such an approach analytically reviews the fact that they are represented as non-ideological tools of protection which transcend political borders; countering this position, the critical approach adopts a sceptical point of view towards the ways in which they appear in political life and everyday discourse, where they are spoken about with particular clarity as if they do not need additional explanation. Although children's rights are often presented as simple fact, which is either respected or violated, they are much more than this. It cannot be disputed that the CRC is used to protect the rights of children, but many authors have highlighted that this does not tell us everything about how children's rights are used, how they appear in international and local relations and what implications they have (e.g. Pupavac 2001, Reynolds, Nieuwenhuys and Hanson 2006, Reynaert *et al.* 2015). Through their writings, these authors have encouraged us to consider the powers that reside within documents such as the CRC and the relations which are supported within it. Although the CRC is viewed as an important document for establishing the rights of the child and the status of children as social agents at a national and international level (Archard 1993; Bourdillon 2004; Freeman 2007; Reynolds *et al.* 2006; Jones and Welch 2010), it has been subject to some sensible critiques.

One of the more common critiques is that the CRC is a typically Western construct (Mayall 2001; Reynolds *et al.* 2006; White 2002) which functions as a form of Western moral imperialism (Harris-Short 2001; White 2002: 727). Being a part of international law, the CRC has great symbolic power which can be used to articulate moral standards and express universalising tendencies based on abstract notions of what is a good and appropriate childhood for all children. For example, the CRC gives priority to *parent–child* relations instead of recognising other extended family and community relations which might be equally important (Mayall 2001: 245); by promoting obligatory schooling, it may impose changes in communities with different education systems; by defining all individuals under 18 years of age as children, the CRC may lead to an invisibility and even 'infantilisation of adolescents' (Reynaert *et al.* 2015); it reflects an image of the dominant urban nuclear middle-class family (Andre 2015: 118) and so on. The rights of a child as put forward in the CRC give a strong message about what childhood should be like, what children need, how they develop and how they should be protected. But imagining the diversity of social organisation in local communities worldwide, it is impossible to accept as true that the CRC reflects a wide variety of cultural communities, inevitably leading to the conclusion that the CRC overrides the diversity of childhood and may be thus recognised as a typically 'Western' document.

In a similar vein, the CRC introduces the child to a wide range of social relations which are vital for reproducing a modernised world order, ideologies and policies. The logic exemplified in the CRC is that a child's well-being depends on protection rights, individual personality rights and human dignity rights, which are in turn grounded in a market economy, economic development and consumer society. For instance, Article 28 obliges states to 'promote and encourage international cooperation in matters relating to education, in particular with a view to contributing to the elimination of ignorance and illiteracy throughout the world and facilitating access to scientific and technical knowledge and modern teaching methods'. In Article 17, the CRC also encourages the use of mass media to disseminate information and material of social and cultural benefit to the child, especially in line with Article 29, which obliges states to achieve the 'development of the child's personality, talents and mental and physical abilities to their fullest potential'. This wording, so typical of a Western world-view, brings us to the understanding that the Convention clearly depicts the needs of children in line with social relations emblematic of the market-driven capitalist and material society, while their well-being is interpreted as dependent upon a modern economic system with its specialists, technology, mass media and standards for living and development as well as rest and leisure, play and recreational activities, and participation in cultural life and the arts.

Applying this view to the rights of a child, one cannot ignore the long history of UNICEF and its innumerable missions around the world, the aim of which is to help the helpless. Although it is difficult to argue with the idea of helping to achieve what is in the best interests of the child, it must be acknowledged that UNICEF typically offers a Western kind of assistance, among other social protection initiatives such as food security programmes, cash transfers to households, guaranteed work schemes and paying school fees, maintaining social expenditures to preserve gains in the realisation of children's rights and long-term national development achievements, promoting economic recovery to raise household living standards, investments in agriculture and food security and employment-generating industry, identifying sources of fiscal space to promote economic recovery, etc. The work of UNICEF clearly adopts the vision of a market economy which is thought to liberate people and bring better respect their rights.

As seen rights are not a neutral medium and not even integrally emancipatory; it all depends on who uses these rights, how and for which purposes (Cowan 2006).

For instance, the children who receive education through UNICEF assistance programmes cannot be regarded as freer than the illiterate children living in traditional communities; in many cases, children are educated to become potential wage workers while still suffering from bad living conditions and limited capacities for their prosperity and development. Likewise, unaccompanied minor migrants who come to the EU cannot be seen as emancipated if they are authorised to stay only until they reach the age of majority. The more critical academics and activists even highlight that although advocacy for children's rights might be conceived of as an ethical, liberating and emancipatory project, in practice these rights do not necessarily contribute to a more just world (Pupavac 2001: 100). This is especially evident in the limited enforceability of the CRC as well as in the fact that the concept of children's rights has no practical value for millions of children who are exposed to extreme poverty, a lack of survival resources, domestic violence, armed conflict or life in refugee camps.

Finally, another critique of the CRC originates from its limiting capacity of children's autonomy, which varies throughout societies. As observed by Andre (2015: 113), the tension implicit in the CRC is the one between building the capacity of children to construct their childhoods and the existing social structures and power relations of the CRC which encapsulate the image of a 'normal' childhood. Children, like many other minority groups, lack a voice. According to the CRC, they have the right to be heard in all decisions and to express their views in all matters affecting them, and their views must be given due weight in accordance with the age and maturity of the child. In many views, however, the CRC and the implementation of rights in practice is often formed by adults' theories about what children need and how they develop (see Mayall 2001). These views often derive exclusively from adult perspectives and their studies of children, which are contextualised and structured by adult social and economic goals. As noted by Pupavac (2001: 99) in the case of the CRC, the rights-holder and moral agent who decides and acts are separate, which essentially raises the question of their agency and the question 'if it is not the child, who then is the moral agent in children's rights who determines the interest of the child?' (ibid.).

In line with the above arguments, it is important to acknowledge that children's rights and the CRC appear within the context of actual events of everyday life and defend and reproduce a particular political world-view, argue for particular values and project a particular image of a child. This means that children's rights are not universal in meaning and do not bring liberation to the rights-bearing subject, but that it is through rights that children are introduced to a particular world-view and a set of values, rules and norms. Children's rights do not have meaning in and of themselves, but only become meaningful within contemporary social organisation. However, that these rights are useless for children, including unaccompanied minor migrants, in order to defend their interests.

The relevance of the Convention on the Rights of the Child for unaccompanied minor migrants

I believe it is not possible to explain children's rights solely in terms of the above-mentioned critiques. Even if one agrees with the criticism developed by several authors, one must acknowledge the significance of international legal documents for the protection of individuals, including children; children's rights have a dual character as they are situated within political state formations and reinforce the power of the state on one hand, while on the other hand children's rights also represent an instrument which has the ability to go beyond that state power or – more accurately – to transform it.

Continuing in line with the above arguments, we must turn to the question: what is the meaning of the CRC for unaccompanied minor migrants? Who interprets and finally decides upon the rights set in the Convention and according to which criteria? Is this document beneficial for unaccompanied minor migrants or is it just another international document mainly used to achieve other goals related to political pragmatism, interventionist politics, global Westernisation and moral imperialism? And, more importantly, what are the interests of nation-states which hinder implementing the rights of the child?

Despite the academic criticism of human and children's rights in contemporary international relations, it is difficult to argue that the CRC has a predominantly negative impact upon unaccompanied minor migrants themselves. There are emancipatory, protective and constraining dimensions of the CRC which come into effect in practice. For instance, according to Article 19 of the CRC, a child who is temporarily or permanently deprived of his or her family environment shall be entitled to special protection and assistance provided by the state. Moreover, the CRC has emancipatory dimensions for unaccompanied minor migrants as it obliges states to ensure the child's right to participation (Article 12) and to respect all other rights set forth in the Convention for each child within their jurisdiction without discrimination of any kind (Article 2). As such, the CRC could be a source of mobilisation and a basis for implementing protection, provision and participation rights. On the other hand, the CRC may have constraining effects for unaccompanied minor migrants should their best interests be interpreted differently from their stated interest or if their life choices significantly differ from what is understood as a 'normal' childhood.

In general, the CRC is very important for unaccompanied minor migrants. Following the principle of non-discrimination, the rights stipulated in the Convention are not limited to children who are citizens and should be available to all minors irrespective of their nationality, immigration status or statelessness – including asylum-seeking, refugee and migrant children (UNCRC 2005: para 12). This principle constructs an obligation on the part of nations for the inclusion and protection of unaccompanied minor migrants who do not have permission to stay and who would otherwise be subjected to the traditional methods of exclusion employed with irregular adult migrants. According to recent data, European states rarely implement return policies when dealing with unaccompanied minor migrants, even if minors do not have permission to enter their territories (ECRE 2011); the analysis shows that they are usually offered basic care and accommodation, and access to education, healthcare services and legal and humanitarian assistance as per the rights set out in the CRC (EMN 2015). Through the principle of non-discrimination, the CRC significantly impacts migration policies and enables unaccompanied minors to stay in destination countries, and therefore offers them additional protection as children, which adults otherwise lack.

Furthermore, the unaccompanied minor migrants arriving in Europe demonstrate that the critique of moral imperialism is somehow false. Through interviews with police, social workers, legal guardians or researchers, unaccompanied minors repeatedly express their wish to be protected by the provisions of the CRC and the safeguard measures that are offered to them due to their age. They often report their traumatic experiences, feelings of anxiety and a lack of safety; they wish to have a 'normal' life, attend schooling, have a job, live with their family, have the ability to develop their personalities, have access to sport and leisure activities (see Chapter 5 in this volume). This is to say that the domains covered and protected by the CRC are found equally important and relevant by unaccompanied minors themselves; from this aspect it is impossible to identify them as subjects upon whom the CRC is imposed. Many identify themselves as bearers of children's rights and find the measures of international law valuable for defending their interests and demanding protection (see e.g. Chapter 7 in this volume).

It is exactly the significance of self-representation in terms of claiming protection of children's rights that is vital for unaccompanied minor migrants as it increases the authenticity and genuineness of their demands. It is through the contextualisation and articulation of their viewpoints, hopes and plans that we can withdraw from the standpoint that 'we' know what is best for 'them'. Giving them the possibility to express their views is a way to empower them; in this way, unaccompanied minor migrants are not represented solely as victims of rights violations but also as speaking subjects capable of defining their interests and forming their own political claims. The importance of the CRC for unaccompanied minor migrants is thus evident from the fact that it can be used for protection and expression of their interests. Although far from witnessing ideal situations in dealing with unaccompanied minor migrants in European migration processes, there is a slow progress of recognising them as a group with special needs for protection. As noted by Smith (2004), there are gradual changes and improvements in legislation, policy and practice regarding the standards of protection and care available to unaccompanied minor migrants, especially in the field of guardianship and recognition of their potential to be victims of trafficking. In this sense, the CRC is a driving force behind the slow changes over the past decades which are evident in the asylum and migration legislation and its implementation across Europe.

Governments are gradually embracing and internalising children's rights within their policies and operations, taking these rights into account in practice when working with unaccompanied minor migrants. Namely, children's rights have a resilient symbolic power which in some views forces states to abide by them. In other words, the responsibility to protect the rights of children has become an evident part of government rationales. Several legal amendments, practical changes and improvements have been introduced in the past decades to asylum and migration policies across Europe. Observation, however, leads one to see that the implementation of the rights of unaccompanied minor migrants is caught in the processes of justification and actualisation of global discourses on children's rights within specific local conditions and continuous negotiations between the meaning of rights and international law on one hand and the national interest on the other. Given this slow and often inadequate response from governments regarding the rights and needs of unaccompanied minors, one can also recognise rights as a notoriously poor instrument for challenging the existing practices and power arrangements in the context of migration law and systems of nation-states.

The power relations manifesting through the implementation of the Convention on the Rights of the Child

The practice in various countries demonstrates that unaccompanied minor migrants are repeatedly exposed to discriminatory treatment by governments in regard to accommodation, care provisions, education, etc. Unaccompanied minor migrants are defined by two fundamental characteristics: first, they are minors and, second, they are either asylum-seeking refugees or economic migrants. Their rights are very much dependent on these factors as each of the two defining characteristics brings with it the potential of some kind of rightlessness (see Chapter 5 in this volume). As I will show in this section, the interpretation and implementation of the rights of unaccompanied minors very much reflects the social power relations stemming from the ideology of nationalism, neoliberalism, bureaucracy and state sovereignty. In order to facilitate this argument, I focus on the questions of age, autonomy, non-discrimination, the best interests of the child and the enforceability of the CRC.

The question of age

The first article of the CRC explains that 'for the purposes of the convention a child is every human being below the age of eighteen years unless under the law applicable to the child, majority is attained earlier'. This means that state parties of the CRC are legally obliged to treat all unaccompanied minor migrants within their jurisdiction as children or young people and provide them additional safeguards and care and appropriate legal protection. It seems that Europeans take their obligations seriously as in the past decades special provisions for unaccompanied minor migrants have been introduced into national migration and asylum policies. In general, European states implement protection measures for minors in accordance with their vulnerability, particularly in the field of legal guardianship, legal representation, accommodation, psychosocial support, detention and repatriation. In practice, however, the restrictiveness of national authorities is revealed as soon as doubt regarding actual age arises; as explained by Bailleul (in Chapter 7 of this volume) more than 50 per cent of the young migrants in France who are initially excluded from the childcare provisions following age assessment regain institutional protection after they appeal and their status as unaccompanied minors is finally recognised.

State authorities attempt to determine the age of minor migrants using various methods including dental, wrist or clavicle X-rays. Problems arise as these methods of age assessment are applied despite the fact that they are unreliable and defined by a wide margin of error (see Chapter 8 in this volume). These mechanisms do not consider the physical variability of children from different social, economic and ethnic backgrounds (Bhabha 2009: 428). The result is that a certain percentage of minor migrants whose age has been disputed are consequently denied the specific protection measures they are entitled to as children. The effect of such policies is problematic from a human rights point of view especially as it prioritises age assessment (and thus the possibility of violating children's rights) over applying the benefit of the doubt (and thus approving child-specific protection to young adults); the young adult migrant will not suffer negative consequences if treated like a child, whereas a child migrant being denied the appropriate protection risks being exposed to unsuitable treatment such as detention and repatriation. Insisting on age assessment rather than applying the benefit of the doubt exhibits the interest of many European states in keeping the number of migrants claiming to be unaccompanied minors as low as possible.

According to the European Migration Network, two-thirds of all asylum-seeking unaccompanied minors from 2009 to 2013 were aged 16–17 years and thus already close to achieving the age of majority. When they reach 18 years of age, the migration status of the individual takes precedence. This has decisive implications in terms of access to rights such as accommodation, education and legality of residence.[2] If a minor has been granted international protection, access to rights does not usually change. When the person in question is a non-asylum-seeking minor, turning 18 years of age without permanent permission to stay, he or she may be treated as an adult migrant with irregular status and may be returned to his or her country of origin. Some countries have introduced measures to support and prepare minors for this transition – for example, moving to new accommodation, individual care or educational plans, or support with the possible return to their country of origin.[3]

In relation to this, it is necessary to focus on the purely formalistic and bureaucratic division between childhood and adulthood. Although used in international law, such an approach does not fulfil the principal aim of children's and human rights law – that is, protection of one's rights, integrity, safety and development. Instead, the formal age division is used in practice as an argument for departure from the obligations set out in the CRC and child protection policies regardless of the actual life circumstances and conditions of each individual. Should a person just over 18, or even 19 or 20 years old, not be protected against detention and repatriation?

This inevitably forces us to question the rigidity of the division between children and adults. How is it possible to determine the boundary between child and adult solely on the basis of turning 18, without also taking into account a person's emotional, psychosocial and physical development as well as his or her world perception, sense of responsibility and capabilities? This is especially relevant in the case of unaccompanied minor migrants who come from various cultural backgrounds and life environments, and have encountered difficult life situations at home, during their migration journey and in the country of destination. For this reason, some young adult unaccompanied migrants should be entitled to greater protection, especially in case of traumatisation due to witnessing or experiencing stressful events. Taking the children's and human rights standpoint, they should all be approached in accordance with their vulnerability, maturity and best interests.

The question of autonomy

Looking at the rights set out in the CRC, one must acknowledge that children's rights as a concept encompass both protection and liberation aspects. A distinction may be observed between children's rights to have their welfare safeguarded by adults (which does not involve children being in control themselves) and children's rights to autonomy and to decide matters for themselves (which involves children as subjects or actors with a set of interests which they can and should define and defend for themselves). There is no straightforward answer as to whether such treatment has more liberating than protective consequences for child right-holders. On the other hand, it is also true that children, including unaccompanied minor migrants, are not a homogeneous group and are not defined by same level of need for autonomy; the needs of a five-year-old child, who is to a great extent dependent on his or her parents, significantly differs from the needs of 17-year-old migrant who might be already rather self-dependent but not yet entirely ready to be on their own.

Although the child acts as a central right-bearer in the Convention, it is stated in its preamble that 'the child, by reason of his physical and mental immaturity, needs special safeguards and care, including appropriate legal protection, before as well as after birth'. The ambivalence about child agency in the CRC is illustrated in provisions which define the child as the competent subject of rights yet needing external advocacy for adequate protection. Even if the child is defined as the holder of the rights set out in the CRC, his or her autonomy is repeatedly moderated through presenting children as persons with limited autonomy according to notions of 'developmentalism', such as the 'evolving capacities of the child' (Alderson, cited in Aitken and Herman 2009: 18). The child as a right-holder is not at the same time also the moral agent who is empowered to act and determine their rights (Pupavac 2001: 99).

Such a stance is problematic from the point of view that it makes rights contingent upon capacity; it prioritises the authority of adults who judge the competency of children and perhaps do so from their own world-view, rather than the child's viewpoint (Aitken and Herman 2009: 18). In a similar manner, Reynolds *et al.* (2006) highlight the contradiction between the child's right to choose and their choice if this choice should clash with what others perceive to be in their best interests. They draw on examples where a child chooses (in response to their circumstances) to live on the streets, live with peers rather than with family, participate in armed conflict, turn to sex work, etc. These decisions may represent conscious choices and demonstrate that a child's wishes can conflict with adults' prevailing conceptions of the child's best interests (Reynolds *et al.* 2006).

Many children, especially unaccompanied minors, are actively and positively engaged in creating a better future for themselves but soon become bound by what others think is in their best interests. In the case that the views and understanding of the child regarding what is in his/her best interest differs from the opinions of adults, there is always the potential that the child will be deemed too immature to know what is in his/her best interests (Aitken and Herman 2009: 18). The same is true for all unaccompanied minors who obviously decided on their best interests before they embarked upon a dangerous migration journey and went in search of better education, employment, safety, etc. European authorities disregard their agency, autonomy, opinion and choice when returning migrants to their home countries, no matter if this is done after they reach the age of majority.

The question in focus here is not the autonomy of a particular child, but rather the closely linked question of child participation offered in the CRC. Article 12 of the CRC may oblige state parties to 'assure to the child who is capable of forming his or her own views the right to express those views freely in all matters affecting the child, the views of the child being given due weight in accordance with the age and maturity of the child'. This is more or less a declarative right which opens a space for adults to decide on the maturity of a child as well as his or her best interests according to adult views. Even if Article 12 provides a right to express views and the right to be heard in any judicial and administrative proceedings, this does not mean that a child has the right to determine his choices and affairs (Pupavac 2001: 99). The rights of a child set out in the CRC imply limited autonomy of underage individuals which could lead to the depersonalisation of children as the objects of adult socialisation; in proposing 'we' know best what is in the best interest of the child, we deny children's rights as well as their right to participate in structuring their childhoods (Mayall 2001: 245). But as Pupavac (2001: 100) interestingly highlights, it is not the power of the adults (e.g. parents) that defines the best interest of a particular child, but the power of institutions, policymakers and professionals, who displace the children and their families as advocates of the child's interests. In this regard, it is important to distinguish 'best interests' from 'stated interests'; the latter consists of what children say they want (Wolozin 2016: 153) and are, in the case of unaccompanied minor migrants, often at odds with what governments and agencies assess and implement as their best interests.

The question of non-discrimination

The lives of unaccompanied minor migrants would be significantly different if governments simply disregarded the fact that they are migrants. They would be treated in the same manner as other underage people. Even if according to the CRC unaccompanied minors should be treated first and foremost as children and not as migrants, this is not the case in practice. Migrant status is one of the most decisive factors for defining the rights and treatment of unaccompanied minors. Most of them are involved in asylum and formal migration processes which determine their rights to a great extent. Because they are migrants, unaccompanied minors may deal with restricted access to the territory of a particular state, restrictions to free movement, long asylum procedures and a lack of child-friendly interview methods. Likewise, because they are migrants they sometimes face limited access to education and the highest attainable standard of health, to an adequate standard of living, to work and leisure activities, etc. The main obstacle to fulfilling their rights is the lack of adequate resident status or nationality, as is the case with undocumented and irregular migrants, trafficked victims and in some cases also asylum seekers. The majority of these situations are unknown and even unimaginable for "national" children. It is through the systematic differentiation between national and foreign children, which seems so obvious and commonsensical today, that states fail to adopt the principle of non-discrimination.

Unaccompanied minor migrants arriving in Europe are usually allowed to enter state territories regardless of whether they meet the entry requirements. Some European states, however, do implement the practice of return at the border. If they apply for asylum, unaccompanied minors gain access to rights, but are at the same time exposed to the uncertainties of the outcome of the asylum application which heavily determines their futures. Non-asylum-seeking minors who do not fulfil the entry conditions may be refused entry and returned to the border immediately or later on in the migration procedures through forced or voluntary return. Some might be allowed a temporary stay under specific conditions. All unaccompanied minors enjoy at best a partial or fractured citizenship, as noted by Bhabha (2009: 415); they may perceive their situation as living between states, so that they can never fully belong where they are. The less fortunate are put in detention despite the fact that Article 37 of the Convention prohibits the deprivation of children's liberty, specifying that 'the arrest, detention or imprisonment of a child shall be in conformity with the law and shall be used only as a measure of last resort and for the shortest appropriate period of time'. Although some states in Europe fulfil this provision accordingly, there are still many countries where the detention of unaccompanied minors is not applied as the last resort but as a regular practice within migration processes.

This confirms that unaccompanied minors are primarily treated as migrants. Although generally protected until they reach the age of majority, unaccompanied minors are well aware that their long-term future plans in their host countries are characterised by a high level of uncertainty. The low percentage of positive asylum decisions, the selectivity of authorised migration and restrictiveness towards irregular migrants severely impact minors' lives and also their decisions. Consider, for example, that up to 50 per cent of unaccompanied migrant children go missing within 48 hours of being placed in certain reception centres in Europe (MCE 2016), or that approximately 60 per cent of unaccompanied minors in France are excluded from institutional care because their age is disputed by authorities (see Chapter 7 in this volume). Additionally, reflect on the numbers of undocumented unaccompanied minors in Europe about whom no official data is available (PICUM 2012) and on the estimations that around 10,000 unaccompanied minors went missing during the refugee crisis in 2015 alone. As exhibited by Bhabha in her account on 'Arendt's children' (2009), such children are faced by rightlessness – that is, living in a liminal space without 'a right to have rights' (Arendt 1962).

It is only through the lens of selective migration policies that we can understand how durable solutions and the best interests of unaccompanied minors are interpreted by governments. As already highlighted, the vital question in regard to the best interests of unaccompanied minor migrants (and other children as well) is who decides what is in the best interests of an individual. Sennovila Hernandez (2011: 151) noted that the authorities in Spain believe that repatriation to their home countries is in the best interests of unaccompanied children and that it complies with the notion of their durable solutions. Although not often realised in practice, it demonstrates the logic of the nation-state authorities, which is generally driven by the objective of controlling migration flows and reducing the numbers of irregular migrants. In a similar vein, a UNICEF (2015) report summarises the perspective of the existing policies, stating that most European countries want asylum seekers whose application has been rejected to return to their country of origin, while some countries also want to make this applicable to children who are in Europe without their families. Their number is hard to estimate but it is assumed that only between 20 and 50 per cent of unaccompanied children are given permanent status in countries such as Belgium, Denmark, the Netherlands, Norway, Sweden and the United Kingdom (UNICEF 2015).

It is true that children's rights laws in some aspects contradict the territorial jurisdiction of the nation-sates and their right to decide on migration policies, but this is the case only when the person in question is still a child. What is problematic in the case of unaccompanied minors is that they do not 'appear' to the state as children to whom rights, obligations and durable solutions are owed. Instead, they are repeatedly regarded as children to whom the state owes only temporary protection, which ceases immediately after the child formally becomes an adult. The protection measures offered to unaccompanied minor migrants are no longer at their disposal as soon as they formally reach the age of majority, in many cases leading to their deportation from the country. Many such children are granted only temporary status which ends when they turn 18. Thereafter they are seen as the transgressors of national borders, uninvited trespassers and deportable aliens who do not have a legitimate basis for the safeguarding of their human rights. In this context it is their migration status that determines their rights, thereby calling into question the right to have rights as a child or a human being. It is because they are migrants and because they (most often) lack regular permanent resident status that their best interests and durable solutions are not far-sighted and do not stretch beyond the age of majority. The result, problematic both in its content and expression, is that nation-states evaluate and determine their international legal obligations mainly through migration and asylum policies – that is, according to the migrant's right to enter the territory of a particular state. In other words, governments mainly operate through the logic of their prerogative to exclude migrants who do not have entry permission, which entirely eclipses the question of state responsibility to protect their human rights.

The question of the best interests of a child

It is intriguing how European governments manoeuvre the concept of the best interests of unaccompanied minor migrants in many ways. It is unquestionably clear that the best interests of the child approach, as set out in the CRC, prioritises the protection of the child's safety, durable solutions and well-being. However, European migration policies and practices evidently show that the best interests of the child are confronted with the 'best interests of the state'. What is in the state's interests? Certainly, it is control of migration and borders and low numbers of asylum seekers and refugees. This is in line with the general myths that prevail in contemporary discourse on migration, where the perception is that refugees are an economic, social and political cost for the host societies; they are perceived as a burden to society to be avoided or at least reduced to a level that has as low an impact on public expenditure as possible.

In the case of unaccompanied minor migrants, 'the best interests of a state' manifest especially through migration law and the standards of removal. For example, in Austria, there were 172 children in detention in 2010; in France, 318 children (in families) were detained pre-removal and 698 unaccompanied children were placed in the border-zone detention centres in 2009. In Slovenia, there were 26 unaccompanied children in the detention centre in 2010, while 1,160 children left detention in the UK in 2009 (ECRE 2011: 34). Only a few EU member states – for example, Hungary, Italy and Ireland – have provisions in their legislation that specifically prohibit the detention of children prior to return. How, then, can governments justify the detention of unaccompanied minor migrants in terms of their best interests? The answer is simple: they do not. Regardless of pursuing their best interests, minor migrants may be detained if they receive a negative decision regarding asylum or a residence permit, if they do not have permission to stay in the county or if the country does not accept responsibility for examining their asylum application according to the Dublin procedures. The reasons used to justify the detention of unaccompanied minor migrants are in fact substantiated in the (best) interests of the state and not of the minor.

From the point of view of children's rights, such policies obviously breach the provisions of the CRC which oblige state authorities to ensure the child protection and care as necessary for his or her well-being. The recent study of the International

Detention Coalition (2012) argues that detention has a profound and negative impact on the well-being of children as it has undesirable consequences on their development and psychological and physical health. Detained children are exposed to circumstances which might lead to depression, anxiety, hopelessness and frustration, and later to violent or self-destructive behaviour. Unaccompanied minor migrants are particularly vulnerable in this regard as detention might aggravate their past traumatic experiences. As reported by the International Detention Coalition, minors express that the detention experience is the worst thing that has happened to them, especially because they are separated from the outside world and do not experience their life as predictable, meaningful and safe. Moreover, detention is exceedingly traumatising for children who are less able to understand explanations as to the reason they have been detained (ibid.). In this respect, detaining unaccompanied minor migrants is apparently used to protect the interest of the state policies regardless of the best interests of a child. Moreover, these procedures are implemented bypassing assessments of the safety and integrity of the child as well as of the possibility of his or her future risk of harm and any other consequences that detention might have for the child's safety and development.

Applying the best interests approach to decision making also means taking into account the child's right to care, protection and safety as well as his or her vulnerability. Governments often regard refugees as an economic and political burden on society and lack the political will to increase public financing to improve reception conditions for immigrants unless absolutely necessary. Unaccompanied minors are no exception in this regard. The neoliberal objectives of the state – to keep the costs of social policies and public expenditure at the lowest possible level – thus result in insufficient support for measures that would adequately respond to the material, educational and emotional needs of unaccompanied minors and their need for affection, safety and a stable environment. The living conditions in reception facilities are often limited or insufficient, evidently showing the lack of political will to comply with the provisions and obligations of the CRC (see Chapter 6 in this volume). The support measures that would contribute to the implementing of the principle of the child's best interests for unaccompanied minor migrants are not at the top of the list of governmental priorities which might lead to maintaining the *status quo* of the inadequate care and protection of unaccompanied minor migrants for several years or even decades.

I would like to draw attention to another view that points to imposing state interest within the implementation of the best interests of a child – that is, the right to family life. As stated in the CRC, a child shall not be separated from his or her parents against their will, except when competent authorities subject to judicial review determine that such separation is necessary for the best interests of the child (CRC Article 9); moreover, the CRC states that in accordance with this obligation, states shall deal with 'applications by a child or his or her parents *to enter or leave* a State Party for the purpose of family reunification [. . .] in a positive, humane and expeditious manner' (CRC Article 10, emphasis added). European governments obviously do not have a problem implementing these provisions when carrying out family reunification by returning unaccompanied minor migrants to their home countries. There seems to be a much greater problem and a lack of interest in guaranteeing family life by reunifying the family in the host society. For instance, the Separated Children in Europe Programme reports in its summer and winter 2016 Newsletters that governments proposed the restriction of family reunification procedures in Cyprus, Denmark and Finland (SCEP 2016a) as well as in Sweden, Norway and Austria (SCEP 2016b).

Unaccompanied minor migrants who cannot return to their home countries for safety reasons may thus face a violation of their right to family life, because governments pursue their interest to control and reduce immigration through procedures of family reunification regardless of what is in the best interests of a child. Preservation of family relations and family reunification is very important for unaccompanied minor migrants. Due to overriding state interests, governments often do not realise that maintaining the separation of a child from his or her parents should only occur as a last resort – that is, when reunification is *not* in the best interest of a child. In all other cases, the family should be reunified either in their home or destination countries.

The question of enforceability and the power of sovereignty

The fundamental rights of unaccompanied minor migrants to protection, which these children have in theory, are often unenforceable in practice. The CRC entrusts the responsibility for monitoring compliance with its provisions to the Committee on the Rights of the Child (the Committee). The Committee does not seek to coerce state parties into complying with the CRC. Instead, it mainly works on the basis of cooperation; it attempts to foster an encouraging and cooperative atmosphere where state parties are not confronted with legally binding and enforceable demands but rather with recommendations and suggestions. As observed by Guilhot (2008: 508), for such reasons international law can hardly be called law, for at best it represents 'positive international morality' without a sufficiently centralised mechanism for its enforcement.

Pursuant to Article 44 of the CRC, state parties oblige themselves to submit periodical reports on the implementation of the Convention to the Committee. The reports are then discussed in open and public meetings of the Committee, during which both the state representatives and Committee members take the floor. Relevant United Nations bodies and agencies, journalists and representatives of non-governmental organisations are also present. The aim of the reporting proceedings is not to enforce changes, but to analyse the achieved progress and identify main difficulties in the implementation of the Convention. As the purpose of the whole process is constructive, it does not legally bind state parties to make changes but puts emphasis on discussing future goals relating to the rights of the child. The Committee designs the concluding observations and assumes that concerns expressed therein will be addressed in a detailed manner by the state party in its next report (see McSweeney 1993). The effectiveness of the Committee is thus limited as it mainly operates on the basis of a structured reporting process and in dialogue with the state parties rather than in a cooperative, methodical and informative manner.

The CRC and the Committee have not given rise to effective mechanisms of judicial protection against state authorities in the international arena, even though this may seem like an obvious function of rights today. Overall, the Committee is powerless to directly enforce compliance with the CRC. While drafting the Convention, negotiators were confronted with the question of whether to set high enforceable standards and risk having a low number of ratifications or to adopt the cooperation model to encourage more states to become parties to the Convention (McSweeney 1993: 482). The negotiators opted for a cooperation model with a proper role to encourage, not compel, compliance with the CRC. Consequently, the UN agencies have limited powers to act in cases of systematic rights violations.

In 2011 the UN General Assembly approved a third Optional Protocol on a communications procedure which introduced the possibility for children to submit individual complaints if they believe their rights as set out in the CRC and its first two Optional Protocols have been violated. The document entered into force in April 2014, but by 2016 there were only 27 state parties and another 28 signatory states to the Protocol. As indicated by Kanics (Chapter 3 in this volume), there has been only one case brought before the Committee, again emphasising the limited enforceability of its final judgments. For this reason it can be concluded that the protection of the rights of the child is highly dependent on the 'human rights culture' in each particular state setting and on the goodwill of each state to cooperate with the Committee. At that level, the legal validity of international law is entirely dependent upon the consent of national governments.

Conclusion

Pointing beyond the instrumentalism of rights as a means of individual protection against the state, the motivation of this chapter was to highlight aspects of the articulation and implementation of children's rights for unaccompanied minor migrants in practice, which reflect the interplay between the 'global' norms of international children's rights law and 'local' migration policies. The analysis focused on particular rationalities, values and norms which decisively impact the implementation and argumentation of children's rights. As I have stated, the responsibility to protect the rights of unaccompanied minor migrants is deeply marked by their status as foreigners in comparison with national children. In many regards they are situated in an unequal position due to the fact that they are migrants.

Despite the criticisms I have presented at the beginning of the chapter, I have tried to show that the CRC and the rights set out therein represent a solid starting point for defending the interests of each child. The power of rights discourse resides in the fact that most of the states undertook to follow and fulfil the principles of international law in domestic legislation and can be held accountable for their actions. Furthermore, international children's rights lay the foundation for the struggle of national NGOs to improve the situation of unaccompanied minor migrants. We have witnessed the introduction of additional protection measures for unaccompanied minor migrants in national migration policies and practices, especially in the last decade, which proves that the discourse of children's rights has the potential to transform the ways in which they are treated by governments. Additionally, many of the unaccompanied minors themselves expressed their aspiration to be protected by the CRC and to be able to put these rights into practice. In this respect, the significance of the CRC in the empowerment of unaccompanied minor migrants cannot be neglected.

As I have shown in this chapter, the rights of the child appear to be very ambiguous, especially when confronted with the interest of a particular state to control migration and reduce the number of irregular immigrants in their territories. To some extent, these rights can be reinterpreted in a manner that does not interfere with 'the best interests of the state'; for example, when the right to family life can be practised only in the country of origin and not also in the country of destination, or when the child's best interests are understood mainly in terms of returning unaccompanied minor migrants to their countries of origin even if the basic conditions for an adequate standard of living are not met, or, even worse, when detaining unaccompanied minor migrants on a regular basis is explained by governments as a measure of last resort. All these examples demonstrate the flexibility of children's rights, which, despite being exactly the same in all CRC signatory states, are implemented differently in each particular setting.

On the other hand, some of the rights of unaccompanied minor migrants are simply ignored by European governments; the principle which practically all states fail to acknowledge is the principle of non-discrimination. To be exact, abiding by this principle would mean that unaccompanied minor migrants are treated primarily as children with particular rights, and not as migrants who, in order to have their rights protected, first need to verify their 'right to be here' through the regular migration processes to which they are all subjected. It might be common sense that minor migrants are treated primarily as migrants; however, this does not speak in favour of the principle of non-discrimination as unaccompanied minor migrants are treated differently from 'national' children just because they happen not to have the 'right' citizenship. What manifests in these relations is the strength of nation-state discourse, according to which each particular state is responsible for protecting only the rights of its citizens and regular residents and not also offering protection to irregular foreigners. One might argue this by highlighting the fact that in some countries forced deportation of unaccompanied minor migrants rarely happens. One must ask, however, whether it is in the interest of the state to protect minors' rights if what actually happens is that they are deported shortly after they reach the age of majority. Clinging to such a bureaucratically justified departure from the obligations of children's rights certainly does not contribute to the better protection of migrants' rights or to a more just world. In the end, it is always the state that determines the rules of the game even if the outcome differs wholly from what unaccompanied minor migrants say they want.

Notes

1 Only three countries have not ratified the Convention: the United States, Somalia and South Sudan.
2 As reported by the European Migration Network, some EU member states might offer support to unaccompanied minor migrants until they reach a certain age (i.e. 21–25 years old), if they are in school, university or employment, or if they are deemed exceptionally vulnerable (Austria, Belgium, Czech Republic, Ireland, Luxembourg, Poland, Sweden, United Kingdom).
3 EU Member States may forcibly return unaccompanied minor migrants. In practice, however, such a procedure is considered on a case-by-case basis and such forced returns are unlikely to take place even where the possibility exists.

Bibliography

Aitken, S. and Herman, T. (2009) *Literature Review on Qualitative Methods and Standards for Engaging and Studying Independent Children in the Developing World.* Available online at www.unicef-irc.org/publications/pdf/iwp_2009_05.pdf (accessed 10 February 2017).

Andre, G. (2015) 'Anthropologists, ethnographers and children's rights: Critiques, resistance and powers', in W. Vandenhole, E. Desmet, D. Reynaert and S. Lembrechts (eds) *Routledge International Handbook of Children's Rights Studies*, New York, NY, and London: Routledge.

Archard, D. (1993) *Children: Rights and Childhood*, New York, NY, and London: Routledge.

Arendt, H. (1962) *Origins of Totalitarianism*, Cleveland. OH, and New York, NY: Meridian Books.

Bhabha, J. (2009) 'Arendt's children: Do today's migrant children have a right to have rights?', *Human Rights Quarterly*, Vol. 31, No. 2, 410–451.

Bourdillon, M. F. C. (2004) 'Children in development', *Progress in Development Studies*, Vol. 4, No. 2, 99–113.

Cowan, J. K. (2006) 'An obligation to "support human rights" unconditionally is misguided moralism', *Anthropology News*, Vol. 47, No. 7, 7.

ECRE (2011) *Comparative Study on Practices in the Field of Return of Minors.* Available online at https://ec.europa.eu/home-affairs/sites/homeaffairs/files/e-library/documents/policies/legal-migration/pdf/general/return_of_children-final.pdf (accessed 7 March 2017).

EMN (2015) *Policies, Practices and Data on Unaccompanied Minors in the EU Member States and Norway.* Available online at https://ec.europa.eu/anti-trafficking/sites/antitrafficking/files/emn_study_2014_uams_0.pdf (accessed 10 February 2017).

Freeman, M. (2007) 'Article 3. The Best Interests of the Child', in A. Alen, J. Vande Lanotte, E. Verhellen, F. Ang, E. Berghmans and M. Verheyde (eds) *A Commentary on the United Nations Convention on the Rights of the Child*, Leiden: Martinus Nijhoff Publishers.

Guilhot, N. (2008) 'Limiting sovereignty or producing governmentality? Two human rights regimes in U.S. political discourse', *Constellations*, Vol. 15, No. 4, 502–516.

Harris-Short, S. (2001) 'Listening to "the other"? The Convention on the Rights of the Child', *Melbourne Journal of International Law*, Vol. 13, No. 2, 304–350.

International Detention Coalition (2012) *Captured Childhood: Introducing a New Model to Ensure the Rights and Liberty of Refugee, Asylum Seeker and Irregular Migrant Children Affected by Immigration Detention*. Available online at http://idcoalition.org/wp-content/uploads/2012/03/Captured-Childhood-FINAL-June-2012.pdf (accessed 7 March 2017).

Jones, P. and Welch, S. (2010) *Rethinking Children's Rights: Attitudes in Contemporary Society*, London and New York, NY: Continuum International Publishing Group.

Mayall, B. (2001) 'The sociology of childhood in relation to children's rights', *The International Journal of Children's Rights*, Vol. 8, No. 3, 243–259.

McSweeney, K. A (1993) 'The potential for enforcement of the United Nations Convention on the Rights of the Child: The need to improve the information base', *Boston College International and Comparative Law Review*, Vol. 16, No. 2, 467–496.

MCE (Missing Children Europe) (2016) *Best practices and key challenges on interagency cooperation to safeguard unaccompanied children from going missing*. Available online at http://missingchildreneurope.eu/Portals/0/Docs/Best%20practices%20and%20key%20challenges%20for%20interagency%20cooperation%20to%20safeguard%20unaccompanied%20migrant%20children%20from%20going%20missing.pdf (accessed 7 March 2017).

OHCHR (2016) *Database of the United Nations Office of Legal Affairs*. Available online at www.ohchr.org/Documents/HRBodies/CRC/OHCHR_Map_CRC-OP-IC.pdf (accessed 10 February 2017).

PICUM (2012) *Undocumented Children: Barriers to Accessing Social Rights in Europe*, presented at UN Committee on the Rights of the Child, Day of General Discussion, Geneva, September 2012. Available online at www.ohchr.org/Documents/HRBodies/CRC/Discussions/2012/Submissions/PICUM.pdf (accessed 10 February 2017).

Pupavac, V. (2001) 'Misanthropy without borders: The international children's rights regime', *Disasters*, Vol. 25, No. 2, 95–112.

Reynaert, D., Desmet, E., Lembrechts, S. and Vandenhole, W. (2015) 'Introduction: A Critical Approach to Children's Rights', in W. Vandenhole, E. Desmet, D. Reynaert and S. Lembrechts (eds) *Routledge International Handbook of Children's Rights Studies*, New York, NY, and London: Routledge.

Return Directive (2008) *Directive 2008/115/ EC of the European Parliament and of the Council on common standards and procedures in Member States for returning illegally staying third-country nationals*. Available online at http://eur-lex.europa.eu/legal-content/EN/TXT/PDF/?uri=CELEX:32008L0115&from=EN (accessed 10 February 2017).

Reynolds, P., Nieuwenhuys, O. and Hanson, K., (2006) 'Refractions of children's rights in development practice: A view from anthropology – Introduction', *Childhood*, Vol. 13, No, 3, 291–302.

SCEP (2016a) *Newsletter No. 45 – Summer 2016*. Available online at www.scepnetwork.org/images/12/296.pdf (accessed 10 February 2017).

SCEP (2016b) *Newsletter No. 44 – Winter 2016*. Available online at www.scepnetwork.org/images/12/291.pdf (accessed 10 February 2017).

Sennovila Hernandez, D. (2011) 'Unaccompanied and Separated Children in Spain: A Policy of Institutional Mistreatment', in J. Bhabha (ed.) *Children Without a State: A Global Human Rights Challenge*, London and Cambridge, MA: MIT Press.

Smith, T. (2004) *Separated Children in Europe: Policies and Practices in European Union Member States: A Comparative Analysis*. Available online at http://scep.sitespirit.nl/images/17/182.pdf (accessed 10 February 2017).

UNCRC (2005) *General Comment No. 6: Treatment of unaccompanied and separated children outside their country of origin*. Available online at www2.ohchr.org/english/bodies/crc/docs/GC6.pdf (accessed 10 February 2017).

UNICEF (2015) *Children's rights in return policy and practice in Europe: A discussion paper on the return of unaccompanied and separated children to institutional reception or family*. Available online at https://ec.europa.eu/anti-trafficking/sites/antitrafficking/files/childrens_rights_in_return_policy_and_practice_in_europe.pdf (accessed 10 February 2017).

White, S. C. (2002) 'From the politics of poverty to the politics of identity? Child rights and working children in Bangladesh', *Journal of International Development*, Vol. 14, No. 6, 725–735.

Wolozin, B. (2016) 'Doing what's best: Determining best interests for children impacted by immigration proceedings', *Drake Law Review*, Vol. 64, 141–188.

3 The best interests of unaccompanied and separated children

A normative framework based on the Convention on the Rights of the Child

Jyothi Kanics

Introduction

Twenty years ago, leading refugee law expert Guy Goodwin-Gill wrote:

> The *Convention on the Rights of the Child* (CRC) uniquely embraces the whole spectrum of children's rights, specifically endorsing the principle of the best interests of the child in a total regime oriented to his or her development and self-fulfilment. Today, the child is subject, not object. International law and international instruments do not alone provide the answers, although the CRC can be used as a model of the achievable, somewhat in the sense of a checklist: a review of its provisions expands the concept of protection, while encouraging focus on the possibilities for effective implementation in any situation of forced migration.
>
> (Goodwin-Gill 1995: 410)

Unfortunately, decades later, much remains to be improved in law, policy and practice to 'expand the concept of protection' for unaccompanied and separated migrant children.

Unaccompanied migrant children are children under 18 years of age outside their country of origin who have been separated from both parents and other relatives and are not being cared for by an adult who, by law or custom, is responsible for doing so (UNCRC 2005: para 7). Similarly, separated children have been separated from both parents, or from their previous legal or customary primary caregiver, but not necessarily from other relatives, and therefore include children accompanied by other adult family members (UNCRC 2005: para 8).

Unaccompanied and separated migrant children have particular needs and special rights under the CRC, regional and national legislation. Yet, as non-nationals, they often face discrimination and violations of their rights. Therefore, it is even more important when aiming for the realisation of their rights to make the best interests of the child a primary consideration in all decisions that may affect the child in order to prevent discrimination, disappearances and exploitation.

The concept of the best interests of the child was introduced well before the drafting of the CRC. For example, it was enshrined in the 1959 *Declaration of the Rights of the Child* (Principle 2 and Principle 7). Yet, even with its inclusion in the CRC, there was neither a precise definition of the concept nor instructions on how to put this important principle into practice. Fortunately, since the adoption of the CRC in 1989 the UN Committee on the Rights of the Child (the Committee) has provided authoritative guidance on the implementation of the principle of the best interests of the child in its General Comments as well as in its recommendations from Days of General Discussion (DGDs) and *Concluding Observations and Recommendations* to States parties.

This chapter will first present a summary of the normative framework at the international level provided in the CRC. It will then examine the role of the Committee as the responsible treaty-monitoring body and in its work concerning the best interests of the child. In particular, the chapter will present authoritative guidance from the Committee that explains how the principle of the best interests of the child should be applied in all measures affecting unaccompanied and separated migrant children. Special attention will be given to the need to identify a durable solution in line with the best interests of each individual child through a formal Best Interests Determination (BID).

The UN Convention on the Rights of the Child and its Protocols

The CRC provides the overarching legal framework for the protection of the rights of all children including unaccompanied and separated migrant children. The CRC is also complemented by its three Optional Protocols, all of which have specific provisions that may be used to strengthen protection for unaccompanied and separated children.

Article 3 of the UN Convention on the Rights of the Child

The CRC is the most widely ratified international treaty, with 196 ratifications since its adoption in November 1989.[1] States parties have agreed to fulfil the rights of the child and every child is entitled to all of the rights in the CRC without exception. The rights of the CRC are intrinsically linked and should be fulfilled in line with the guiding principles of the CRC: the principle of non-discrimination (article 2); the right of the child to be heard and to have his or her views given due weight (article 12); the right to survival and development (article 6); and the principle of the best interests of the child (article 3). Article 3.1 of the CRC states that:

> In all actions concerning children, whether undertaken by public or private social welfare institutions, courts of law, administrative authorities or legislative bodies, the best interests of the child shall be a primary consideration.

As noted above, the best interests of the child is one of the four general principles of the CRC (UNCRC 2003: para 12; UNCRC 2009a: para 2). As a general principle of the Convention, States parties should strive to ensure that the interpretation and implementation of all other rights incorporated in the CRC are guided by it (UNCRC 2009a: para 17). The principle of the best interests of the child has a close relationship with the other general principles of the CRC, which will be described in the following section.

Relation of the best interests of the child to other general principles of the CRC

The non-discrimination principle requires that all the rights guaranteed by the CRC should be recognised for all children within the jurisdiction of States (UNCRC 2005: para 12). This principle not only prohibits all forms of discrimination, but also requires proactive measures to ensure equal treatment and equal opportunities (UNCRC 2013a: para 41). For unaccompanied and separated children, this may include important safeguards and supports such as guardians and interpreters, who can enable them to access and to participate fully in procedures that will assess and determine their best interests.

With regard to the child's right to be heard and to have his or her views given due weight, the Committee has clearly stated that 'there can be no correct application of article 3 if the components of article 12 are not respected' (UNCRC 2009a: para 74). Indeed, this right is inextricably linked with the complementary principle of the best interests of the child (UNCRC 2013a: para 43). In particular, the assessment of the best interests of the child must include respect for the child's right to express their views freely and to have such views given due weight in all matters affecting the child (UNCRC 2013a: para 43).

This means that the State must put in place child-friendly procedures to solicit the views of the child and mechanisms to give due weight to those views (UNCRC 2013a: para 19). Additionally, States should ensure remedies and access to justice through complaints procedures and mechanisms for appeal and redress (UNCRC 2013a: para 47). States must take into consideration not only the age but also the maturity (CRC article 12) and evolving capacities of the child (CRC article 5) when assessing the best interests of the child (UNCRC 2013a: para 44). The greater the maturity of the child, the more weight should be given to his or her views in the assessment of his or her best interests (UNCRC 2013a: para 44).

In order for an unaccompanied and separated child to be able to express an informed view on a matter, he or she should be provided with the assistance of an interpreter when necessary and with child-friendly information concerning his or her 'entitlements, services available including means of communication, the asylum process, family tracing and the situation in their country of origin' (UNCRC 2005: para 25).

Finally, the Committee has underscored the importance of respect for the child's inherent right to life, survival and development in any assessment or formal determination of the child's best interests (UNCRC 2013a: para 42). The safety and security as well as the future development prospects of unaccompanied and separated migrant children are key elements to consider in a BID as will be described below (UNCRC 2013a; UNHCR and UNICEF 2014: 42).

Additional provisions of the CRC with particular relevance for unaccompanied children

In addition to the general principles, it is important to be aware that there are several additional provisions in the CRC that relate to special protection and important rights for separated and unaccompanied children. When making decisions concerning the fulfilment of these rights, States should make the best interests of the child a primary consideration.

According to article 20 of the CRC, children who are deprived of their family environment are entitled to special protection and assistance provided by the State. Such children should be provided with alternative care in accordance with national laws (CRC article 20(2)) and the standards set out in the *UN Alternative Care Guidelines* (UNGA 2010). This means that unaccompanied or separated migrant children should enjoy the same level of protection and care as national children deprived of parental care (UNGA 2010: para 141).

Concerning the treatment of asylum-seeking and refugee children, article 22 of the CRC notably requires States to take appropriate measures to ensure that such children receive appropriate protection and humanitarian assistance in the enjoyment of applicable rights set forth in the CRC and in other international human rights or humanitarian instruments ratified by the State (CRC article 22(1)). States shall cooperate with the UN and international organisations to protect and assist such children as well as to trace the parents and family members of such children (CRC article 22(2)).

With respect to maintaining family contact and facilitating family reunification, articles 9 and 10 of the CRC call on States to respect the right to maintain personal relations and direct contact on a regular basis (CRC article 9(3)) as well as to deal with applications for family reunification in a 'positive, humane and expeditious manner' (CRC article 10(1)). Furthermore, submission of a request for family reunification shall entail no adverse consequences for the applicants and for the members of their family (CRC article 10(1)).

Finally, concerning alternatives to detention, according to article 37 of the CRC, States parties should ensure that no child shall be subjected to torture or other cruel, inhuman or degrading treatment or punishment and that no child shall be deprived of his or her liberty unlawfully or arbitrarily. This provision also includes important safeguards as any detention shall be in conformity with the law and shall be used only as a measure of last resort and for the shortest appropriate period of time. Furthermore, detained children have the right to legal aid and other assistance 'as well as the right to challenge the legality of the deprivation of his or her liberty before a court or other competent, independent and impartial authority, and to a prompt decision on any such action' (CRC article 37).

Provisions of the Optional Protocols to the CRC

The three Optional Protocols to the CRC all contain important provisions that are relevant to the protection of unaccompanied and separated migrant children.

Unfortunately, due to their vulnerability, some unaccompanied children are trafficked for sexual exploitation, transfer of organs, forced labour or other abuses. *The Optional Protocol on the sale of children, child prostitution and child pornography* (OPSC) includes provisions to criminalise and to punish offences related to those acts as well as measures to protect the rights of child victims. It stresses that the bests interests of the child victim shall be a primary consideration in the child's treatment by the criminal justice system (OPSC article 8(3)).

The *Optional Protocol on the involvement of children in armed conflict* (OPAC) includes provisions that require States parties to accord children affected by armed conflict 'all appropriate assistance for their physical and psychological recovery and their social reintegration' (OPAC article 6) including through technical cooperation and financial assistance (OPAC article 7). These provisions are important for many unaccompanied migrant children who become separated from their families in the context of or fleeing from armed conflict. In reviewing the implementation of this Protocol as well as articles 38 and 39 of the CRC, the Committee has drawn attention to the need to identify former child soldiers and other children affected by conflict not only in their regions of origin but also in the countries where they seek asylum (UNCRC 2015a: para 54(b)), and to ensure that they receive rehabilitation and integration support.

The Optional Protocol to the CRC on a Communications Procedure (OPIC), which entered into force in April 2014, has already been ratified by 29 States and signed by 27 more.[2] This Protocol establishes new possibilities for unaccompanied and separated children and those advocating on their behalf to challenge violations of their rights and to ensure respect for and consideration of their best interests. The communication procedure enables children to bring complaints about violations of their rights to the Committee on the Rights of the Child, if they have not been able to secure a remedy at the national level (OPIC article 7(e)). The Committee can hear complaints made by or on behalf of individual children or groups of children against any State that has ratified OPIC. The Committee is also able to launch investigations into grave or systematic violations of children's rights. Finally, States are able to submit communications to the Committee concerning alleged violations of children's rights by other States when the State concerned has accepted the inter-State communications procedure as outlined in the Protocol (OPIC article 12). For example, a State might raise concerns about the treatment of unaccompanied children who are its nationals and who have migrated to another country.

The work of the Committee on the Rights of the Child

This section outlines the main activities of the Committee on the Rights of the Child and how this work has resulted in greater awareness of and further guidance concerning the best interests of unaccompanied and separated migrant children. Through its General Comments as well as its *Concluding Observations and Recommendations* to States parties, the Committee advises governments on how to fully respect and fulfil children's rights including the rights of the most vulnerable and marginalised.

The Committee publishes its interpretation of the content of child rights provisions and provides authoritative guidance on the implementation of the CRC in its General Comments on thematic issues. The Committee sheds light on the meaning and fulfilment of the best interests principle in its *General Comment No. 14 (2013) on the right of the child to have his or her best interests taken as a primary consideration (art. 3, para 1)*. In *General Comment No. 14*, the Committee distinguishes the best interests of the child as a threefold concept (UNCRC 2013a: para 6):

a A substantive right: Every child has the right to have his or her best interests assessed and taken as a primary consideration in every decision that may affect him or her. This right is directly applicable and can be invoked before a court.
b A fundamental, interpretative legal principle: 'If a legal provision is open to more than one interpretation, the interpretation which most effectively serves the child's best interests should be chosen' (UNCRC 2013a: para 6).
c A rule of procedure*:* Strict procedural guarantees are required whenever a decision may affect a child. The decision-maker must assess both the positive and negative possible impacts on the child concerned. The decision should be provided in a written reasoned statement including justification demonstrating how the best interests of the child have been taken into account. In particular, it should be made clear which criteria were assessed to determine the best interests and how the best interests have been weighed against other considerations.

In addition to *General Comment No. 14*, the Committee has issued other General Comments that provide guidance that relates to the framework for ensuring respect for the rights and best interests of unaccompanied and separated children. When considering the overall child protection system, this includes *General Comment No. 2 on the role of independent national human rights institutions in the promotion and protection of the rights of the child* (2002) and *General Comment No. 5, General measures of implementation of the Convention on the Rights of the Child* (2003). Most recently, the Committee has also adopted *General Comment No. 19 (2016) on public budgeting for the realization of children's rights (art. 4)*, which makes recommendations on how to realise all children's rights through 'effective, efficient, equitable, transparent and sustainable public budget decision-making' (UNCRC 2016a: para 1). Finally, with regard to procedural safeguards, *General Comment No. 12 (2009) on the right of the child to be heard* provides detailed guidance. Finally, *General Comment No. 6 on the treatment of unaccompanied and separated children outside their country of origin* addresses many issues specific to the identification, reception and care of such children as well as concerning the identification and implementation of a durable solution that will end the child's cycle of displacement, discrimination and neglect.

In addition to the guidance it provides in General Comments, as noted above, since the adoption of the third Optional Protocol to the CRC, the Committee may consider complaints alleging violations of the CRC or the OPAC and OPSC by States parties to the OPIC. As separated and unaccompanied children often face barriers in accessing justice due to discrimination as well as their lack of legal capacity, this procedure may allow their representative to bring a complaint at the international level when they have been unable to secure a remedy at the national level.

Notably, the first and only complaint (UNCRC 2014a) considered by the Committee thus far concerned an individual who claimed to be an unaccompanied Ghanaian child who had been denied protection from the Spanish authorities following an allegedly unreliable age assessment procedure. Unfortunately, the case was deemed inadmissible by the Committee because the events had occurred before the Protocol came into force in Spain (OPIC article 7(g)).

Furthermore, unaccompanied and separated children may also bring complaints to other UN treaty-monitoring bodies. For example, unaccompanied children have brought complaints to the Human Rights Committee in the past and claimed specific violations against their best interests. For example, in the case of X.H.L. (UNHRC 2011) the Committee decided that the Dutch government's decision to return the child to China violated his rights under the Covenant, specifically article 24 concerning the child's right to protection and article 7 which prohibits torture and cruel, inhuman or degrading treatment or punishment. Unfortunately, the Dutch government refused to take any measures that would give effect to the Committee's views, but the decision has been used in follow-up advocacy work at the national and international level.

In addition, the Committee currently organises Days of General Discussion (DGDs) biannually. The purpose of the DGDs is to foster a deeper understanding of the contents and implications of the Convention as they relate to specific articles or topics. For example, the best interests of migrant children were a focus of the 2012 DGD on the rights of all children in the context of international migration. Other special DGDs have addressed issues relevant for unaccompanied and separated children, such as the 2006 DGD on the child's right to be heard. Interested individuals or organisations are invited to make written submissions in preparation for each DGD and there is the possibility to register to participate, which is then confirmed by the Secretariat to the Committee.

Finally, as part of its mandate the Committee monitors States parties' compliance and implementation of the CRC. Following the reporting and dialogue with the State party, the Committee issues specific *Concluding Observations and Recommendations* in order to guide the State party in its future efforts to meet its obligations under the CRC.

The Committee regularly notes concern that States parties have not yet applied the principle of the best interests of the child as a primary consideration in all areas affecting children including in matters affecting unaccompanied and separated migrant children such as asylum and immigration legislation and decision-making procedures (UNCRC 2012c and 2013b).

The Committee has noted a lack of awareness of the principle as well as gaps in its application. For example, it has expressed concern

> that the principle of the best interests of the child is not widely known, appropriately integrated and consistently applied in all legislative, administrative

> and judicial proceedings and in policies, programmes and projects relevant to and with an impact on children. In this context, the Committee is particularly concerned at the inadequate understanding and application of the principle of the best interests of the child in asylum-seeking, refugee and/or immigration detention situations.
>
> (UNCRC 2012c: para 31)

Furthermore, the Committee has often expressed concern that 'those responsible for taking the child's best interests into account are not always sufficiently trained to conduct a thorough case-by-case assessment of the best interests of the affected child' (UNCRC 2010a: para 22).

The Committee's *Concluding Observations and Recommendations* are a very useful tool for monitoring and advocacy work. In between Committee sessions, civil society at the national level uses the *Recommendations* for targeted advocacy work. Progress on the *Recommendations* is then normally reviewed in subsequent sessions between the State party and the Committee. In this way, the Committee's work contributes to changes in law and practice at the national level that promote the full implementation of the CRC.

Authoritative guidance regarding putting the best interests into practice

Guidance from *General Comments* as well as *Recommendations* from the Committee's DGD reports and *Concluding Observations* and *Recommendations* to States parties are reflected in the section below and explain in great detail how the principle of the best interests of the child may be operationalised in practice to better protect unaccompanied and separated children.

Principles of the Convention

In its *Concluding Observations and Recommendations*, the Committee systematically comments on the implementation of the principles of the CRC. In doing so, they have specifically noted the interrelated nature of the general principles and the importance of the best interests of the child.

In this regard, the Committee has emphasised the principle of non-discrimination and reminded States parties that the rights enshrined in the CRC should be guaranteed to all unaccompanied and separated children, be they asylum-seeking, refugee or migrant children and irrespective of their nationality, immigration status or statelessness (UNCRC 2005: para 12).

With regard to the child's rights to be heard, the Committee has stressed that the analysis of the unaccompanied child's individual circumstances should bear in mind both the best interests of the child and the child's right to be heard (UNCRC 2010b). Additionally, the Committee often refers to its *General Comment No. 14* and reminds States parties of the obligation to provide for remedies in cases of violation of the right to be heard (UNCRC 2014c).

The Committee also addresses the child's right to life, survival and development throughout its *Concluding Observations* and *Recommendations.* This principle and the child's right to maximum development are particularly linked with rights such as the right to health and the right to an adequate standard of living as well as the right to education and the right to play. Unaccompanied and separated children often face discrimination and barriers in exercising and realising such rights. Additionally, article 6 also includes protection from violence and exploitation such as trafficking, which disproportionately affects unaccompanied migrant children (UNCRC 2005: para 23). With this in mind, the Committee makes *Recommendations* to States parties to prevent trafficking and to strengthen protection for trafficked children.

CRC General Measures of Implementation

Article 4 of the CRC requires States parties to undertake all appropriate legislative, administrative and other measures for the implementation of the rights recognised in the CRC. This provision allows States to fulfil children's economic, social and cultural rights to the maximum extent of their available resources and, where needed, encourages States to do so within the framework of international cooperation. In *General Comment No. 5*, *General Comment No. 2* and *General Comment No. 19* the Committee specifies in great detail which General Measures of Implementation States should take and how they should be fulfilled.

The Committee has repeatedly drawn attention to how CRC General Measures of Implementation can advance respect for the best interests of the child – for example, by stressing that States parties strengthen measures to raise awareness of the meaning and practical application of the principle of the best interests of the child (UNCRC 2015a). For example, the Committee has recommended:

> that the State party strengthen its efforts to ensure that the right of the child to have his or her best interests taken into account as a primary consideration, is appropriately integrated and consistently applied in all legislative, administrative and judicial proceedings as well as in all policies, programmes and projects relevant to and with an impact on children, particularly those deprived of a family environment, or in asylum-seeking, refugee and/or in immigration situations, including detention. In this regard, the State party is encouraged to develop procedures and criteria to provide guidance for determining the best interests of the child in every area related to children, and to disseminate this to the public, including Social Work Centres, courts of law, administrative authorities and legislative bodies.
>
> (UNCRC 2013c: para 29)

With regard to legislative reform measures, article 3 of the Convention should be duly reflected in its legislation and administrative measures (UNCRC 2015a). The Committee has recommended that States parties introduce the right of the child to have his or her best interests taken into account as a primary consideration in its Constitution (UNCRC 2013c: para 29). Furthermore, the Committee has advocated that 'States should make clear in their legislation, policy, and practice that the principle of the child's best interests takes priority over migration and policy or other administrative considerations' (UNCRC 2012a: para 73). Specifically, the Committee has urged States parties to bring immigration and asylum laws into full conformity with the CRC and 'to ensure that its migration and asylum legislation and procedures have the best interests of the child as the primary consideration in all immigration and asylum processes' (UNCRC 2012c: para 81).

The Committee also recommends that the States parties 'undertake mandatory child rights impact assessments to determine the impact of any proposed policy, legislative, regulatory, budget, international cooperation or other administrative decision which affects children and their enjoyment of their rights' (UNCRC 2013a, 2015a and 2016b). The results of such child rights impact assessments should be made publicly available and include recommendations for amendments, alternatives and improvements (UNCRC 2013a: para 99).

With regard to training, the Committee recommends that States parties 'train asylum and migration officials in the application of the legislation governing asylum and complementary protection, including training in taking into consideration child-specific forms of persecution' (UNCRC 2011a: para 68). The Committee also recommends that States elaborate practicable directions for how to operationalise the best interests principle and train all those involved in the determination of the best interests of a child (UNCRC 2010a: para 23). The determination of the best interests of the child should be 'consistently conducted by professionals who have been adequately trained on best-interests determination procedures' (UNCRC 2012c: para 81). While the implementation of the Committee's *Recommendations* in this regard may depend on the State's commitment to children's rights and its available resources, specific *Recommendations* offer the possibility for civil society, including international organisations, to follow up and to advocate for necessary legislative reform and improved training measures as well as to offer the necessary training to relevant State authorities.

General Comment No. 2 highlights the potential role of national human rights institutions such as national ombudspersons for children in monitoring and addressing the situation of unaccompanied and separated migrant children. In line with the principle of non-discrimination, such institutions should be accessible to all children and should proactively reach out to the most vulnerable and disadvantaged such as refugee and migrant children as well as children in detention (UNCRC 2002: para 15). National legislation should ensure the right of such institutions to have access in conditions of privacy to children in all forms of alternative care including detention (UNCRC 2002: para 15).

Furthermore, *General Comment No. 2* recognises that children's rights issues are not constrained by national borders and that it is necessary for national human rights institutions to devise appropriate regional and international responses to issues such as the situation of refugee and migrant children. Exchange of experience and good practice can strengthen common positions and contribute to resolving problems at both the national and regional levels (UNCRC 2002: para 29).

Safeguards and Best Interests Assessments

The framework below follows the typical journey of an unaccompanied or separated child and draws upon the process outlined in the *Statement of Good Practice* (SCEP 2009) of the Separated Children in Europe Programme, which provides further references and guidance for international obligations and standards in this field.

At the 2012 DGD on the rights of all children in the context of international migration, the Committee recommended that:

> States should conduct individual assessments and evaluations of the best interests of the child at all stages of and decisions on any migration process affecting children, and with the involvement of child protection professionals, the judiciary as well as children themselves.
>
> (UNCRC 2012a: para 72)

Therefore, during all phases of the child's displacement cycle, their best interests must be taken as a primary consideration (UNCRC 2005: para 19).

Best Interests Assessments (BIA) should be undertaken for every decision that may affect the child such as deciding on a care placement or whether to initiate family tracing. A BIA describes a simple procedure for making decisions about immediate actions such as which care interventions are in an individual child's best interests (UNHCR and UNICEF 2014: 20). The child should be consulted and additional information should be gathered as needed by professionals with the required expertise, knowledge and skills in child protection (UNHCR and UNICEF 2014: 20). Applying the best interests principle should start with the first encounter with a child, which may in many cases occur at the border. The Committee's guidance has expressly addressed the importance of access to territory and appropriate reception for at-risk migrant children. While many unaccompanied and separated children are first encountered on the territory or when making an application for asylum, some are also intercepted or identified at State borders. Therefore, child protection measures should begin at the border and there must be a BIA to decide whether to allow the child access to the territory. For an unaccompanied child, such a BIA would likely result in a decision to allow access to the territory in order to carry out a more thorough assessment of the child's situation. In this regard, the Committee has stressed that 'State obligations under the Convention apply within the borders of a State, including with respect to those children who come under the State's jurisdiction while attempting to enter the country's territory' (UNCRC 2005: para 12).

Another important step to ensure protection for children is registration. The Committee's guidance has expressly addressed the importance of access to territory, registration, documentation and appropriate reception for at-risk migrant children. As soon as possible, a guardian should be appointed for every unaccompanied and separated child. In its *Recommendations*, the Committee has emphasised that the timely appointment of a trained guardian upon the child's arrival or identification can be a practical and appropriate measure for preventing disappearances (UNCRC 2011b: para 58(b) and UNCRC 2015a: para 50(d)). Therefore, the guardian should be appointed as soon as the child is identified (UNCRC 2005: paras 24 and 33). Furthermore, the guardian serves as a key procedural safeguard to ensure respect for the best interests of an unaccompanied or separated child (UNCRC 2005: para 21) throughout various procedures from any initial procedures such as age assessment through to decisions concerning international protection procedures and the identification of a durable solution.

Additionally, children should receive the support of free legal aid in order to be advised on their legal options and assisted through any necessary procedures. The Committee provides clear guidance in its *General Comment No. 6*, stating that unaccompanied and separated children, who are involved in asylum procedures or any other proceedings, should be provided with timely and free access to legal assistance and assigned a qualified legal representative in addition to a guardian (UNCRC 2005: paras 36, 63 and 69). The Committee notes that in particular this includes cases where unaccompanied and separated children are deprived of their liberty as well as cases where their asylum application may be processed under the normal procedure for adults (UNCRC 2005: paras 63 and 69).

Respecting the best interests of the child means that age assessment procedures should not be mandatory for every individual, but rather only carried out in cases of doubt where the individual's age is disputed. Such measures should be conducted in a child- and gender-sensitive manner with respect for human dignity, avoiding any risk to the physical integrity of the individual (UNCRC 2005: para 31). The best interests principle should ensure that any margin of error is recognised and applied in the favour of the individual and that the individual is given the benefit of the doubt and treated as a child in case of any remaining uncertainty (UNCRC 2005: para 31).

With regard to reception standards and alternative care arrangements, it is never in the best interests of unaccompanied and separated children to be subjected to immigration detention (UN Human Rights Council 2015: para 80). This is because detention can have extremely negative effects on a child's physical and psychological well-being and further increase their vulnerability (UNHCR Executive Committee 2007). Following its 2012 DGD on Migration, the Committee strongly recommended that States should expeditiously and completely cease the detention of children on the basis of their immigration status (UNCRC 2012a: para 78). The Committee has also urged States around the world to end the immigration detention of children in its recent *Concluding Observations and Recommendations.* Additionally, the Committee has highlighted the role of consular services abroad in monitoring detention and assisting those detained as well as recommended that States take measures to end the administrative detention of children awaiting repatriation (UNCRC 2015e: para 76(b)).

The choice of a care placement for an unaccompanied and separated child should be subject to a BIA and meet the standards of article 20 of the CRC. In particular, 'due regard shall be paid to the desirability of continuity in a child's upbringing and to the child's ethnic, religious, cultural and linguistic background' (CRC article 20). As with national children placed in care, unaccompanied and separated migrant children also have the right to a periodic review of the treatment provided to them and to all other circumstances relevant to the care placement (CRC article 25). Family tracing, re-establishing family links and carrying out a family assessment are essential components in the search for a durable solution for an unaccompanied child and should be prioritised unless it is not in the child's best interests or would endanger the child or those being traced (UNCRC 2005: para 80).

With regard to access to services, unaccompanied and separated children should have the same access to healthcare as national children (CRC article 2 and 24; UNCRC 2005: para 46). During the DGD on the rights of children in the context of international migration, the Committee recommended that States should ensure adequate and accessible measures for addressing trauma experienced by children during migration including specialised care and mental health services (UNCRC 2012a: para 89). This is also in line with article 39 of the CRC, according to which States have a duty to provide rehabilitation services to children who have been victims of any form of abuse, neglect, exploitation, torture, cruel, inhuman and degrading treatment or armed conflicts. For unaccompanied migrant children, it is crucial that such services are culturally appropriate and gender sensitive in order to facilitate recovery and reintegration (UNCRC 2005: para 48).

All children have the right to free primary education. The Committee further affirms that States should ensure access to education without discrimination during all phases of the displacement cycle to all children including those with special needs and disabilities (UNCRC 2005: para 41). It is also in the best interests of most children to continue their education and to have access to opportunities for skills building. As many unaccompanied and separated children are above the age of obligatory schooling, it is important to stress that States should ensure access (UNCRC 2005: para 40) to vocational and professional training to adolescents (UNCRC 2005: para 42).

Finally, provision of social assistance may be necessary to ensure that children are able to have an adequate standard of living. This is particularly true for unaccompanied and separated children, who do not have a family to support them and who may not be allowed to work. The Committee has recommended to States that they raise family and child allowances and benefits to correlate with the cost of living including for asylum-seeking, refugee and migrant children (UNCRC 2015b: para 65 and UNCRC 2016c: para 66(c)).

Special measures for child victims of trafficking

Child victims of trafficking are most often unaccompanied children whose separation from family has made them vulnerable to exploitation. The Committee has specifically recommended that States parties to

> enhance the efforts to raise awareness and competency of family court judges and prosecutors on existing national and international standards as well as on how to respect the best interests of the child in the legal proceedings relevant to human trafficking, taking into consideration the specific protection needs of child victims of trafficking.
>
> (UNCRC 2015d: para 51(c))

With respect to National Action Plans to address trafficking in human beings, the Committee has called on States parties to integrate 'comprehensive measures to identify, protect and support child victims of trafficking which reflect their best interests and special needs' (UNCRC 2015d: para 51(d)). The Committee has also addressed the risk of re-trafficking for vulnerable children and urged States parties to take due consideration of the best interests of the child to ensure 'that children in need of international protection and at risk of being re-trafficked, are not returned to the country where this danger exists' (UNCRC 2009b: para 86(d)). Such risks and protection responses are also noted in the *UNHCR Trafficking Guidelines* (UNHCR 2006: para 19), which advise that the best interests principle should be scrupulously applied when assessing claims for international protection from trafficked children (UNHCR 2006: para 20).

Determination of international protection needs and the asylum procedure

Unaccompanied and separated children may be fleeing forms of child-specific persecution or situations of conflict such as civil war. Child-specific forms of persecution include: under-age recruitment, female genital mutilation, domestic violence, forced or under-age marriage, child trafficking and hazardous forms of child labour (UNHCR 2009: para 178). For these children, it may be deemed in their best interests to make an application for asylum or international protection on humanitarian grounds.

The Committee has raised concerns with States parties when relevant laws in this field do not include gender-related persecution as a legitimate ground for asylum and when laws do not reflect the principle of the best interests of the child (UNCRC 2011a: para 67). The Committee has stressed that States should take account of manifestations of persecution experienced by children (UNCRC 2011a: paras 15–17) when assessing claims for refugee status (UNCRC 2005: para 74). Such an assessment should of course be made on a case-by-case basis (UNCRC 2005: para 72) as with any assessment of the child's best interests (UNCRC 2013a: paras 32, 39 and 48).

The Committee has criticised the situation where some States only provide such children with a temporary subsidiary form of protection (UNCRC 2013c: para 67(c)) that does not ensure a durable solution and future stability for the child's development. Instead, applications for international protection for unaccompanied and separated children should be prioritised and States should carry out a thorough process in which the best interests of the child is a primary consideration (UNCRC 2013c: para 67(c); 2011b: para 35; 2011a: para 68(a); 2012c: para 32; 2015a). Such procedures should result in information gathering and a decision that will inform the subsequent choice of durable solution for the child (SCEP 2009: 32).

Best interests determinations and durable solutions

When considering the situation of migrant children, the Committee has recommended: 'In particular, primary consideration should be given to the best interests of the child in any proceeding resulting in the child's or their parents' detention, return or deportation' (UNCRC 2012a: para 72). Indeed, it is particularly important to consider the best interests of the child when aiming to identify a durable solution for a separated or unaccompanied child. A durable solution in the case of an unaccompanied and separated child has been defined as:

> a sustainable solution that ensures that the unaccompanied or separated child is able to develop into adulthood, in an environment which will meet his or her needs and fulfil his or her rights as defined by the CRC and will not put the child at risk of persecution or serious harm.
>
> (UNHCR and UNICEF 2014:22)

Therefore, a durable solution encompasses a broader concept of child rights-based protection in comparison with the traditionally narrow refugee definition. It is not only aiming to identify international protection needs and to secure a legal residence status for the child, but it is also concerned with long-term care arrangements and prospects for the child's future development.

As identifying a durable solution is a significant decision that will have a fundamental impact on a child's future development prospects, it requires a Best Interests Determination (BID). A BID is a formal procedure with strict procedural safeguards such as a written reasoned decision and the right to appeal the decision with the assistance of legal aid.

Notably, UNHCR's Executive Committee recommends in its *Conclusion No. 107 on Children at Risk* that States, UNHCR and other relevant agencies and partners:

> Within the framework of the respective child protection systems of States, utilize appropriate procedures for the determination of the child's best interests which facilitate adequate child participation without discrimination: where the views of the child are given due weight in accordance with age and

> maturity; where decision makers with relevant areas of expertise are involved; and where there is a balancing of all relevant factors in order to assess the best option.
>
> (UNHCR Executive Committee 2007: para (g))

In recent years, the Committee has called on States parties to 'create a national BID procedure that is complemented by procedural safeguards, in order to guide public and private institutions and administrative authorities in their actions affecting third-country national children' (UNCRC 2012e: para 63(c)).

Minimum procedural guarantees and criteria for a BID

As noted above, the best interests principle is a rule of procedure and in this regard the Committee has recommended that States guarantee due process in legislation, policies, measures and practices including in all migration procedures and judicial proceedings that may affect migrant children (UNCRC 2012a: para 75). In addition to the procedural safeguards listed below, this also means that unaccompanied and separated children should have 'access to administrative and judicial remedies against decisions in order to guarantee that all decisions are taken in their best interests' (UNCRC 2012a: para 75).

As stressed in *General Comment No. 14*, a BID is a formal procedure that requires strict procedural safeguards (UNCRC 2013a: para 47). Such safeguards include a professional, independent guardian, legal aid and an interpreter as well as child-friendly procedures that enable meaningful child participation, mechanisms for complaint, written reasoned decision and the right to appeal (UNHCR and UNICEF 2014: 16; UNCRC 2013a: paras 85–99).

The written legal reasoning of all judicial and administrative decisions should be based on the principle of the best interests of the child, specifying the criteria used in the individual assessment (UNCRC 2012d: para 35). The criteria or elements (UNHCR and UNICEF 2014: 42; UNCRC 2013a: paras 52–79) considered in a BID will vary case by case, but should include the care, protection and safety of the child; situation of vulnerability; child's views; child's identity; parent or (current) caregiver's views; preservation of the family environment, maintaining or restoring relationships; child's right to health; and access to education.

In weighing these different elements, it is critical to bear in mind that the purpose of determining the best interests of the child is 'to ensure the full and effective enjoyment of the rights recognized in the Convention and its Optional Protocols, and the holistic development of the child' (UNCRC 2013a: para 82). As already mentioned, the Committee also notes that the more mature the child, the more weight should be given to his or her views in determining his or her best interests (UNCRC 2013a: para 44).

Family reunification

As noted above, one aspect of the BID is to consider which custodial and care arrangements will be most appropriate for the child in the future. Therefore, the

BID should consider whether family reunification is possible, under which conditions and whether it would be in the best interests of the child. In line with article 10 of the CRC, the Committee has recommended that States parties 'ensure that the family reunification procedure is dealt within a positive, humane and expeditious manner, taking into account the best interests of the child' (UNCRC 2012b: para 46(b)). When family reunification in the country of origin is decided not to be in the best interests of the child because this would lead to a violation of the child's rights, or when there are legal obstacles to return, the host country should fulfil its obligations under articles 9 and 10 of the CRC and facilitate family reunification on their territory (UNCRC 2005: paras 82–83).

Integration in the host country

When a BID recommends that a child should remain in the host country, measures should be taken to foster their integration. Integration should be based on a secure legal status (UNCRC 2005: para 89). Therefore, States should provide possibilities for unaccompanied children to regularise their residence status when this would be in their best interests (UNCRC 2012a: para 84). The Committee has recommended that States ensure in law and practice that 'the best interests of the child will always be of paramount consideration in deciding on residence permits for foreigners' (UNCRC 2012a: para 84). Finally, unaccompanied and separated children who are stateless should have access to facilitated naturalisation and be assisted to realise their right to acquire a nationality (CRC article 7).

Return to country of origin or third-country resettlement or transfer

Return should only take place when it is determined to be in the best interests of the child (UNCRC 2005: para 84). If there is a risk that return will result in a violation of the fundamental rights of the child concerned, then return is not an option (UNCRC 2005: para 84). In this regard, the Committee has raised concerns about expulsions and recommended that all necessary measures be taken to prevent irregular procedures in the expulsion of unaccompanied children (UNCRC 2010b: para 60(a)). Furthermore, States are urged to respect the principle of non-refoulement (UNCRC 2015a: para 50) and to establish safeguards against refoulement as well as child- and gender-sensitive procedures for decision making in cases concerning unaccompanied and separated children (UNCRC 2014b: para 62).

However, the Committee acknowledges that in rare cases other rights-based considerations may outweigh the best interests of the child and result in a decision to return the child. In its *General Comment No. 6*, the Committee provides clear guidance:

> Exceptionally, a return to the home country may be arranged, after careful balancing of the child's best interests and other considerations, if the latter are rights-based and override best interests of the child. Such may be the case

> in situations in which the child constitutes a serious risk to the security of the State or to the society. Non rights-based arguments such as those relating to general migration control, cannot override best interests considerations.
>
> (UNCRC 2005: para 86)

Still, in any case of return, the Committee emphasises that concrete care arrangements and custodial responsibilities must be in place in the country of return prior to the child's return (UNCRC 2005: para 85). States should also respect the best interests of the child when they carry out the return and should ensure this by signing bilateral agreements containing appropriate safeguards (UNCRC 2011a: para 68(c)). Protocols between States for the voluntary return of migrant children should contain guarantees of due process (UNCRC 2015c: para 64(b)).

Conclusion

When the concept of the best interests of the child was included as a general principle in the CRC, there remained much debate about its meaning and scope as well as about how it should be applied in practice. Fortunately, the Committee on the Rights of the Child has worked to address this gap in understanding and has devoted its attention to elaborating relevant guidance such as its *General Comment No. 14*. Additionally, the Committee continues to provide specific targeted *Recommendations* both on advancing the best interests of the child and on improving protection for unaccompanied and separated children in its detailed *Concluding Observations and Recommendations* to States parties. Currently, the Committee is drafting a new *Joint General Comment on the human rights of children in the context of international migration* together with the Committee on the Rights of Migrant Workers. The Committees have affirmed that, as a substantive right, legal principle and rule of procedure, the best interests of the child will be applied to the analysis and interpretation of all the themes to be addressed by the *Joint General Comment*.[3] Child rights advocates can use such principled and practical guidance to make further progress in their efforts to advocate for and to monitor protection for unaccompanied and separated children.

However, there remain many gaps between the obligations found in the international normative framework and State practices. As the implementation of the CRC varies greatly from country to country, advocacy and monitoring efforts are crucial to addressing these remaining gaps and challenges. With regard to the international legal framework, there is a need for continued advocacy to encourage States parties to remove reservations to the CRC, especially those that specifically affect migrant children such as reservations to the non-discrimination principle or to provisions relating to family reunification. There are also significant challenges with regard to the establishment and functioning of BID procedures in industrialised countries, where asylum and children protection systems are often quite developed and working in separate silos. It is hoped that, based on the guidance from the Committee, States will begin to bridge this gap and to establish a more multidisciplinary approach to determining the best interests of the child within existing procedures. Courts will also continue to play a key role in safeguarding the best interests of unaccompanied and separated children in many jurisdictions (OHCHR and UNICEF 2012).

Notes

1 https://treaties.un.org/Pages/showDetails.aspx?objid=08000002800007fe (accessed 15 February 2017).
2 As of 9 October 2016: https://treaties.un.org/Pages/ViewDetails.aspx?src=TREATY&mtdsg_no=IV-11-d&chapter=4&clang=_en (accessed 15 February 2017).
3 Committee on the Rights of the Child, *Concept Note for CMW-CRC Joint General Comment on the Human Rights of Children in the Context of International Migration*, available at http://tbinternet.ohchr.org/_layouts/treatybodyexternal/Download.aspx?symbolno=CRC/CMW General Comment&Lang=en (accessed 15 February 2017).

Bibliography

Goodwin-Gill, G. (1995) 'Unaccompanied refugee minors: The role and place of international law in the pursuit of durable solutions,' *International Journal of Children's Rights*, Vol. 3, 405–416.

OHCHR and UNICEF (2012) *Judicial Implementation of Article 3 of the Convention on the Rights of the Child in Europe: The case of migrant children including unaccompanied children*. Available online at www.refworld.org/docid/5135ae842.html (accessed 15 February 2017).

Separated Children in Europe Programme (SCEP) (2009) *Statement of Good Practice*. Available online at www.scepnetwork.org/p/1/91/translations-statement-of-good-practice (accessed 15 February 2017).

UN Committee on the Rights of the Child (UNCRC) (2002) *General Comment No. 2: The role of independent national human rights institutions in the promotion and protection of the rights of the child*, 15 November 2002, CRC/GC/2002/2. Available online at http://tbinternet.ohchr.org/_layouts/treatybodyexternal/Download.aspx?symbolno=CRC%2FGC%2F2002%2F2&Lang=en (accessed 15 February 2017).

UNCRC (2003) *General Comment No. 5: General measures of implementation of the Convention on the Rights of the Child*, 27 November 2003, CRC/GC/2003/5. Available online at http://tbinternet.ohchr.org/_layouts/treatybodyexternal/Download.aspx?symbolno=CRC%2fGC%2f2003%2f5&Lang=en (accessed 15 February 2017).

UNCRC (2005) *General Comment No. 6: Treatment of unaccompanied and separated children outside their country of origin*, 1 September 2005, CRC/GC/2005/6. Available online at http://tbinternet.ohchr.org/_layouts/treatybodyexternal/Download.aspx?symbolno=CRC%2fGC%2f2005%2f6&Lang=en (accessed 15 February 2017).

UNCRC (2009a) *General Comment No. 12: The right of the child to be heard*, 20 July 2009, CRC/C/GC/12. Available online at http://tbinternet.ohchr.org/_layouts/treatybodyexternal/Download.aspx?symbolno=CRC%2fC%2fGC%2f12&Lang=en (accessed 15 February 2017).

UNCRC (2009b) *Concluding observations on the combined third and fourth periodic report of France*, CRC/C/FRA/CO/4. Available online at http://tbinternet.ohchr.org/_layouts/treatybodyexternal/Download.aspx?symbolno=CRC%2FC%2FFRA%2FCO%2F4&Lang=en (accessed 15 February 2017).

UNCRC (2010a) *Concluding observations on the fourth periodic report of Norway*, CRC/C/NOR/CO/4. Available online at http://tbinternet.ohchr.org/_layouts/treatybodyexternal/Download.aspx?symbolno=CRC/C/NOR/CO/4&Lang=En (accessed 17 February 2017).

UNCRC (2010b) *Concluding observations on the combined third and fourth periodic reports of Spain*, CRC/C/ESP/CO/3-4. Available online at http://tbinternet.ohchr.org/_layouts/treatybodyexternal/Download.aspx?symbolno=CRC/C/ESP/CO/3-4&Lang=En (accessed 17 February 2017).

UNCRC (2011a) *Concluding observations on the combined third and fourth periodic report of Belarus*, CRC/C/BLR/CO/3-4. Available online at http://tbinternet.ohchr.org/_layouts/treatybodyexternal/Download.aspx?symbolno=CRC/C/BLR/CO/3-4&Lang=En (accessed 15 February 2017).

UNCRC (2011b) *Concluding observations on the fourth periodic report of Denmark*, CRC/C/DNK/CO/4. Available online at http://tbinternet.ohchr.org/_layouts/treatybodyexternal/Download.aspx?symbolno=CRC/C/DNK/CO/4&Lang=En (accessed 15 February 2017).

UNCRC (2012a) *Report of the 2012 Day of General Discussion: The Rights of all Children in the Context of International Migration*. Available online at www2.ohchr.org/english/bodies/crc/docs/discussion2012/2012CRC_DGD-Childrens_Rights_InternationalMigration.pdf (accessed 15 February 2017).

UNCRC (2012b) *Concluding observations on the second periodic report of Andorra*, CRC/C/AND/CO/2. Available online at http://tbinternet.ohchr.org/_layouts/treatybodyexternal/Download.aspx?symbolno=CRC/C/AND/CO/2&Lang=En (accessed 15 February 2017).

UNCRC (2012c) *Concluding observations on the fourth periodic report of Australia*, CRC/ C/AUS/CO/4. Available online at http://tbinternet.ohchr.org/_layouts/treatybodyexternal/Download.aspx?symbolno=CRC/C/AUS/CO/4&Lang=En (accessed 15 February 2017).

UNCRC (2012d) *Concluding observations on the combined third and fourth periodic report of Canada*, CRC/C/CAN/CO/3-4. Available online at http://tbinternet.ohchr.org/_layouts/treatybodyexternal/Download.aspx?symbolno=CRC/C/CAN/CO/3-4&Lang=En (accessed 15 February 2017).

UNCRC (2012e) *Concluding observations on the combined second and third periodic report of Greece*, CRC/C/GRC/CO/2-3. Available online at http://tbinternet.ohchr.org/_layouts/treatybodyexternal/Download.aspx?symbolno=CRC/C/GRC/CO/2-3&Lang=En (accessed 15 February 2017).

UNCRC (2013a) *General Comment No. 14 on the right of the child to have his or her best interests taken as a primary consideration (art. 3, para 1)*, 29 May 2013, CRC/C/GC/14. Available online at http://tbinternet.ohchr.org/_layouts/treatybodyexternal/Download.aspx?symbolno=CRC%2fC%2fGC%2f14&Lang=en (accessed 15 February 2017).

UNCRC (2013b) *Concluding observations on the second periodic report of Malta*, CRC/C/MLT/CO/2. Available online at http://tbinternet.ohchr.org/_layouts/treatybodyexternal/Download.aspx?symbolno=CRC/C/MLT/CO/2&Lang=En (accessed 15 February 2017).

UNCRC (2013c) *Concluding observations on the combined third and fourth periodic reports of Slovenia*, CRC/C/SVN/CO/3-4. Available online at http://tbinternet.ohchr.org/_layouts/treatybodyexternal/Download.aspx?symbolno=CRC/C/SVN/CO/3-4&Lang=En (accessed 15 February 2017).

UNCRC (2014a) *Committee Decision concerning Communication No. 1/2014*, CRC/C/69/D71/2014. Available online at www.ohchr.org/EN/HRBodies/CRC/Pages/TableJurisprudence.aspx (accessed 15 February 2017).

UNCRC (2014b) *Concluding observations on the combined fourth and fifth periodic reports of the Russian Federation*, CRC/C/RUS/CO/4-5. Available online at http://tbinternet.ohchr.org/_layouts/treatybodyexternal/Download.aspx?symbolno=CRC/C/RUS/CO/4-5 (accessed 15 February 2017).

UNCRC (2014c) *Concluding observations on the combined third, fourth and fifth periodic reports of Hungary*, CRC/C/HUN/CO/3-5. Available online at http://tbinternet.ohchr.org/_layouts/treatybodyexternal/Download.aspx?symbolno=CRC/C/HUN/CO/3-5&Lang=En (accessed 15 February 2017).

UNCRC (2015a) *Concluding observations on the fifth periodic report of Sweden*, CRC/C/SWE/CO/5. Available online at http://tbinternet.ohchr.org/_layouts/treatybodyexternal/Download.aspx?symbolno=CRC/C/SWE/CO/5&Lang=En (accessed 15 February 2017).

UNCRC (2015b) *Concluding observations on the combined second to fourth periodic reports of Switzerland*, CRC/C/CHE/CO/2-4. Available online at http://tbinternet.ohchr.org/_layouts/treatybodyexternal/Download.aspx?symbolno=CRC/C/CHE/CO/2-4&Lang=En (accessed 15 February 2017).

UNCRC (2015c) *Concluding observations on the combined third to fifth periodic reports of the Dominican Republic*, CRC/C/DOM/CO/3-5. Available online at http://tbinternet.ohchr.org/_layouts/treatybodyexternal/Download.aspx?symbolno=CRC%2fC%2fDOM%2fCO%2f3-5&Lang=en (accessed 15 February 2017).

UNCRC (2015d) *Concluding observations on the combined third and fourth periodic reports of Poland*, CRC/C/POL/CO/3-4. Available online at http://tbinternet.ohchr.org/_layouts/treatybodyexternal/Download.aspx?symbolno=CRC/C/POL/CO/3-4&Lang=En (accessed 15 February 2017).

UNCRC (2015e) *Concluding observations on the combined fourth and fifth periodic reports of Honduras*, CRC/C/HND/CO/4-5. Available online at http://tbinternet.ohchr.org/_layouts/treatybodyexternal/Download.aspx?symbolno=CRC/C/HND/CO/4-5&Lang=En (accessed 15 February 2017).

UNCRC (2016a) *General Comment No. 19 (2016) on public budgeting for the realization of children's rights (art. 4)*, 20 July 2016, CRC/C/GC/19. Available online at http://tbinternet.ohchr.org/_layouts/treatybodyexternal/Download.aspx?symbolno=CRC%2fC%2fGC%2f19&Lang=en (accessed 15 February 2017).

UNCRC (2016b) *Concluding observations on the fifth periodic report of France*, CRC/C/FRA/CO/5. Available online at http://tbinternet.ohchr.org/_layouts/treatybodyexternal/Download.aspx?symbolno=CCPR/C/FRA/CO/5&Lang=En (accessed 15 February 2017).

UNCRC (2016c) *Concluding observations on the combined third and fourth periodic reports of Ireland*, CRC/C/IRL/CO/3-4. Available online at http://tbinternet.ohchr.org/_layouts/treatybodyexternal/Download.aspx?symbolno=CRC/C/IRL/CO/3-4&Lang=En (accessed 15 February 2017).

UN General Assembly (UNGA) (2010) *Guidelines for the Alternative Care of Children: Resolution adopted by the General Assembly*, 24 February 2010, A/RES/64/142.

Available online at www.refworld.org/docid/4c3acd162.html (accessed 15 February 2017).

UNHCR (2006) *Guidelines on International Protection No. 7: The Application of Article 1A(2) of the 1951 Convention and/or 1967 Protocol Relating to the Status of Refugees to Victims of Trafficking and Persons At Risk of Being Trafficked*, 7 April 2006, HCR/GIP/06/07. Available online at www.unhcr.org/en-us/publications/legal/443b626b2/guidelines-international-protection-7-application-article-1a2-1951-convention.html (accessed 15 February 2017).

UNHCR (2009) *Guidelines on International Protection No. 8: Child Asylum Claims under Articles 1(A)2 and 1(F) of the 1951 Convention and/or 1967 Protocol relating to the Status of Refugees*, 22 December 2009, HCR/GIP/09/08. Available online at www.refworld.org/docid/4b2f4f6d2.html (accessed 15 February 2017).

UNHCR and UNICEF (2014) *Safe & Sound: What States can do to ensure respect for the best interests of unaccompanied and separated children in Europe*. Available online at www.refworld.org/docid/5423da264.html (accessed 15 February 2017).

UNHCR Executive Committee (2007) *Conclusion on Children at Risk*, 5 October 2007, No. 107 (LVIII) – 2007. Available online at www.refworld.org/docid/471897232.html (accessed 15 February 2017).

UN Human Rights Committee (UNHRC) (2011) Views on Communication No. 1564/2007, CCPR/C/102/D/1564/2007. Available online at http://tbinternet.ohchr.org/_layouts/treatybodyexternal/Download.aspx?symbolno=CCPR%2FC%2F102%2FD%2F1564%2F2007&Lang=ru (accessed 15 February 2017).

UN Human Rights Council (2015) *Report of the Special Rapporteur on torture and other cruel, inhuman or degrading treatment or punishment*, 5 March 2015, A/HRC/28/68. Available online at www.refworld.org/docid/550824454.html (accessed 15 February 2017).

4 Methodology for the assessment of the best interests of the child for recently arrived unaccompanied refugee minors

Carla van Os, Elianne Zijlstra, Erik J. Knorth, Wendy Post and Margrite Kalverboer

Introduction

This chapter aims to provide an insight into the development of a methodology for the assessments of the best interests of recently arrived unaccompanied minor refugees. The assessment reports provide evidence and child rights-based information to the migration authorities, which should be taken into account when the asylum decision is made. In the introduction we describe why it is necessary to perform a best interests of the child (BIC) assessment for unaccompanied minors in migration procedures and how those BIC assessments are performed by the Study Centre for Children, Migration and Law (Study Centre). The Study Centre had been mainly practising BIC assessments with refugee children who had been residing in the Netherlands for a long time. This chapter describes the process of how those BIC assessments were adjusted to the situation of recently arrived unaccompanied refugee minors and how this adjusted BIC assessment was practised in the case of an unaccompanied minor from Eritrea. In the conclusion we reflect on the process and discuss the implications for practice and policy.

Unaccompanied children who ask for asylum in a host country are entitled to an asylum decision that prioritises of their best interests. This right is laid down in Article 3 of the Convention on the Rights of the Child (CRC), implying that the best interests of the child should be a primary consideration whenever a decision is made that affects a child. The Committee on the Rights of the Child (the Committee) states that the best interests principle, like all rights laid down in the CRC, has equal meaning for all children, irrespective of their nationality or residential status (UNCRC 2005: para 12; see Chapter 3 of this volume). However, in the field of migration law it is often seen that decision-makers ignore the interests of refugee children[1] (Beltman and Zijlstra 2013).

The best interests of the child principle has been criticised for being too vague and therefore lacking practical importance for children (Beltman *et al.* 2016). Decision-makers and judges in migration law in the Netherlands are reluctant to apply the best interests of the child principle because they think that migration law is not meant to protect this principle but to provide rules for regulation of migration (Van Os and Beltman 2012: 735). Their counterparts in family law seem to feel much more comfortable with applying the concept. For example, in decisions in child protection cases the best interests of the child are assessed by answering the question whether the child's safety is protected in the current living circumstances (Van Nijnatten *et al.* 2001).

In response to the concerns raised about article 3 of the CRC, the Committee published *General Comment No. 14 on the right of the child to have his or her best interests taken as a primary consideration* (UNCRC 2013). The Committee describes a non-exhaustive list of areas of concern that should be part of every best interests assessment: the child's views; the child's identity; the family environment and the child's relations; the care, protection and safety of the child; the state of vulnerability; and the child's right to health and education (ibid.: paras 53–79). For each decision that affects a child, a best interests assessment should be undertaken (ibid.: para 32) in accordance with well-established scientific methodologies (ibid.: para 95).

In this chapter we describe how the BIC assessments are performed by the Study Centre and how this methodology was adapted to the situation of recently arrived refugee children. With the case of Elsa, we illustrate how the adapted methodology for recently arrived refugee children is practised. We conclude with some general observations and suggestions for further research.

Best interests of the child assessment in migration procedures

In this section we describe the theoretical framework and elements of the BIC assessment and how it has been practised with migrant children with long-term residency. The BIC assessments are meant to influence decisions in migration procedures: from the first decision on the request for a residence permit until the final court case. The Study Centre developed a scientific methodology to assess the best interests of the child in decision-making processes, which is fully in line with the guidelines of the Committee (Kalverboer 2014: 15). As will be shown in the following paragraphs, the BIC assessment is compiled from different elements, which are of great importance for minor migrants.

The theoretical framework of the BIC assessment of the Study Centre is based on a comprehensive international social science literature review compiled in the BIC-Model which interprets the best interests of the child as the child's right to live in an environment that ensures his or her holistic development (UNCRC 2013: para 42; Zijlstra 2012). The BIC-Model identifies which rearing environment best guarantees the development of the child (Kalverboer and Zijlstra 2006; Zijlstra 2012: 70) by taking into account the cumulative and interactive effects of stress factors on the child's development (Zijlstra 2012: 53). The BIC assessment has been practised in all stages of migration procedures – for example, before a decision is taken or in the appeal phase in a court case in order to provide the decision maker with information about the child's interests at stake including protection needs, access to education and health care, family ties and vulnerability of the child. Migrant and refugee children face an increased risk for internalising mental health problems due to stressful experiences before, during and after migration (Fazel *et al.* 2012; Kalverboer 2014: 17–26). Therefore, the current stage of development, mental health and other factors that may increase the vulnerability and resilience of the child are also part of the BIC assessment (Zijlstra *et al.* 2013). The outcomes of the BIC assessment in migration procedures indicate which interests of the child should be considered when a decision about a future rearing environment is made and which decision in the migration procedure would serve best the interests of the child (Zijlstra 2012: 71).

In accordance with the Committee's standpoints, the Study Centre likewise aims to analyse the socio-cultural context of the child, taking into account the individual characteristics of the child (e.g. age, sex, level of maturity) as well as the social and cultural context surrounding the child (the quality of social and familial relationships, whether they are unaccompanied, environmental safety) (Kalverboer and Zijlstra 2006; Zijlstra 2012; UNCRC 2013). Correspondingly, the BIC-Model comprises 14 conditions for the development of the child (Zijlstra 2012), which reflect the quality of the environment the child is raised in and concern the family situation, as well as the conditions for development in society. All conditions of the BIC-Model are linked to children's rights and to different elements of *General Comment No. 14* (see Table 4.1).

Table 4.1 The Best Interests of the Child-Model with reference to the related Articles in the Convention on the Rights of the Child (CRC) and to the paragraphs of the *General Comment No. 14* (GC 14) of the UN Committee on the Rights of the Child on the best interests of the child assessment and determination

Best Interests of the Child-Model	
Current situation	
Family	*Society*
1. Adequate physical care Adequate physical care refers to the care for the child's health and physical well-being by parents or care-providers. They offer the child a place to live, clothing to wear, enough food to eat and (some) personal belongings. There is a family income to provide for all of this. In addition, the parents or care-providers are free of worries about providing for the child's physical well-being. CRC Articles 24, 26, 27. GC 14 paras 70, 71, 77, 78, 84.	*8. Safe wider physical environment* The neighbourhood the child grows up in is safe, as well as the society the child lives in. Criminality, (civil) wars, natural disasters, infectious diseases, etc. do not threaten the development of the child. CRC Articles 33, 34, 35, 36, 37. GC 14 paras 70, 71, 73, 74, 77, 78, 84.

(continued)

Table 4.1 (continued)

Best Interests of the Child-Model	
Current situation	
Family	*Society*
2. Safe direct physical environment A safe direct physical environment offers the child physical protection. This implies the absence of physical danger in the house or neighbourhood in which the child lives. There are no toxic or other threats in the house or neighbourhood. The child is not threatened by abuse of any kind. CRC Articles 19, 24. GC 14 paras 61, 70, 71, 73, 74, 77, 78, 84.	*9. Respect* The needs, wishes, feelings and desires of the child are taken seriously by the child's environment and the society the child lives in. There is no discrimination because of background, race or religion. CRC Articles 2, 13, 14, 15, 16, 30, 37. GC 14 paras 56, 70, 73, 74, 79, 84.
3. Affective atmosphere An affective atmosphere implies that the parents or care-providers of the child offer the child emotional protection, support and understanding. There are bonds of attachment between the parent(s) or care-giver(s) and the child. There is a relationship of mutual affection. CRC Article 19. GC 14 paras 70, 71, 72, 84.	*10. Social network* The child and his family have various sources of support in their environment upon which they can depend. CRC Articles 20, 37, 31. GC 14 para. 70, 73, 84.
4. Supportive, flexible childrearing structure A supportive, flexible childrearing structure encompasses several aspects such as: enough daily routine in the child's life; encouragement, stimulation and instruction to the child and the requirement of realistic demands; rules, limits, instructions and insight into the arguments for these rules; control of the child's behaviour; enough space for the child's own wishes and thoughts, enough freedom to experiment and to negotiate on what is important to the child; no more responsibilities than the child is capable of handling. CRC Articles 13, 14. GC 14 paras 70, 71, 84.	*11. Education* The child receives a suitable education and has the opportunity to develop his personality and talents (e.g. sport or music). CRC Articles 17, 28, 29, 31. GC 14 paras 70, 73, 84.

Best Interests of the Child-Model	
Current situation	
Family	*Society*
5. Adequate example by parents The parents or care-providers offer the child the opportunity to incorporate their behaviour, values and cultural norms that are important, now and in the future. CRC Article 10. GC 14 paras 70, 71, 84.	*12. Contact with peers* The child has opportunities to have contact with other children in various situations suitable to his perception of the world and developmental age. CRC Article 31. GC 14 paras 70, 73, 84.
6. Interest in the child The parents or care-providers show interest in the activities and interests of the child and in his perception of the world. CRC Article 31. GC 14 paras 70, 71, 84.	*13. Adequate examples in society* The child is in contact with children and adults who are examples for current and future behaviour and who mediate the adaptation of important societal values and norms. CRC Articles 2, 8, 13, 14, 15. GC 14 paras 70, 73, 84.
Future and past	
7. Continuity in upbringing conditions, future perspective The parents or care-providers care for the child and bring the child up in such a way that attachment bonds develop. Basic trust is to be continued by the availability of the parents or care-providers to the child. The child experiences a future perspective. CRC Articles 5, 6, 9, 10, 18. GC 14 paras 65, 66, 67, 70, 72, 74, 84.	*14. Stability in life circumstances, future perspective* The environment in which the child is brought up does not change suddenly and unexpectedly. There is continuity in life circumstances. Significant changes are prepared for and made comprehensible for the child. Persons with whom the child can identify and sources of support are constantly available to the child, as well as the possibility of developing relationships by means of a common language. Society offers the child opportunities and a future perspective. CRC Articles 6, 9, 10, 20. GC 14 paras 65, 70, 74, 84.

In general, the BIC assessment at the Study Centre is requested by lawyers and occasionally also by guardians, social workers or children themselves. The assessment builds upon the documents of the migration procedure, which are sent by the lawyer in agreement with the child and his or her guardian, as well as upon information gathered from external professionals working with the child such as mental health professionals. In addition to this, the diagnosticians also collect information on the situation in the home country from human rights reports and country reports of the ministry of foreign affairs.

The child and the guardian are always informed about the goals and the process of the assessment. They need to give written consent for the whole procedure to start as well as after receiving the draft report of the interests assessed. The BIC assessment is performed by two diagnosticians: academically schooled experts in child development and child rearing who are trained to assess the emotional, social and cognitive development of the child and any psychosocial problems the child may have. The child and caregivers come to the Study Centre or the diagnosticians visit the child 'at home', usually an asylum seekers' centre. The semi-structured interview is based on a list of issues concerning the 14 conditions for development. The child fills in various self-report measures.

The diagnosticians follow the general guidelines for interviewing of vulnerable children (Saywitz, Lyon and Goodman 2011) and work on the basis of the best interests of the child principle. First, they try to make contact and build trust with the child as much as possible, adapting the language to the development and age of the child. They are aware of cultural dilemmas and loyalty problems that may hamper the child from speaking freely. Nevertheless, they never put pressure on the child but repeatedly reassure the child that his or her story is always 'good', compliment the child and show a positive and respectful attitude. External professionals such as teachers, care professionals or mentors in the reception centre who know the child well are interviewed, in a semi-structured manner, about their observations on the development and mental health of the child (Zijlstra *et al.* 2013).

The diagnosticians record their observations, analysis and conclusions on the best interests of the child in a diagnostic report of the BIC assessment (Zijlstra *et al.* 2013). Depending on the phase of the procedure, the lawyer sends the report to the immigration authorities (*Immigratie en Naturalisatie Dienst*, IND) or to the administrative judge. The court assesses whether the IND decision is based on a sound reasoning and shows a proportional balancing of interests.

Based on the BIC-Model, researchers at the Study Centre have developed the Best Interests of the Child-Questionnaire (BIC-Q) (Zijlstra *et al.* 2013). The BIC-Q consists of 24 questions that provide guidance for a diagnostician when identifying the 14 conditions for a child's development within the family and society (Zijlstra *et al.* 2013). After analysing the information from the diagnostic interview with the child and the information from the interviews with external professionals, the interviewers fill in the BIC-Q with one of five possible answers: 'unsatisfactory', 'moderate', 'satisfactory', 'good' or 'unknown'. By comparing the BIC-Q scores for different outcomes of a decision (e.g. prolonged stay in the host country or return to the home country) the diagnosticians can discern which decision serves the child's best interests (Kalverboer 2014: 13). The BIC-Q is a reliable and valid instrument to assess and predict concerns about the development, mental health and well-being of a child (Zijlstra 2012) and has been evaluated as a culturally sensitive measure in a study with returnees in Kosovo (Zevulun *et al.* 2015).

In order to assess the vulnerability and resilience of the child, the diagnosticians use the Strengths and Difficulties Questionnaire (SDQ) within the BIC assessment. The SDQ is a behavioural screening questionnaire with 25 questions, giving an indication of the pro-social strength of the child and the presence of internalising and externalising problems (Goodman 1997). The SDQ is available in 84 languages and dialects. The reliability and validity of the SDQ is sufficient in different versions and languages (Achenbach *et al.* 2008). The child and the parent(s) or guardian(s) both complete the SDQ. Depending on the description of the child's development and current difficulties, other instruments may be added to the assessment, such as the Teacher's Report Form (TRF) and the Child Behaviour Checklist (CBCL).

So far, the BIC assessment of the Study Centre has been employed mainly with migrant and refugee children facing deportation after having resided in the Netherlands for some years. Therefore, those BIC assessments focus on the development of the child during their stay in the Netherlands, the level of child integration in Dutch society and the expectations about the development of the child after return to the home country of the parents. Generally, these BIC assessments conclude that the child's development would be endangered if the child were to be deported after a residence period of more than five years (Kalverboer, Zijlstra and Knorth 2009). The lawyers who request a BIC assessment at the Study Centre use the diagnostic report as a means of last resort when asylum or other procedures have failed. The immigration authorities do not perform a BIC assesment before the first asylum decision is made (Beltman and Zijlstra 2013). To fill this gap, we began new research on the necessary adjustments of the BIC assessment for recently arrived refugee children, which can be used in the first phase of the asylum procedure in 2014.

BIC assessment adjusted for recently arrived refugee children

The Study Centre investigates which adjustments of the BIC assessment are necessary when it is applied to recently arrived refugee children, unaccompanied or accompanied by family members. These children differ in certain aspects from asylum-seeking children who have resided in the host country for a long period. The recently arrived children fled war or other forms of violence just a couple of weeks or months before. Most of them feared for their lives during the journey, walked vast distances or used fragile boats to cross a sea. The recently arrived children are often confused about the roles of the different people involved in the procedures, such as migration authorities, lawyers, guardians and social workers. They do not speak the Dutch language, and they experience instability in their lives (Van Os *et al.* 2016). Instead of focusing on the development of the child in the Netherlands, the diagnostic questions in the BIC assessments focus on the extent of the vulnerability of the child, as well as the degree to which the child's development was protected or endangered in their country of origin.

This section describes the development process of the adjustments of the BIC assessment and the results of the different stages in this process.

Methodological outline of the research on the adjusted BIC assessment

This process of adjustment of the BIC assessment to the situation of recently arrived refugee children went through three phases: (1) exploration and theoretical research; (2) consultation with mental health professionals and lawyers; and (3) pilot of the BIC assessments with nine recently arrived refugee children. This section describes the research methods practised during these phases.

The first phase included explorative interviews with guardians working with recently arrived refugee minors and two systematic reviews. First, we interviewed the guardians at reception centres where unaccompanied refugee minors spend the first weeks of their asylum procedure. We choose to focus on guardians because of their special appointment to defend the best interests of the unaccompanied child. During open interviews based on a topic list, we explored the guardian's views on the task to defend the best interests of the child in relation to the children and the asylum procedure (Verhoeven 2015: 142). The interviews took one hour on average. At the time of information gathering (February to April 2015) three such centres existed in the Netherlands, all of which were visited for one day. Eleven guardians of unaccompanied minors were interviewed, representing 55 per cent of the guardians working at these locations at that time. We also asked four guardians for permission to be a 'fly on the wall' during their meetings with recently arrived minors to observe the interactions between the guardian and the minor.

The exploration and theoretical research also involved two systematic reviews (Petticrew and Roberts 2006). The first review analysed existing social science knowledge concerning the mental health and development of recently arrived refugee children (Van Os *et al.* 2016). There is a vast amount of literature about the mental health of refugee children who have resided for several years in the

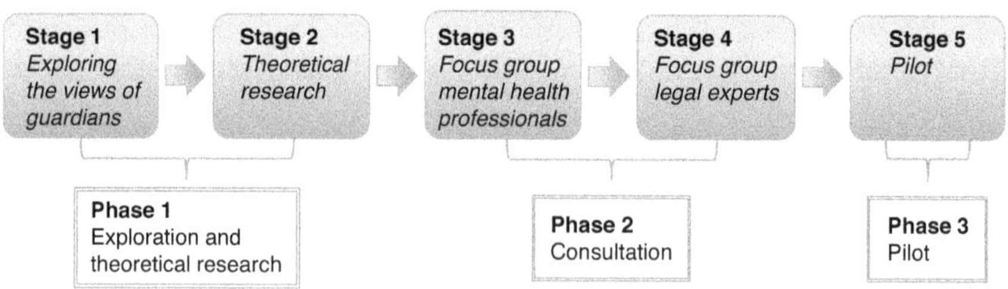

Figure 4.1 Stages in the study on adjustments of the BIC assessment

host country (Kalverboer *et al.* 2009; Montgomery 1998; Vervliet *et al.* 2014). However, the knowledge about recently arrived refugee children in a host country is rather limited. This review aimed to provide relevant material elements for the assessment of the best interests of this specific group of minors.

Many unaccompanied children experience a deeply rooted distrust of figures of authority, including social workers and other professionals (De Haene, Grietens and Verschueren 2010). Therefore, they often keep silent when professionals inquire about their lives and opinions (Kohli 2006a, 2006b, 2011). However, for the BIC assessment, it is indispensable to hear the views of the minors concerning their desire for protection, as well as their views on the effect on their lives of return to their home country or prolonged stay in the host country (Kalverboer 2014: 21; UNCRC 2013: paras 53–54). For this reason, the second review within the theoretical research was aimed at gaining insights about the elements that support or hamper refugee children in sharing their life stories with the interviewer. This research provided the procedural guidelines for implementing diagnostic interview within the BIC assessment (Van Os *et al.* 2017).

Based on the explorative and theoretical stages, a diagnostic BIC assessment was drafted. The draft included relevant aspects of the previously existing BIC assessment, which we found applicable to recently arrived refugee children too, in addition to new aspects on *what* should be assessed, as well as on *how* the assessment should be performed. The BIC assessment draft was discussed and consulted upon in focus groups with mental health professionals in the third stage of the research and with legal experts in the fourth stage. The selection of the participants was purposively sampled, seeking a balance of expertise in the participants' backgrounds (Verhoeven 2015: 186).[2]

Based on the exploration and theoretical research and the consultation with professionals, a revised design for the individual BIC assessment was tested in a pilot study. The main research question for the pilot study was: Is the adjusted BIC assessment valid and complete, feasible and achievable for the cases of recently arrived refugee children? Furthermore, we asked the children to evaluate the interviews using a short questionnaire about the way the interview was conducted and the different methods employed.

The cases for the pilot study were selected via snowball sampling through the lawyers and guardians who participated in the first two phases of the research and lawyers who had worked with the Study Centre before (Verhoeven 2015: 186). They were asked to bring cases of recently arrived refugee children awaiting the first decision on their asylum claims. Nine cases were brought by the intermediaries and were admitted to the pilot study. The cases were analysed according to the research questions of the pilot study, with the aim being to find out whether the assessments provided answers to the diagnostic questions.

Development of the adjustment process for the BIC assessments

This section presents the main results of the different phases of the development of the adjusted BIC assessment to the situation of recently arrived refugee children.

It focuses on (1) the main conclusions from the interviews with the guardians and the theoretical research, (2) on the results from the focus groups with professionals and (3) on the results of the pilot study.

Results of phase 1: exploration and theoretical research

The first part of the preliminary research showed that the guardians believe their views on the best interests of the child do not have a significant meaning in the asylum procedure, especially because the immigration authorities focus on asylum-related arguments and on the consistency and credibility of the asylum story. Therefore, the guardians do not make an explicit BIC assessment and do not bring their views to the attention of the immigration authorities. As can be concluded from their experiences, the guardians are often confronted with non-communicative minors who face difficulties in sharing details of their past and seem to mistrust all people in their environment, including the guardians. The guardians indicate that for many of the minors under their care, talking about their previous family environment is a 'no go area'. They suppose that children think they have to be persistent in the story they tell to the authorities upon their arrival and therefore hesitate to give more or different details later in the procedure. Overall, the guardians underlined the need for a tool to perform a systematic BIC assessment for unaccompanied minors. Moreover, the obtained results confirmed the importance of the focus in the research design on methods that could support unaccompanied minors in disclosing their life stories.

The second part of the preliminary research (systematic review of social science knowledge) showed that children who have recently arrived in the host country have been exposed to a disproportionately high number of stressful life events. Experiences mentioned most concerned exposure to violence and war, persecution, loss of family members, hardship and experiencing fear for their life during their flight (Van Os *et al.* 2016). A considerable percentage of the recently arrived children have mental health problems; most prevalent are anxiety disorders, ranging from 30 per cent (Goldin *et al.* 2001) to 67 per cent (Montgomery 1998); traumatic stress and post-traumatic stress disorder (PTSD), ranging from 18 per cent (Almqvist and Brandell-Forsberg 1997) to 57 per cent (Rothe *et al.* 2002); and depression, ranging from 9.4 per cent (Jakobsen, Demott and Heir 2014) to 45 per cent (Ekblad 1993). Significant risk factors for the mental health of these children are the number, intensity and duration of the stressful life events (Abdalla and Elklit 2001; Jensen *et al.* 2015; Vervliet *et al.* 2014); exposure to violence (Geltman *et al.* 2000; Montgomery 1998); loss of a close family member (Geltman *et al.* 2000; Montgomery 1998); duration of the journey (Abdalla and Elklit 2001) and experiencing fear for their life during the flight (Rothe *et al.* 2002).The results of this review were combined with the material elements from *General Comment No. 14* and the BIC-Model. These elements should be considered for the assessment of the best interests of recently arrived refugee children (Van Os *et al.* 2016). See Table 4.2 for an overview.

Table 4.2 Elements of the best interests of the child assessment based on *General Comment No. 14* of the UN Committee on the Rights of the Child, the Best Interest of the Child-Model and risk factors (*italic*)

Elements of the best interests of the refugee child assessment upon arrival			
Individual characteristics		*Family and social environment*	
Identity	*Situation of vulnerability*	*Conditions for development in the family*	*Conditions for development in society*
Gender Sexual orientation Nation of origin Religion and beliefs Culture Age	Being refugee, asylum seeker, migrant *Pre existing vulnerability: development illnesses, extreme poverty* *Being unaccompanied* *Number, severity and duration of stressful life events* *Exposure to violence* *Witnessing violence* *Dangerous and/or long flight* *Having stayed in refugee camps* *Number of separations* Mental health: PTSD, anxiety, depression	Care, protection, safety of the child and rearing conditions within the family *Extreme poverty* *Poor parental support* *Death and loss of close relatives* *Separations*	Safe environment *Exposure to violence* *Witnessing violence* *Feeling of being in danger* Social environment *Experience of discrimination* *Lack of social support* *Lack of opportunities to play* Education
Prospects in the future			
Possibility to preserve identity	Possibility to address special needs, including (mental) health care	Preservation of the family environment *Drastic changes in family* *Death and loss of close relatives* *Separations* *Poor parental support*	Stability and future perspectives in society on safety, protection, possibility to address educational needs, preservation of social ties
The child's views on all elements and on his/her need for protection			

Based on this first systematic literature review, two instruments were added to the existing BIC assessment with the aim to screen the traumatic stress of recently arrived refugee children: the Stressful Life Events (SLE) and the Reactions of Adolescent on Traumatic Stress (RATS) questionnaires. Both instruments were adjusted to the situation of refugee adolescents by Bean (2006) for her research on the mental health of unaccompanied minors in the Netherlands. The SLE is a checklist of 12 dichotomous (yes/no) questions about whether the refugee has experienced certain stressful life events – for example, separations and losses within the family, experiencing or witnessing violence and experiencing war or natural disasters.[3] The RATS is a self-report questionnaire and includes 22 items on a four-point scale ranging from 'not at all' to 'very much'. The items on the RATS reflect the criteria for PTSD: intrusion, avoiding and hyper-arousal in the *Diagnostic and Statistical Manual of Mental Disorders*. The SLE and RATS are short self-report instruments with good validity and reliability (Bean *et al.* 2004a, 2004b). The instruments are culturally sensitive and available in the main languages of refugees. Together, these instruments give an indication of the level of traumatic stress the refugee adolescent experiences and whether the refugee may suffer from PTSD (Bean 2006: 110).

The second part of the theoretical review focused on the barriers and facilitators of refugee children's disclosure of their life stories and provided deeper insight into the reasons why refugee children often experience mistrust (for an overview see Ní Raghallaigh 2014). The main facilitators that can support the children in sharing their life stories are related to the interviewer's positive and respectful attitude – for example, by providing emotional closeness (Sourander 1998) and respecting the wish of the child for non-disclosure (De Haene *et al.* 2012). The interviewers need to take time to build trust with the child (Hodes 2000; Katsounari 2014; Sourander 1998) – for example, by eating or playing together (Adams 2009; Due, Riggs and Augoustinos 2014), meeting the child on more than one occasion (Chase 2010; Jaffa 1996) and by introducing themselves to the child (Servan-Schreiber, Le Lin and Birmaher 1998). Children should be provided agency during the interview. This can be done by giving the children a say in the logistics of the interview (Oh 2012; Thomas *et al.* 2004) and by giving children the lead in choosing subjects that can be talked about in more depth, as well as those subjects that should only be touched upon briefly or even ignored (Chase 2010; Kohli and Mather 2003). Non-verbal methods are useful to facilitate the interview – for example, through drama, art, free drawing and drawing lifelines and social circles to identity the supportive network of the child (Schauer *et al.* 2004; St. Thomas and Johnson 2002; Warr 2010). Involving trained interpreters is a facilitator to promote the refugee children's speaking about difficult experiences (Keselman *et al.* 2010; Vickers 2005).

The required positive and respectful attitude was already a matter of course in the existing BIC assessment; so too was the encouragement of the children to make drawings to explain or sustain their story. However, we considered more time is needed for the interviews with recently arrived refugee children than with their longer-residing counterparts. For this reason the interview was extended from two to four hours, including breaks. During the breaks, the interviewers and the child may go for a walk or eat together. If necessary, the assessment is divided over two meetings. At the beginning of the interview, extra time is taken to build trust by speaking about informal or less sensitive subjects and by letting the diagnosticians introduce themselves – for example, by drawing their own houses and explaining a bit about their private lives. Furthermore, the children are given agency about the interview – for example, by letting them decide where and during which part of the day the interview should take place and who should be present during the interview. Finally, drawing lifelines and social circles was added to the non-verbal methods.

Results of consultation with professionals

A draft design of the diagnostic assessment aiming to provide an individual BIC assessment in the asylum procedure was presented to professionals during two focus group discussions. The main diagnostic question for the assessment was formulated as follows: Is the development of the child endangered in the country of origin? Two sub-questions were formulated as: (1) Is the child especially vulnerable due to traumatic experiences? (2) Are the conditions for development sufficiently fulfilled in the country of origin? The theoretical framework of the BIC-Model and instruments (BIC-Q, SDQ, SLE and RATS) were explained to the participants of the focus groups. The discussion revolved mostly around the proposed procedures with emphasis on the facilitators for the children's disclosure of their life stories.

The results of the first focus group showed that the mental health professionals generally supported the design for the diagnostic assessment. However, they advised adjusting the terminology of the diagnostic questions to conform to practised child protection law, such as in cases where it has to be decided if the child's development is endangered in the current living circumstances. Furthermore, the professionals recommended the addition of an assessment of protective factors in the question about vulnerability. The experts advised waiting to conduct the diagnostic assessment until the child is stabilised as much as possible. They thought an acclimation period of at least four weeks after arrival is necessary before children are able to talk about their experiences. Finally, the experts highlighted the importance of the diagnostician's awareness about the intercultural differences in communication, memory and the interpretation of events in collective or individual terms.

After the first focus group with mental health professionals, it was decided to rephrase the diagnostic questions in the individual assessments as follows: (1) To what extent is the child particularly vulnerable and what protective factors are present? (2) To what extent were the conditions for development within the family and society in the country of origin fulfilled before departure? (3) What is expected on the fulfilment of the conditions for development in the country of origin upon their return? Furthermore, we decided not to perform the BIC assessments earlier than four weeks after the arrival of the refugee child in the Netherlands.

The result of the second focus group with legal experts revealed that in their opinion an additional diagnostic assessment is hardly possible in the current formal asylum process given that the procedure starts after just a few days of rest after arrival and takes only eight days. These days are fully booked with appointments with the immigration authorities and the lawyer. However, because of the high influx of asylum seekers in 2015, the waiting period before the start of the process is extended about six to eight months. Therefore, due to the extraordinary circumstances there is sufficient time for the diagnostic assessment before the asylum procedure starts. Furthermore, the legal experts thought that the most important contributions of the diagnostic report to the asylum process are the diagnosis of psychological complaints and statements on the children's ability to tell their asylum story in a coherent, consistent and chronological way. However, they doubted whether considerations of the development of the child will be seen as relevant by the immigration authorities. Finally, the experts emphasised that it is important to distinguish the child's specific position due to individual circumstances from the general situation of all children in the country of origin. Based on the main findings of the focus group, researchers recognised that it is necessary to write guidelines for lawyers on how the diagnostic report about the BIC assessment should be translated in legal terms that make sense in the current asylum system.

Results of phase 3: pilot to test the revised design for the BIC assessments

The adjusted BIC assessment for recently arrived refugee children was tested in a pilot study, which involved implementing nine BIC assessments. Among these, four cases concerned children who came to the Netherlands with their parent(s). However, due to the scope of this book we will solely focus on the five unaccompanied minors who participated. In this section we will expound the results along the research questions of the pilot study, while the whole procedure of the diagnostic assessment will be described in the next section about Elsa, one of the participants in the pilot study.

Five participants (four male and one female) in the pilot study were unaccompanied minor refugees. They came from Afghanistan, Benin, Eritrea, Iraq and Mauritania, and were 16 to 17 years old. At the time of the assessments, they had been in the Netherlands for between four and 23 weeks.

First, after it was concluded that the revised design for the BIC assessment provides an answer to the diagnostic questions, the diagnosticians were able to formulate a conclusion about whether the development of the child was endangered in the home country before departure. In two of the five cases, the diagnosticians stated that more diagnostic study and time was needed to formulate conclusions as to whether the family environment could be expected to protect the development of the child after return. The diagnostic interview appeared to be the most informative element of the assessment for answering the diagnostic questions. The BIC-Q provided a thorough and systematic analysis of the rearing conditions and the development opportunities and risks, while the SDQ, SLE and

RATS proved to be useful to confirm the observations on the vulnerability and resilience of the child.

Second, we assessed whether the methods to promote the children's disclosure of their life stories worked sufficiently. The refugee minors told the diagnosticians that they felt supported sufficiently to communicate what they thought was important and that they liked the fact that they did not feel pressured. During the pilot period, two unaccompanied minors shared fewer details of their life stories than the other three. This might be attributed to the fact that with the latter the diagnosticians took more time to build trust and provided them more agency. The use of drawings, lifelines and social circles seemed to be useful methods to facilitate the interviews. Some minors used drawings to explain certain situations in more detail. Others just used the pencils to put dots on a piece of paper as a means of concentration and focus. The diagnosticians noticed that for some minors it was difficult to provide a detailed picture of their family life before departure. However, the main risks for development could be explained sufficiently for the diagnosticians to assess the overall quality of the rearing conditions in the country of origin. The assessment of the current resilience and vulnerability of the child can be done satisfactorily. The adjusted BIC assessment is expected to provide sufficient information to make an assessment of the developmental risks.

Third, we assessed whether the adjusted BIC assessment is feasible and achievable within the planned four hours. The five assessments with unaccompanied minors took three hours on average. However, through the pilot period the later assessments took more time because the diagnosticians increased the time that was spend on building trust. Therefore, four hours' planning seems to be necessary. With one participant, the assessment was divided over two days in advance as advised by the guardian. With the other, this was decided during the first meeting because his attention span was short. The other three assessments could be performed in one meeting because the minors felt well enough to continue the interview in one session while providing enough information to enable the diagnosticians to answer the diagnostic questions. The results of the pilot study show that in cases where the guardian foresees the child will face extraordinary difficulties with trusting the diagnosticians or when the diagnosticians notice the child is losing concentration, it seems to be necessary to divide the assessment over two meetings.

Fourth, we assessed whether it is feasible to give the children a level of agency in the logistic aspects of the interview. Overall, it was possible to offer the child different options for places, dates and times for the interview. Providing a completely free choice was not possible due to the commitments of the interpreters and the availability of the locations where the interviews took place. The children nevertheless indicated that they enjoyed having a say in how the interview was conducted.

Fifth, we asked the participants how they evaluated the interviews. Overall, the refugees expressed positive views about the assessment. However, it was difficult to determine if these answers were more than just assumptions of what was socially desirable. In their opinion, everything was 'just fine'. Two refugees were more specific in explaining that drawing helped them to tell their story. They said this method was useful, for example, in explaining the division of rooms in the family house or indicating the position of people involved in stressful events.

The results of the pilot study show that the adjusted BIC assessment is a valid and achievable tool to provide answers to the diagnostic questions that are relevant when an asylum decision had to be made. No further adjustments were made.

The case of Elsa

In this section, the case of Elsa[4] illustrates how the adjusted BIC assessment for recently arrived refugee children is performed. We describe the process of the BIC assessment as well as the content, and the results on various instruments: the BIC-Q, SDQ, SLE and RATS. We focus the description of the diagnostic interview with Elsa on the procedural methods the diagnosticians used to support Elsa in sharing important details about what happened to her. In the final part we show how the results of the BIC assessment were described in the assessment report.

Registration at the Study Centre

Elsa is an unaccompanied Eritrean asylum seeker who came to the Netherlands at the age of 16. She failed to give the reason for her leaving Eritrea in a coherent and consistent way. Therefore, the immigration authorities did not believe she came from Eritrea and made a draft negative decision on her asylum request. On Elsa's behalf, her lawyer had to present her views on the draft decision. At that moment, Elsa's guardian asked the Study Centre to conduct a diagnostic assessment to find out what happened to her, and why she was not able to tell about her life in Eritrea. The report could be sent to the IND as a professional analysis of the best interests of Elsa to sustain the views of the lawyer on the draft negative decision. The lawyer asked the IND to delay their final decision and wait for the diagnostic research report, to which they agreed. The diagnosticians obtained the transcripts of the asylum hearings and the draft negative decision of the IND and written information from the guardian about Elsa, which will be summarised below.

Like all refugees, Elsa was checked by a health professional to determine whether she was able to participate in the IND hearings. The health professional declared that Elsa could participate in the hearings with the IND but she would need a break every 20 to 30 minutes due to her concentration problems. The first interview about her identity and travel route took from 9 a.m. till 4 p.m. After a few hours, it became obvious that Elsa was starting to get nervous about the detailed questions about the landscape and school buildings in Eritrea, which she had difficulty in answering. She complained about a headache and told the interviewer she was confused and did not feel well.

During the second interview with the IND, which concerns the motivation for an asylum claim, most of the questioning was again spent on discerning details about her neighbourhood and school buildings. The part of the hearing questioning her reasons for fleeing Eritrea was relatively short. In summary, Elsa told the interviewer that she fled Eritrea because she had a difficult life and she feared she would be forced to join the army. During a first attempt to leave the country, she was arrested and brought to a prison where she was severely physically abused.

In the draft negative decision, the IND wrote that Elsa could not prove her identity and Eritrean nationality. Because she did not provide any documents that could prove her identity, the IND had to rely on the details given by Elsa about her home country in order to find out whether she was telling the truth about her Eritrean nationality. With satellite photos, the IND showed that Elsa was not accurate in her description of the school buildings and the landscape. Since the IND did not believe Elsa had Eritrean nationality, they did not consider the motivations for asylum. About the stress complaints, the IND stated that Elsa only received headache painkillers and was not referred for medical treatment. Consequently, according to the IND, there was no reason to suggest that she was traumatised in a degree that could explain the incorrect details she provided in the hearings.

The guardian wrote in her reports that she felt very worried about Elsa, noting that Elsa was sad, had sleeping problems, cried a lot and generally gave the impression that she was stressed. The guardian believed that Elsa might have had more traumatic experiences than she had talked about. Elsa told the guardian that it was difficult for her to remember things that happened before she fled.

After reading the file, one of the diagnosticians called the guardian to guide her in preparing Elsa for the diagnostic interview. Considering the concentration problems and the difficulties Elsa faced in talking about her past, it was decided in advance to divide the interview over two meetings of a maximum of two hours each. The diagnostician asked the guardian to speak with Elsa about how the interview setting could be as comfortable as possible, what was the best time for her to speak, what location she preferred and whether she thought it would be supportive for her to take someone she trusts with her to the interview. Elsa chose to come to the Study Centre at the University and bring her best friend with her because she was the only person 'who knows everything'. The friend had accompanied her during a part of the migration journey. Elsa was very precise in indicating what she expected from the guardian during the interview. She asked her to travel with her to and from the University, to be around, but not to be present at the interview, 'just being available'. It was decided that during the interview, the guardian would wait in the diagnostician's workspace, located in the same building.

The diagnosticians spend the first session almost completely on building trust with Elsa. By way of introducing themselves, the diagnosticians made drawings of their houses and the people who live there. During the first meeting, the diagnosticians concentrated on the current situation of Elsa and the happy period in her life – before the age of 12. Elsa told the diagnosticians about the people who lived in her neighbourhood, the games she played with her friends, the tradition of storytelling within the family and the bonds she felt with her family members. Elsa seemed to leave the first session quite relaxed. Afterwards, the guardian confirmed that on the way back home Elsa told her, 'You have brought me to a good place.' The second meeting, one week after the first, Elsa stated at the beginning that she had been thinking a lot about the previous session and that she felt it would be important for her to talk about more difficult things, too. Two traumatic experiences, about which she could not talk before, became the central themes of the session. Both happened during the flight. Elsa could tell the diagnosticians the smallest details about these events.

During the first meeting Elsa had told the diagnosticians she misses her mother a lot. She could reach her mother by phone only occasionally. The interviewers asked Elsa if she thought it was a good idea to try to call her mother during the second meeting. She agreed to this plan. Calling Elsa's mother together seemed a way for Elsa to become closer with the diagnosticians. She shared her fear of crying when she spoke with her mother. She refused the offer of privacy during part of the phone call and wanted the diagnosticians to speak with her mother, too.

As far as necessary to assess her best interests, Elsa could share her life story with the diagnosticians. Being asked why that was not possible for her at the asylum hearings, Elsa said:

> They only asked me 13 things and I had 27 things to tell them. When I did not remember things well and replied with 'might so' or 'maybe' they said they needed clear answers. They wanted exact dates all the time. Every time I started to tell something I had to stop because they wanted more details. Then I forgot all the things I wanted to say. It was really hard, I could not do anything well.

Elsa explained who the important people in her life were at various moments: in the reception centre, in the Netherlands and in Eritrea. This was useful in being able to analyse whether the crucial people in her life were and are able to guarantee her safety and development. Elsa drew her own house in Eritrea roughly. She took more time to draw the hill besides the house and stated – without being asked for explanation – that this was an important place for her, where she went whenever she had to think about something or felt sad. During the two meetings, the hill remained an important reference point. Whenever difficult topics were touched upon, Elsa went back to the hill in her thoughts, pointed at the hill and could tell what she thought while she was sitting there.

Elsa made schematic drawings of the two scenes that represent the central traumas she experienced during her migration journey. She used the drawings to point out who was standing where at the crucial moments. While talking about these stressful times in her life, it seemed to help her to look at the drawing and point to the people involved in the events. The diagnosticians drew a lifeline together with Elsa, marking the crucial points in the story she told. They decided whether the crucial moments and periods were 'happy' or 'sad' by adding 'emoticons'. While working on the lifeline, Elsa decided that she needed to talk more about the period when she was detained. She gave detailed information about the ill-treatment and the general living circumstances in the prison.

After the two sessions with Elsa, and with her agreement, the diagnosticians held an interview by phone with three professionals working with Elsa. Elsa's guardian described her as being insecure and shy, while sometimes being enthusiastic and amicable. The guardian thinks Elsa has difficulty expressing her feelings. When the guardian tries to speak about emotions, Elsa's thoughts seem to drift away. According to the guardian, Elsa experiences a lot of stress due to the uncertainty about the outcome of the asylum procedure. Elsa is beautiful and is happy when she gets compliments about her appearance. She is popular within her living group at the reception centre and gets along with everyone well. The teacher described Elsa as often enthusiastic and alert at school. She has the impression that Elsa wants to look happy but that she hides her true feelings. The teacher expressed a strong feeling that Elsa is affected by traumatic experiences but did not want to speak with her about them. The teacher thinks Elsa is intelligent; her school results are good despite the fact that she faces difficulties with her concentration. Her work tempo is extremely slow; sometimes she falls asleep during the lessons or does not attend the lessons at all. The mentor believes Elsa prefers to keep people she does not know at a distance. If she knows someone, Elsa becomes more open. The mentor observed that Elsa seems to feel sad often. She was greatly disturbed when her group mates had to move to another reception centre. It was difficult for her to say goodbye. The mentor is worried about the fact that Elsa withdraws from the group and thinks a lot on her own. She does not want to talk at these moments. However, at other times, she can be social and helpful.

Outcomes of the instruments

Elsa reported having experienced eight stressful life events (SLE). The average number of stressful life events reported by unaccompanied minors is 6.5. This high number of stressful events and the intensity of the traumatic experiences puts Elsa at risk for developing psychological problems. Elsa had a 'very high' score on the RATS total scale, as well as on the three subscales: intrusion, avoiding and hyper-arousal. Elsa has nightmares very often. She feels very upset and sad when she has to think about her traumatic memories. Although she tries to avoid thinking about the experiences, Elsa does not succeed in doing so. She is hyper-aroused and jumps at loud or unexpected noises. She has intensive problems with her concentration. Elsa feels desperate about the future. The outcomes on the SLE and RATS taken together indicate that Elsa might suffer from PTSD.

Elsa filled in the self-report version of the SDQ. She had a 'very high' total score and on the subscale on emotional symptoms, a 'slightly higher' score on attention/hyper-activity problems, a 'high score' on social problems and a 'near average' score on conduct problems and pro-social behaviour. The emotional and attention problems highlighted by the SDQ confirm the information found during the interview and other instruments. The social problems give a more ambiguous

Table 4.3 Scores on the Best Interests of the Child-Questionnaire for Elsa

Conditions for development	*Before departure from Eritrea*	*Expected after return to Eritrea*
Family		
1. Adequate physical care	Satisfactory	Satisfactory
2. Safe direct physical environment	Satisfactory	Satisfactory
3. Affective atmosphere	Good	Good
4. Supportive, flexible childrearing structure	Satisfactory	Satisfactory
5. Adequate example set by parents	Unknown	Unknown
6. Interest	Unknown	Unknown
7. Continuity in upbringing conditions, future perspective	Unsatisfactory	Unsatisfactory
Society		
8. Safe wider environment	Unsatisfactory	Unsatisfactory
9. Respect	Unsatisfactory	Unsatisfactory
10. Social network	Satisfactory	Unsatisfactory
11. Education	Unsatisfactory	Unsatisfactory
12. Contact with peers	Satisfactory	Moderate
13. Adequate example set in society	Unsatisfactory	Unsatisfactory
14. Stability in life circumstances, future perspective	Unsatisfactory	Unsatisfactory

picture. Elsa feels insecure about what other children think about her despite being well liked, according to others.

With the BIC-Q, it was concluded that due to social circumstances, Elsa's environment in Eritrea could not ensure her safety and development prior to her departure and the situation is expected to be the same or worse if she were forced to return to Eritrea. Table 4.3 shows the scores on the BIC-Q.

Diagnostic report

In order to provide insight into how the BIC assessment was described in Elsa's case, we include below some fragments of the concluding answers to the diagnostic questions as they were formulated in the report.

Elsa is extremely vulnerable due to a number of factors (GC 14, paras 75–77). She has experienced a disproportionally high number of stressful life events and has mental health problems that are likely associated with PTSD. Elsa's reactions to the traumatic stress show she is struggling to cope with her experiences. This makes it remarkably difficult for Elsa to think about her flight and time in Eritrea and to tell others her story about this period. It is important that time and energy is spent on winning her confidence before she is able to share details of her life story.

Elsa has always been a reserved child, not willing to share her feelings with others. The traumatic experiences reinforced this personality trait and made it even more difficult for her to speak openly. Research with traumatised children confirms it is difficult for them to tell a story coherently, consistently and chronologically (Christianson 1992). For Elsa, this is especially true. In general, traumatised children are known to be able to describe in detail the key events surrounding the trauma, but all details and events before and after the trauma may be difficult to retrieve or even lost. A focus on details, time and spatial concepts may disturb the child's ability to unlock a story (Saywitz *et al.* 2011). The diagnosticians observed this confusing effect of talking about details not related to the central traumas with Elsa. Elsa's social behaviour is a factor that promotes her resilience. She has one very good friend whom she trusts fully. Children at the reception centre and at school like her to join activities. She is quite popular and even admired.

Elsa's parents offered her an affective atmosphere at home and could fulfil the basic conditions for development. However, her parents could not protect Elsa against the risks in Eritrean society, threatening her development. She experienced fear she would have to join the army. She was ill-treated in prison. Elsa's story about her experiences in prison is supported by various sources. The inhumane treatment of prisoners, the torture during interrogations and the underground prisons are a known phenomenon in Eritrea. The prisons are notorious for the ill-treatment of detainees (UN Human Rights Council 2015: 11). Elsa had no stability in her life and no future prospects in Eritrea. The conditions for development in Eritrean society were insufficiently fulfilled (UNCRC 2013: paras 71–73).

Elsa fears for her life if she has to return to Eritrea because she has fled the country twice (ibid.: para 53–54). This fear is realistic given the current situation in Eritrea. There is a high risk of being detained again and being forced to join the military (European Asylum Support Office 2015: 42). The army in Eritrea is known to be particularly unsafe for women; they are regularly exposed to rape and sexual abuse (UN Human Rights Council 2015: 13). Political and social conditions in Eritrean society do not guarantee the safety and development of Elsa. Due to these circumstances, Elsa's family is not able to provide security and Elsa will not experience continuity and stability in living circumstances. The conditions for development will be insufficiently fulfilled if she has to return (UNCRC 2013: para 74). For Elsa's development, it is important that she is able to envision a future for herself, that she feels safe in her environment and that she can build a life without life-threatening risks. Given the current situation in Eritrea, the expectation is that she will not be able to experience this in her country of origin (ibid.: para 82).

Elsa's lawyer sent the BIC report together with her views on the draft negative decision to the immigration authorities. The IND withdrew the draft negative decision and took a positive decision instead. Elsa was offered protection as a refugee in the Netherlands.

Conclusions

The aim of this chapter was to determine which adjustments to the BIC assessment were necessary to meet the specific needs of recently arrived refugee children and to achieve the specific objective of providing a BIC assessment to immigration authorities who ultimately decide on the child's asylum claim. More attention is given to the mental health problems of the newly arrived refugee children and to various methods to support the children sharing their life stories. The development procedure of the adjustments of the BIC assessment went through three phases: exploration and theoretical research, consultation and a pilot study.

Our findings show that the adjusted BIC assessment is a useful tool to assess the best interests of recently arrived unaccompanied minors. The assessment provides the immigration authorities with scientifically and clinically based information that should be taken into account when a decision about an asylum claim is made. The process described in this study focuses on providing information that has to be taken into account with the asylum decision. We think this assessment could facilitate other decisions concerning unaccompanied minors – for example, about which reception facility is the most suitable for them (Kalverboer *et al.* 2016). Moreover, this BIC assessment could be used to facilitate decisions in the return process. The results on the BIC-Q provide the guardian with valuable information about which conditions in the rearing environment need to be improved in the country of origin to guarantee the development of the minor (Zevulun *et al.* 2015). Further research to tailor the BIC assessment to those kinds of decisions is recommended.

Two limitations of the process to adjust the BIC assessment to the situation of recently arrived refugee children should be explained. First, although significant attention was paid during the development process to how to facilitate the minors in sharing their life stories, it was not possible to prove any causal relationship between the methods and the extent of the disclosure of life stories. The small number of participants in the pilot study is one reason for this limitation, but even with a higher number of cases it will always be difficult to know whether the minor would have told the diagnosticians less when the methods to promote the disclosure of life stories had not been practised. Second, because the immigration authorities could not share information on whether the diagnostic reports had supported them in the asylum decisions, it is not possible to measure the impact of the BIC assessment on the decision.

The theoretical framework of the BIC assessment is based on scientific knowledge on what *all* children need for their development (Kalverboer and Zijlstra 2006). Those conditions for development, comprising the BIC-Model, do not differ for refugee children. The process of adjustments in the details of the assessment we made for the group of refugee children who are recently arrived in the host country could also be undertaken for other vulnerable groups of children. The development procedure took about 18 months and all stages provided the researchers with an increased knowledge about the material and procedural elements that should be taken into account. Reflecting on the procedure, we believe no elements were missed. The BIC methodology developed at the Study Centre is tailored to facilitate decisions on which rearing environment best serves the interests of the child.

The case of the Eritrean refugee Elsa illustrated how the adjusted BIC assessment was applied in her asylum procedure. We chose the case of Elsa because it demonstrates how the different approaches in interviewing refugee children between immigration authorities and diagnosticians may provide different information on the child. Taking time to build trust, a positive attitude, providing agency and the use of non-verbal methods seemed to be helpful tools to facilitate Elsa in telling her life story during the diagnostic interview. Immigration authorities could practise those methods as well, in order to build asylum decisions on more differentiated and reliable information that better conforms to the guidelines provided by the UN Committee on the Rights of the Child (2013). Likewise, guardians and social workers at reception centres could benefit from the results of the review on how refugee children could be supported to share information they think is important (Van Os *et al.* 2017).

The results of the interviews with guardians showed that the guardians feel there is no room in the asylum process to present their assessment of the interests of the child. The legal experts in the focus group stated that it is difficult for them to translate pedagogical information on the development of the child into the legal terms of the asylum procedure. However, the BIC assessment is in line with the guidelines of the UN Committee on the Rights of the Child (Kalverboer 2014: 15). Therefore, we think it is necessary to implement the best interests principle in the asylum procedure as an independent source of international protection (Pobjoy 2015).

Notes

1 We use the term 'refugee children' for unaccompanied children and children accompanied by their parents or caregivers who are *forced* to leave their home country and seek protection in another country. When these children ask for asylum, they are asylum-seeking children in the legal sense. Legally, these children are called refugees once their asylum claim has been accepted. Working from our pedagogical point of view, we prefer to call these children *refugees* seeking protection, whether on the grounds of being a refugee in the sense of the 1951 Refugee Convention or because of other forms of perceived danger in the home country (UNHCR 1994: 70).

2 The meetings lasted four hours each and were audio-taped with the permission of the participants. The tapes were transcribed. The transcriptions were structured and analysed by the first author according to the main issues raised during the expert meetings.

3 The average number of stressful life events unaccompanied refugee children report is 6.5, whereas for Dutch children the average is three (Bean *et al.* 2004b).

4 To protect the privacy of the child, Elsa is not her real name. Personally identifiable details in her life story are not included.

Bibliography

Abdalla, K. and Elklit, A. (2001) 'A nationwide screening survey of refugee children from Kosovo', *Torture*, Vol. 11, No. 2, 45–49.

Achenbach, M. T., Becker, A., Döpfner, M., Heiervang, E., Roessner, V., Steinhauzen, H. C. and Rothenberger, A. (2008) 'Multicultural assessment of child and adolescent psychopathology with ASEBA and SDQ instruments: research findings, applications, and future directions', *The Journal of Child Psychology and Psychiatry*, Vol. 49, 251–275. doi: 10.1111/j.1469-7610.2007.01867.x.

Adams, M. (2009) 'Stories of fracture and claim for belonging: Young migrants' narratives of arrival in Britain', *Children's Geographies*, Vol. 7, No. 2, 159–171. doi:10.1080/14733280902798878.

Almqvist, K. and Brandell-Forsberg, M. (1997) 'Refugee children in Sweden: Post-traumatic stress disorder in Iranian preschool children exposed to organized violence', *Child Abuse & Neglect*, Vol. 21, No. 4, 351–366.

Bean, T. M. (2006) *Assessing the psychological distress and mental health care needs of unaccompanied refugee minors in the Netherlands.* PhD Dissertation, Leiden University.

Bean, T., Eurelings-Bontekoe, E. H. M., Derluyn, I. and Spinhoven, P. (2004a) *RATS User's Manual*, Oegstgeest: Stichting Centrum '45.

Bean, T., Eurelings-Bontekoe, E. H. M., Derluyn, I. and Spinhoven, P. (2004b) *Stress Life Events. User's Manual*, Oegstgeest: Stichting Centrum '45.

Beltman, D., Kalverboer, M. E., Zijlstra, A. E., Van Os, E. C. C. and Zevulun, D. (2016) 'The Legal Effect of Best Interests of the Child Reports in judicial Migration Proceedings. A Qualitative Analysis of Five Cases', in T. Liefaard and J. Sloth-Nielsen (eds) *The United Nations Convention on the Rights of the Child: Taking Stock after 25 Years and Looking Ahead* (pp. 655–680), Leiden: Brill Nijhoff.

Beltman, D. and Zijlstra, A. E. (2013) 'De doorwerking van "het belang van het kind" ex artikel 3 VRK in het migratierecht: vanuit een bottom-up benadering op weg naar een top-down toepassing' ['The impact of "the best interests of the child" pursuant to Article 3 CRC in migration law: from a bottom-up approach towards a top-down application'], *Journaal Vreemdelingenrecht*, Vol. 12, No. 4, 286–306.

Chase, E. (2010) 'Agency and silence: Young people seeking asylum alone in the UK', *British Journal of Social Work*, Vol. 40, No. 7, 2050–2068. doi:10.1093/bjsw/bcp103.

Christianson, S. (1992) 'Emotional stress and eyewitness memory: A critical review', *Psychological Bulletin*, Vol. 112, No. 2, 284–309. doi:10.1037/0033-2909.112.2.284.

De Haene, L., Grietens, H. and Verschueren, K. (2010) 'Holding harm: Narrative methods in mental health research on refugee trauma', *Qualitative Health Research*, Vol. 20, No. 12, 1664–1676. doi:10.1177/1049732310376521.

De Haene, L., Rober, P., Adriaenssens, P. and Verschueren, K. (2012) 'Voices of dialogue and directivity in family therapy with refugees: Evolving ideas about dialogical refugee care', *Family Process*, Vol. 51, No. 3, 391–404.

Due, C., Riggs, D. W. and Augoustinos, M. (2014) 'Research with children of migrant and refugee backgrounds: A review of child-centered research methods', *Child Indicators Research*, Vol. 7, No. 1, 209–227.

Ekblad, S. (1993) 'Psychosocial adaptation of children while housed in a Swedish refugee camp: Aftermath of the collapse of Yugoslavia', *Stress Medicine*, Vol. 9, No. 3, 159–166. doi:10.1002/smi.2460090306.

European Asylum Support Office (2015) *EASO Country of Origin Information Report Eritrea Country Focus*, Luxembourg: Publications Office of the European Union.

Fazel, M., Reed, R. V., Panter-Brick, C. and Stein, A. (2012) 'Mental health of displaced and refugee children resettled in high-income countries: Risk and protective factors', *Lancet*, Vol. 379, 266–282. doi:10.1016/S0140-6736(11)60051-2.

Geltman, P. L., Augustyn, M., Barnett, E. D., Klass, P. E. and Groves, B. M. (2000) 'War trauma experience and behavioral screening of Bosnian refugee children resettled in Massachusetts', *Journal of Developmental and Behavioral Pediatrics*, Vol. 21, No. 4, 255–261. doi:10.1097/00004703-200008000-00001.

Goldin, S., Levin, L., Persson, L. A. and Hägglof, B. (2001) 'Stories of pre-war, war and exile: Bosnian refugee children in Sweden', *Medicine, Conflict, and Survival*, Vol. 17, No. 1, 25–47.

Goodman, R. (1997) 'The Strengths and Difficulties Questionnaire: A research note', *Journal of Child Psychology and Psychiatry*, Vol. 38, 581–586.

Hodes, M. (2000) 'Psychological distressed refugee children in the United Kingdom', *Child Psychology & Psychiatry Review*, Vol. 5, No. 2, 57–68.

Jaffa, T. (1996) 'Case report: Severe trauma in a teenage refugee', *Clinical Child Psychology and Psychiatry*, Vol. 1, No. 3, 347–351. doi:10.1177/1359104596013004.

Jakobsen, M., Demott, M. A. M. and Heir, T. (2014) 'Prevalence of psychiatric disorders among unaccompanied asylum-seeking adolescents in Norway', *Clinical Practice and Epidemiology in Mental Health*, Vol. 10, 53–58. doi:10.2174/17450 17901410010053.

Jensen, T. K., Fjermestad, K. W., Granly, L. and Wilhelmsen, N. H. (2015) 'Stressful life experiences and mental health problems among unaccompanied asylum-seeking children', *Clinical Child Psychology and Psychiatry*, Vol. 20, No. 1, 106–116. doi:10.1177/1359104513499356.

Kalverboer, M. E. (2014) *The Best Interests of the Child in Migration Law: Significance and Implications in Terms of Child Development and Child Rearing*, Amsterdam: SWP Publishers.

Kalverboer, M. E. and Zijlstra, A. E. (2006) *Het belang van het kind in het Nederlands recht: Voorwaarden voor ontwikkeling vanuit een pedagogisch perspectief [The interests of the child in Dutch law: Conditions of child development from a pedagogical perspective]*, Amsterdam: SWP Publishers.

Kalverboer, M. E., Zijlstra, A. E. and Knorth, E. J. (2009) 'The developmental consequences for asylum-seeking children living with the prospect for five years or more of enforced return to their home country', *European Journal of Migration and Law*, Vol. 11, No. 1, 41–67. doi:10.1163/157181609X410584.

Kalverboer, M., Zijlstra, E., Van Os, C., Zevulun, D., Ten Brummelaar, M. and Beltman, D. (2016) 'Unaccompanied minors in the Netherlands and the care facility in which they flourish best', *Child & Family Social Work*, doi:10.1111/cfs.12272.

Katsounari, I. (2014) 'Integrating psychodynamic treatment and trauma focused intervention in the case of an unaccompanied minor with PTSD', *Clinical Case Studies*, Vol. 13, No. 4, 352–367. doi:10.1177/1534650113512021.

Keselman, O., Cederborg, A., Lamb, M. E. and Dahlström, Ö. (2010) 'Asylum-seeking minors in interpreter-mediated interviews: What do they say and what happens to their responses?' *Child & Family Social Work*, Vol. 15, No. 3, 325–334. doi:10.1111/j.1365-2206.2010.00681.x.

Kohli, R. K. S. (2006a) 'The sound of silence: Listening to what unaccompanied asylum-seeking children say and do not say', *British Journal of Social Work*, Vol. 36, No. 5, 707–721. doi:10.1093/bjsw/bch305.

Kohli, R. K. S. (2006b) 'The comfort of strangers: Social work practice with unaccompanied asylum-seeking children and young people in the UK', *Child & Family Social Work*, Vol. 11, No. 1, 1–10. doi:10.1111/j.1365-2206.2006. 00393.x.

Kohli, R. K. S. (2011) 'Working to ensure safety, belonging and success for unaccompanied asylum-seeking children', *Child Abuse Review*, Vol. 20, No. 5, 311–323. doi:10.1002/car.1182.

Kohli, R. and Mather, R. (2003) 'Promoting psychosocial well-being in unaccompanied asylum seeking young people in the United Kingdom', *Child & Family Social Work*, Vol. 8, No. 3, 201–212.

Montgomery, E. (1998) 'Refugee children from the Middle East', *Scandinavian Journal of Social Medicine. Supplementum*, Vol. 54, 1–152.

Neuman, W. L. (2011) *Social Research Methods: Qualitative and Quantitative Approaches*, Boston, MA: Allyn & Bacon.

Ní Raghallaigh, M. (2014) 'The causes of mistrust amongst asylum seekers and refugees: Insights from research with unaccompanied asylum-seeking minors living in the Republic of Ireland', *Journal of Refugee Studies*, Vol. 27, No. 1, 82–100.

Oh, S. (2012) 'Photofriend: Creating visual ethnography with refugee children', *Area*, Vol. 44, No. 3, 282–288.

Petticrew, M. and Roberts, H. (2006) *Systematic Reviews in the Social Sciences: A Practical Guide*, Malden, MA: Blackwell.

Pobjoy, J. M. (2015) 'The best interests of the child principle as an independent source of international protection', *International & Comparative Law Quarterly*, Vol. 64, No. 2, 327–363. doi:10.1017/S0020589315000044.

Rothe, E., Lewis, J., Castillo-Matos, H., Martinez, O., Busquets, R. and Martinez, I. (2002), 'Posttraumatic stress disorder among Cuban children and adolescents after release from a refugee camp', *Psychiatric Services*, Vol. 53, No. 8, 970–976. doi:10.1176/appi.ps.53.8.970.

Saywitz, K. J., Lyon, T. D. and Goodman, G. S. (2011) 'Interviewing Children', in J. E. B. Myers (ed.) *The APSAC Handbook on Child Maltreatment* (pp. 337–360), Thousand Oaks, CA: SAGE Publications.

Schauer, E., Neuner, F., Elbert, T., Ertl, V., Onyut, L. P., Odenwald, M. *et al.* (2004) 'Narrative exposure therapy in children: A case study', *Intervention: International Journal of Mental Health, Psychosocial Work & Counselling in Areas of Armed Conflict*, Vol. 2, No. 1, 18–32.

Servan-Schreiber, D., Le Lin, B. and Birmaher, B. (1998) 'Prevalence of posttraumatic stress disorder and major depressive disorder in Tibetan refugee children', *Journal of the American Academy of Child and Adolescent Psychiatry*, Vol. 37, No. 8, 874–879.

Sourander, A. (1998) 'Behavior problems and traumatic events of unaccompanied refugee minors', *Child Abuse and Neglect*, Vol. 22, No. 7, 719–727. doi:10.1016/S0145-2134(98)00053-2.

St. Thomas, B. and Johnson, P. (2002) 'In their own voices: Play activities and art with traumatized children', *Groupwork: An Interdisciplinary Journal for Working with Groups*, Vol. 13, No. 2, 34–48.

Thomas, S., Thomas, S., Nafees, B. and Bhugra, D. (2004) '"I was running away from death": The pre-flight experiences of unaccompanied asylum seeking children in the UK', *Child: Care, Health and Development*, Vol. 30, No. 2, 113–122.

UN Committee on the Rights of the Child (2005) *General Comment No. 6. (2005) Treatment of unaccompanied and separated children outside their country of origin.* CRC/C/GC/6. Available online at www2.ohchr.org/english/bodies/crc/docs/GC6.pdf (accessed 15 February 2017).

UN Committee on the Rights of the Child (2013) General comment No. 14 (2013) *The right of the child to have his or her best interests taken as a primary consideration (art.3, para 1)*. CRC/C/GC/14. Available online at www2.ohchr.org/English/bodies/crc/docs/GC/CRC_C_GC_14_ENG.pdf (accessed 15 February 2017).

UNHCR (1994) *Refugee Children: Guidelines on Protection and Care*. Geneva: UNHCR. Available online at www.unhcr.org/3b84c6c67.html (accessed 15 February 2017).

UN Human Rights Council (2015) *Report of detailed findings of the Commission of Inquiry on human rights in Eritrea*. A/HRC/29/42. Available online at https://documents-dds-ny.un.org/doc/UNDOC/GEN/G15/114/50/PDF/G1511450.pdf? (accessed 15 February 2017).

Van Nijnatten, C., Boesveldt, N., Schilperoord, A. and Mass, M. (2001) 'The construction of parental authority and co-operation in reports to the Dutch Court', *International Journal of the Sociology of Law*, Vol. 29, No. 3, 237–252. doi:10.1006/ijsl.2001.0149.

Van Os, C. and Beltman, D. (2012) 'Kinderrechten in het migratierecht' ['Children's Rights in Migration Law']. In M. Blaak, M. Bruning, M. Eijgenraam, M. Kaandorp and S. Meuwese (eds) *Handboek Internationaal Jeugdrecht [Handbook on International Youth Law]*, Leiden: Defence for Children, 647-818.

Van Os, E. C. C., Kalverboer, M. E., Zijlstra, A. E., Post, W. J. and Knorth, E. J. (2016) 'Knowledge of the unknown child: A systematic review on the elements of the Best Interests of the Child Assessment for recently arrived refugee children', *Clinical Child and Family Psychology Review*. doi: 10.1007/s10567-016-0209-y.

Van Os, E. C. C., Zijlstra, A. E., Kalverboer, M. E., Post, W.J. and Knorth, E. J. (2017). Finding keys: A systematic review of barriers and facilitators for refugee children's disclosure of their life stories (submitted).

Verhoeven, N. (2015) *Doing Research. The Hows and Whys of Applied Research*, Amsterdam: Boom Lemma.

Vervliet, M., Meyer Demott, M. A., Jakobsen, M., Broekaert, E., Heir, T. and Derluyn, I. (2014) 'The mental health of unaccompanied refugee minors on arrival in the host country', *Scandinavian Journal of Psychology*, Vol. 55, No. 1, 33–37.

Vickers, B. (2005) 'Cognitive model of the maintenance and treatment of post-traumatic stress disorder applied to children and adolescents', *Clinical Child Psychology and Psychiatry*, Vol. 10, No. 2, 217–234.

Warr, S. (2010) 'Counseling refugee young people: An exploration of therapeutic approaches', *Pastoral Care in Education*, Vol. 28, No. 4, 269–282.

Zevulun, D., Kalverboer, M. E., Zijlstra, A. E., Post, W. J. and Knorth, E. J. (2015) 'Returned migrant children in Kosovo and Albania', *Cross-Cultural Research*, Vol. 49, No. 5, 489–521. doi:10.1177/1069397115608173.

Zijlstra, A. E. (2012) *In the best interest of the child? A study into a decision-support tool validating asylum-seeking children's rights from a behavioural scientific perspective*. PhD dissertation, University of Groningen.

Zijlstra, A. E., Kalverboer, M. E., Post, W. J., Ten Brummelaar, M. D. C. and Knorth, E. J. (2013) 'Could the BIC-Q be a decision support tool to predict the development of asylum-seeking children?', *International Journal of Law and Psychiatry*, Vol. 36, 129–135. doi:10.1016/j.ijlp.2013.01.005.

5 Asylum experiences in Austria from the perspective of unaccompanied minors

Best interests of the child in reception procedures and everyday life

Ayşe Dursun and Birgit Sauer

Introduction

An increasing number of unaccompanied minors escape war and poverty in their countries of origin and set out on a dangerous and uncertain journey in pursuit of security and protection. Austria is both a common transit country and destination of unaccompanied minors who have either lost family members on the way to Europe or left home alone. In 2015, 8,277 applications were lodged by unaccompanied minor refugees in Austria.[1] Overall, 88,340 asylum applications were lodged in Austria in 2015 which signify the most dramatic increase in the last decade (Bundesministerium für Inneres 2015) and represent an enormous challenge in terms of resources and capacity for state authorities both on national and subnational levels. The federal reception centre in Traiskirchen, Lower Austria, reached full capacity in the summer of 2015 and pictures of asylum seekers sleeping in tents and in the open circulated through the media.[2] However, this obvious state failure reflects not only Austria's reluctant approach to refugees, but also the country's unwillingness to admit third-country migrants. The Austrian provinces (*Länder*) failed to provide adequate accommodation for the rapidly growing number of asylum seekers who were admitted to the asylum process, which further contributed to the overcrowding at the initial reception centre. The Austrian UNHCR described the situation in Traiskirchen as 'unbearable, dangerous and degrading'.[3] Similarly, Member of the Austrian Ombudsman Board, Günther Kräuter, warned that the current situation in Traiskirchen was unbearable for unaccompanied minors in particular. Reportedly, around 1,800 unaccompanied minor refugees were accommodated in Traiskirchen *de facto* without any special child support. In late July 2015, the Lower Austrian governor announced a freeze on admissions to Traiskirchen due to the deteriorating hygiene and medical conditions in the facility. Around the same time, the *Bund* – the Austrian federal government – announced that 1,100 new accommodation places would be provided for asylum seekers. The City of Vienna, one of the nine Austrian provinces, took over the unaccompanied girls from the initial reception centre in

Traiskirchen. Further asylum seekers were moved to *Länder* facilities to relieve Traiskirchen.

This chapter analyses the experiences of unaccompanied minor refugees from their own perspective. How do they – implicitly and explicitly – describe, define and construct their best interests? What are their needs and wishes in the process of migration, at the time of arrival in Austria and during the asylum procedure? The chapter considers unaccompanied minors' agency as constitutive of their definition of what is in their best interests. Or, put differently, minor refugees' agency rests on their ability to define and negotiate what is in their best interests. The aim of the chapter is to contextualise international and national norms of the best interests of the child in experiences of unaccompanied minor refugees and hence to demonstrate how unaccompanied minor refugees despite the adverse conditions of migration and discriminatory practices of the Austrian state claim at least some rights and construct liminal situations between childhood, dependency and the 'right to rights'.

In the following, we elaborate first the theoretical considerations and method that have guided this research. Then we outline the Austrian asylum regime in terms of national and international laws and institutions involved in the asylum procedure, ranging from the Federal Office for Asylum to child and youth welfare services at the *Länder* level. In a third step, we present our data collected through field research and discuss our findings by distinguishing between three stages of asylum: escape, reception and everyday life. Finally, we discuss the main findings of our research in the light of our theoretical lens.

Theoretical considerations and method

The Austrian asylum regime displays a complex composition of national, supranational and international laws and regulations, which are complementary and at times contradictory to each other. This is due to the fact that the various institutions entrusted with the implementation of asylum law and integration measures pursue different logics (see Giner 2007). For example, while the child and youth care services and social workers at care facilities for unaccompanied minors are guided by protection and support concerns, the Ministry of the Interior, the aliens police and the labour market service are driven by national security and labour market protection concerns. Therefore, unaccompanied minor asylum seekers, as minors *and* asylum seekers, are caught at the interface between inclusive childcare policies and exclusive migration and asylum policies (see Giner 2007; Heidbrink 2014; Vitus and Lidén 2010). The social position of unaccompanied minor refugees is the outcome of political negotiations and debates over the (re)distribution and allocation of resources, which condense in legal norms. For instance, while unaccompanied minor refugees, as minors, enjoy additional rights compared with adult asylum seekers, such as child-friendly accommodation, guardianship and legal representation in the asylum procedure, as asylum seekers they face restrictions in access to vocational training and the labour market. For the same reason, unaccompanied minor refugees do not enjoy the same care standards as do Austrian children without parents and under the guardianship of the child and youth welfare services (Glawischnig 2014; Fronek 2010). This is unmistakably manifested in the lower daily rates for unaccompanied minor refugees compared with Austrian children without parents or legal guardian. Hence, unaccompanied minors are treated as 'half children' only – that is, their status as children in need of special care and recognition is thwarted by their status as asylum seekers who are treated with 'institutionalized suspicion' (Giner 2007). This is especially true for unaccompanied minors who are assumed to make false statements (e.g. about their age and the background from which they have escaped).

Asylum is not only a condition that imposes itself on unaccompanied minor refugees, nor is migration a mere reaction (e.g. to immediate danger), but it is a 'movement' to live a life on one's own (Papadopoulos and Tsianos 2013: 185; see Mezzadra 2011; Karakayali and Tsianos 2005). This approach does not consider unaccompanied minor refugees as mere victims and a vulnerable group with special needs, but is interested in exploring their narratives and experiences of migration. Also, migration and escape are not perceived as processes with a clear end – for instance, integration, assimilation or citizenship – but as ongoing processes which might challenge clear-cut notions of belonging, of borders and citizenship as well as of age. The authenticity of the narrative is an integral part of every asylum procedure where the unaccompanied minor is expected by authorities to tell a plausible story of their escape background which will legitimise their application for international protection in accordance with the definitions provided by the law (see Kohli 2009). Thus, minors are urged to tell a 'thin' and 'rational' version of their personal story, which does not do justice to the complexity of migration and the often contradictory experiences of young refugees (ibid.: 112). Different from 'official' escape stories, narratives help minors to position themselves in their present and past environments. The self-positioning includes reflection on past experiences as well as the articulation of expectations and hopes, of fear and dissatisfaction.

Although the concept of the best interests of the child appears in legal documents, which regulate the reception, asylum and care procedures after the minors' arrival in the host country, minors prove to have a solid understanding of their best interests. Their best interests have at least two dimensions. On one hand, the concept of best interests is reactive and aims to avoid immediate danger and threats such as war, forced enlistment and violence, and entails the prevention of harm to the minors' physical and psychological integrity. This dimension is relatively well acknowledged by national and international law and lends legitimacy to asylum applications. On the other hand, the proactive dimension of unaccompanied minors' best interests includes long-term goal setting, which goes beyond survival and avoidance of physical and psychological harm. Yet these two dimensions are inherently related to one another and therefore inseparable. Austrian legal norms and enforcement authorities appear to distinguish strictly between asylum seekers who flee their homes for survival and those who come to Europe to improve their living conditions. Furthermore, the latter have been increasingly accused by right-wing political parties – not only in Austria – of exploiting the asylum regime and are pejoratively called 'economic refugees' (*Wirtschaftsflüchtlinge*). In the same vein, unaccompanied minor refugees are labelled 'anchor children' (*Ankerkinder*) whose parents are accused of instrumentalising their children in order to travel to Europe safely through family reunification. These distinctions show that unaccompanied minors' interests are insufficiently defined by law, leading to arbitrary hierarchies of minors' needs. Minors are forced to figure out how to deal with these hierarchies, which do not reflect their experiences.

Within the framework of the EU-funded research project 'In Whose Best Interests? Exploring Unaccompanied Minors' Rights through the Lens of Migration and Asylum Procedures', the Austrian team conducted in-depth interviews with 17 experts working with and on behalf of unaccompanied minors and with 12 (former) unaccompanied minor refugees. Among the experts were two managers and two care workers in a care facility for unaccompanied minor refugees, one officer from the Ministry of the Interior, two officers from the child and youth welfare services in two Austrian *Länder*, two legal advisors/ representatives to (unaccompanied minor) asylum seekers in the asylum process, one officer of the Children's Ombudsman in one of the *Länder*, one national politician, the manager of a non-profit organisation which works, among others, with unaccompanied minor refugees, one expert on unaccompanied minors from an NGO dealing with asylum, a lawyer at a network project which provides legal advice and representation services for asylum seekers, an expert from the UNHCR, an activist and a voluntary godfather to an unaccompanied minor.

Furthermore, two former unaccompanied minors and ten unaccompanied minors were interviewed. Their ages ranged between 14 and 23. The youngsters came from Afghanistan, Syria, Iran, Pakistan, Chechen Republic, Republic of Dagestan and Somalia.[4] All but one of the unaccompanied minors (a girl from Somalia) were male, which matches the overall gender distribution among unaccompanied minors in Austria. All interviews were transcribed, coded and interpreted according to our general questions.

The Austrian asylum regime: unaccompanied minor refugees at the interface between childcare and asylum law

Austria ratified the UN Convention on the Rights of the Child (UNCRC) in 1992 with a reservation for fulfilment, which did not allow its direct implementation through courts and administrative bodies. The Convention did not have constitutional ranking, but only that of a simple law. In 2011, the National Council passed the Federal Constitutional Act on the Rights of Children (*Bundesverfassungsgesetz über die Rechte von Kindern*, BGBl. I No. 4/ 2011) which involved some but not all paragraphs of the UNCRC. The Constitutional Act established the 'welfare of the child' (*Wohl des Kindes* or *Kindeswohl*), the German equivalent to the 'best interests of the child', as a guiding principle in all measures to be taken by public and private authorities (Article 1). According to this, all children have a right to regular personal contacts, child labour is prohibited and every child has a right to participation and consideration of his/her opinion, to a non-violent upbringing and protection against abuse and exploitation as well as care that corresponds to his/her needs. Moreover, the Austrian Civil Code (*Allgemeines Bürgerliches Gesetzbuch*, JGS No. 946/1811) establishes the best interests of the child as a guiding principle, which should be considered and ensured in every matter, in particular guardianship and personal contacts, concerning a minor (Article 138). A child's best interests entail, among other things, providing the child with adequate food, medical care, accommodation, upbringing and security, protection of his/her physical and mental integrity, and observance of his/her rights, demands and interests. In the case of a child whose parents are unknown, the child and youth welfare services are by law entrusted with the guardianship of the child (Article 207).

Despite existing legal ground, the guardianship for unaccompanied minor refugees remained a mostly unregulated area (Fronek and Rothkappel 2013) until 2005 when the Supreme Court ruled that unaccompanied minor refugees also need to have a legal guardian at all times (OGH 19.10.2005, 7 Ob 209/05v). In its explanation, the Court noted that no distinction can be made between Austrian citizens and non-citizens when it comes to the basic rights established in the Civil Code, and that beyond the satisfaction of basic needs such as food, accommodation, clothing, schooling and medical care, the minor needs support for physical, mental, spiritual and moral development, which can only be assured through guardianship.

Despite enduring structural shortcomings, Austria has a relatively comprehensive system of basic care for asylum seekers. In 2003, the Council of the European Union laid down in its directive (2003/9/EC) the minimum standards for the reception of asylum seekers and urged Member States to bring into force legal regulations and administrative provisions necessary to comply with the directive by 6 February 2005. The Austrian *Bund* and the *Länder* had to restructure the basic care system for asylum seekers comprehensively in accordance with this directive. They concluded a Basic Welfare Support Agreement (BGBl. I Nr. 80/2004, *Grundversorgungsvereinbarung*) in 2004 in order to establish a division of labour and costs between the *Bund* and the *Länder* as well as to unify services throughout Austria and avoid regional overload. According to the agreement, the *Bund* is responsible for providing initial reception centres and care facilities for asylum seekers in the admission process, whereas *Länder* are responsible for the care and support of asylum seekers who have been admitted to the asylum process. *Bund* and the *Länder* may outsource these services to church and private institutions and organisations. Basic Welfare Support includes board and lodging, monthly pocket money for persons in accommodation facilities, medical examination at the reception centre, health insurance, information about legal procedures, consultation and tutoring by qualified personnel such as translators, schooling and transport costs for school attendance and school supplies as well as providing structure to the daily routine. The agreement acknowledges unaccompanied minors as a vulnerable group among asylum seekers, compared with adult asylum seekers or minor asylum seekers with parents, and lays down further standards for unaccompanied minor refugees. Depending on their degree of self-reliance and autonomy, minors are accommodated in care facilities with a staff-to-child ratio of 1:10, 1:15 or 1:20; 1:10 is currently the most common ratio in Austria (Glawischnig 2016). Special provisions for unaccompanied minor refugees include psychological support, a suitable daily routine, support with the processing of questions related to age, identity, country of origin, residence of family members, family reunification if possible, the development of an integration plan and measures for schooling and professional training to acquire necessary skills for self-preservation.

Despite significant improvements in the welfare support system for unaccompanied minors in the last decade, this group does not enjoy the same resources and standards as Austrian children without parents under the guardianship of child and youth welfare services. Some aspects of the discrimination faced by unaccompanied minors are immediate, resulting directly from their legal definition as 'non-citizens' and 'asylum seekers'. For example, unaccompanied minor refugees are granted lower daily rates than their Austrian counterparts who are cared for by the child and youth welfare services. Other aspects are more complex, displaying an interplay of factors such as scarce resources, the high workload of enforcement officers and lack of political will. Despite being systematic, discrimination against unaccompanied minors is mitigated by childcare laws, committed care workers and critical civil society organisations which push the public debate away from nationalist security or labour market concerns and towards children's human rights. Most importantly, the agency of unaccompanied minors who take the initiative to 'violate' the nation-state's borders in pursuit of survival, safety and self-fulfilment represents the greatest challenge to discriminatory practices towards this group of minors.

Unaccompanied minor refugees and their best interests in Austria – a long migration journey

Escape

Minors escape from immediate danger in search of safety in terms of physical and psychological integrity. (Civil) War is one of the primary sources of flight for unaccompanied minors (Adam, 16; Hamed, 17; Khalid, 16; Karim, 14). Adam (16) from Syria explains that it had become increasingly difficult for him to stay in Syria because he was forced to fight in the ranks of one or other of the conflicting armed groups, but he did not want to fight at all. He travelled to Lebanon and Egypt, and crossed the Mediterranean to Italy, finally arriving in Austria. The journey took him around 20 days. Hamed (17) came to Austria from Syria via Turkey, Greece, Macedonia, Serbia and Hungary. He travelled for around two and a half months. It was a tough and sad journey, Hamed told us. He even had to spend 25 days in a sort of 'jail' in Serbia because he did not have a passport with him. It took Ehsan (23) five months to arrive in Austria. He is a member of the ethnic-religious minority Hazaras and lost his brother and friends in religiously motivated assassinations.

Also, high rates of crime and poverty represent threats to minors in their countries of origin. Asif (16) from Afghanistan was robbed twice on the street and felt increasingly unsafe in his home town. To this day, when walking to his care facility at night, he feels insecure, turns and looks back frequently because he is afraid that someone might be following him. Besides common threats, unaccompanied minor refugees face gender-specific threats. For example, male youngsters are more likely to face conscription, whereas female minors are threatened by violent patriarchal practices. Aasiya (17) moved from Dubai to her father's home country Somalia after her father lost his job. In Somalia, her relatives and the broader community put Aasiya's father under increasing pressure to allow Aasiya to be subjected to genital mutilation and forced marriage. Aasiya's father decided to send his daughter to Europe where she would be safe. Our respondents also told us that, contrary to common prejudice, not every minor is sent away by his or her parents. One example is Asif (16) who had started receiving threats from the Taliban, who were searching for his brother after he had managed to escape them. After they had kidnapped Asif's father to make him tell them where his son was, Asif decided to leave. Malik (18) is traumatised by leaving his family behind and having to live thousands of kilometres away from them. However, after six months of migration he decided that it was also a chance for him to start a new life and learn a new language and about a new culture. He embraced this challenge.

Only one minor, Rasheed (17), left Iran with his parents. However, he lost them at the Turkish–Iranian border and had to continue the journey alone. Since then, he has had no contact with his family. In order to afford the journey to Europe, Rasheed had to make a stopover in Greece to earn money. He stayed with a migrant family and had to do housework for the family in return for his accommodation. Besides labour exploitation, he had to face widespread racism after witnessing the murder of a migrant boy by a racist group in a park. The migration journey is not only long and dangerous, but it is also expensive. Back in 2007, traffickers demanded around $7,000 for a journey per person from Afghanistan to Austria; currently, it is around $10,000, as reported by Ehsan (23).

Unaccompanied minor refugees try to organise a 'calm' (Tahir, 17) and 'normal' life (Karim, 14) throughout their migration journey. This life includes first and foremost living with their families, schooling, a regular job and self-fulfilment. But when Karim (14) and Khalid (16) arrived in Bulgaria, they were put in a jail-like place where the brothers had to spend around 30 days with other unaccompanied minors from Afghanistan and Syria. They were only allowed to leave the room, which did not have any outside view, for one hour a day. In Hungary, the brothers were put into a very dirty facility; the younger brother Karim (14) is convinced that this infringed their human rights. When the brothers arrived in Austria, they were positively surprised by how different Austria was from Bulgaria and Hungary with regard to resources and treatment.

In some cases, the decision to leave is encouraged by the already precarious residence status of the minors and their families in the country of origin. Rasheed (17) grew up in Iran, but he and his parents did not have a residence permit in Iran. Afghanistan, where his parents were originally from, did not grant the family such a permit either. In both countries, Afghanistan and Iran, Rasheed feared deportation to the other. Austria has granted Rasheed subsidiary protection – that is, protection from deportation despite having been denied asylum. For the first time in his life, Rasheed explains, he possesses an official document with his name on it and he finally feels like a human, as he puts it in the interview.

Also, the escape to Europe for unaccompanied minors is sometimes an open-ended journey with no predetermined destination. Some unaccompanied minors had sophisticated criteria to determine whether to stay or not in a country, such as human rights. For example, when Karim (14) and his 16-year-old brother left Afghanistan for Europe, they decided to terminate their journey in a country where human rights are recognised and respected. Majeed (17) originally wanted to go to France, but then stayed in Austria. Also, through their asylum networks, unaccompanied minors acquire information to compare the living conditions in different European countries. Adam (16), for instance, originally wanted to go to Sweden. When he arrived in Italy, his father convinced him on the phone that he should go to Austria, which he did. However, Adam keeps hearing from his friends that Sweden and Germany are much better than Austria.

Overall, war, crime, poverty, lack of a permanent residence permit in the country of origin and patriarchal practices such as genital mutilation and forced marriages are among the common reasons why minors leave their homes. Beyond immediate threats, minors are proactively motivated by the idea of a peaceful life in another country, given the lack of any such prospect in their own country. Finally, unaccompanied minor refugees make use of their vast experiences and networks to judge the quality of life among the countries in Europe, which shapes their decision to apply for asylum in one specific country. This also helps them to develop a sense of what their needs and rights are.

Reception and asylum procedure

Almost all unaccompanied minor refugees who have contact with state authorities apply for asylum in Austria (interview: Officer at child and youth welfare services 1). In order to qualify as a refugee, however, unaccompanied minors pragmatically 'thin down' their stories vis-à-vis state authorities (see Kohli 2009). Ehsan (23) from Afghanistan says that during his asylum interview he had to tell the officer stories about humiliating situations in order to prove the credibility of the threats from which he had fled. Ehsan had four such interviews where he had to tell his story over and over again. Ehsan complains that nobody asks a minor from Syria why he has come to Austria because the degree of destructiveness that the Syrian civil war has reached is commonly acknowledged. However, minors from Afghanistan who similarly escape (civil) war are expected to name a personal reason for their entry to Austria, Ehsan remarks critically. Although Ehsan had no contact with his family for five months while he was on his way to Europe, he did not dare to call them immediately after his arrival because he feared that having a family could impact the outcome of his asylum application negatively. He says there is too much pressure on asylum seekers by state authorities, which causes a feeling of 'paranoia'. Karim (14) from Afghanistan tells about his experience when he was interviewed by the Federal Office for Immigration and Asylum (*Bundesamt für Fremdenwesen und Asyl*). Karim and his brother had a tough journey which took them through numerous countries, including Bulgaria, Serbia and Hungary, during which they spent three days in the mountains and 30 days in a prison-like place in Bulgaria together with other minors from Afghanistan and Syria. Karim wanted to tell the officer conducting the interview more about his terrible journey and about the bad experiences he had had on his way. However, he was often interrupted; the officer did not care about his feelings and was primarily interested in the questions of why and how he came to Austria. Karim then briefly told the officer that his life was in danger because of the Taliban. Other minors' stories, too, confirm that the reception and admission procedures for asylum allow only a very thin version of their multilayered stories, let alone their interests. 'Thin' should be understood in a double sense. First, state officials are interested only in specific parts of the migration story. Second, minors learn to tell only pieces of their experiences because they do not know what the state official wants to hear, and therefore in telling 'thick' stories they might be inconsistent.

Similarly, Majeed (17) was asked at the initial reception centre how and why he came to Austria. He was not asked, at any time, about his feelings, experiences and opinions. Aasiya (17), the only minor who travelled by plane to Austria, applied for asylum at the airport. After that, she was taken to a place which was 'like a jail' with a bed and a toilet; the officers locked the door behind her. She was very cold and very scared, and wondered whether she was being punished for something she had done. In the morning, she was brought to the initial reception centre in Traiskirchen. Although the police officers were very kind to her, the reception procedure was rather scary and, because minors are poorly informed on the process, incomprehensible for her.

Another important but humiliating and also frightening experience is the age assessment procedure. When Asif (16) arrived in Traiskirchen, he informed the gateman of his intention to apply for asylum. The gateman informed a female officer who came to the door to pick up Asif. She took him to the police station in Traiskirchen where his fingerprints and picture were taken. To prove his identity and age, he submitted a copy of his national ID, which was not considered credible by the officer. Even after his sister sent him the original ID, the officer still doubted its authenticity and ordered an age assessment. Due to the age assessment procedure and the suspicion with which he was confronted, Asif had to stay in Traiskirchen two months longer than expected. Nevertheless, the result of the age assessment confirmed Asif's statement. Adam (16), Hamed (17) and Salim (17), on the other hand, did not have to undergo an age assessment because they had their IDs from Syria and Afghanistan with them.

Age assessment is a highly controversial procedure among experts with regard to both its ethical legitimacy and its scientific reliability. According to the Federal Office for Immigration and Asylum Procedures Act (BGBl. I No. 87/2012, *BFA-Verfahrensgesetz*), an age assessment can be ordered by the Federal Office for

Asylum or the Federal Administrative Court when a person has failed to prove his/her minority by means of credible documents. A multifactorial method including radiological examination, particularly X-ray, is used. Although it is defined by law as a last resort, an expert from the Ministry of Interior confirmed during the interview that age assessment is a very common practice. Minors are either poorly informed on their right to decline the assessment or they fear that non-participation may be considered unwillingness to cooperate and thus impact the application outcome negatively. In this sense, age assessments demonstrate institutionalised suspicion against asylum-seeking minors. For example, the expert from the Ministry remarked during the interview that minor applicants 'strategically' claim to be 16 years old so that there is still enough time to bring their families to Austria after they are granted subsidiary protection.

The experiences of minors at the initial reception facility in Traiskirchen are mostly bad. Overall, experts agree that Traiskirchen is an inappropriate place to accommodate unaccompanied minors who have no or only very limited access to personal care and assistance, education and leisure activities. Adam (16) reports that in Traiskirchen they were not allowed to leave the building after 9 p.m. and the officers would shout at them. Rasheed (17) confirms that it is 'like a jail' where people leave their rooms to eat and return to their rooms as soon as they are finished. Every day many new people arrive in Traiskirchen and others leave without anyone knowing where they are going. In describing his feelings about Traiskirchen, Rasheed wondered when and to where he would be going from here. Also, minors report that the accommodation in Traiskirchen is very overcrowded (Salim, 17), which sometimes leads to tension and competition among asylum seekers. Majeed (17) had a fight with another asylum seeker who cut in line and pushed himself forward while at the queue for food. One of the parties was badly injured during the fight and Majeed received a warning from the police as a consequence. Experts agree that the long waiting time in Traiskirchen, often on grounds of inadequate care facilities in the *Länder*, is not in the best interests of the minors, and lacks such infrastructure as individual care and mentoring (interviews: Legal advisor to asylum seekers; Manager at care facility 1).

However, one best-practice example is *Drehscheibe*, a pedagogical care facility of the Child and Youth Welfare Services of the City of Vienna, which temporarily accommodates unaccompanied minor refugees. Once unaccompanied minors are identified (e.g. by the police at train stations), they are brought to *Drehscheibe*. A *Drehscheibe* employee then accompanies the minor to Traiskirchen where he/she applies for asylum. After the application, the minor is taken back to *Drehscheibe* the same day without the minor having to stay in Traiskirchen (interview: Manager care facility 2). Two minors we have talked to were accommodated in *Drehscheibe* and confirmed that they only spent a couple of hours in Traiskirchen. After initial reception procedures, minors are moved from *Drehscheibe* to a permanent care facility where they stay until they turn 18. Experts in *Drehscheibe* assess, depending on a minors' level of autonomy and need for assistance, whether he/she can be accommodated in a Basic Welfare Support facility or, in the case of a greater need for assistance, in a facility of the child and youth welfare services (interview: Expert from an NGO dealing with asylum). Intervention centres like *Drehscheibe* are particularly important for underage minors – that is, those of 14 or younger according to Austrian law – who otherwise would have to be accommodated in Traiskirchen until they are admitted to the asylum procedure or until a permanent care facility is provided by one of the *Länder* (interview: Officer at child and youth welfare services 1). Experts encourage the establishment of such clearing centres in every *Land* because clearing, in most cases, remains an act of good will rather than institutionalised common practice (interview: Expert from an NGO dealing with asylum).

The asylum process normally take a very long time, which is a clear violation of the best interests of children who are forced to live in a state of uncertainty for long periods (interview: Legal advisor to asylum seekers). Malik (18), who had been living in Austria for two years, was still waiting for the outcome of his asylum application at the time of our interview. Although he submitted a complaint against the Federal Office for Asylum for failing to meet the legal deadline more than once, he did not receive any answer. Malik remembers being very depressed during that long time of waiting. Majeed (17) and Asif (16) had been living in Austria for over a year at the time of our interview and were still waiting for a decision. However, minors were not only upset about their situation; they were at the same time well informed about the Office's legal duties and their own rights. For example, Asif (16) and his legal representative filed a complaint against the Federal Office for Asylum, which had failed to meet the legal deadline of six months after the application was made to assign Asif an appointment. Asif notes that the Office failed to meet the legal deadline for a second time when it did not respond to the complaint within three months. Despite the Office's intense workload, Asif thinks that rules should be followed, especially when the affected party is a minor. Similarly, Salim (17) had lodged his asylum application over a year ago and was still waiting for a letter from the Federal Office for Asylum at the time of our interview. Salim says that he did not cause any problems whatsoever and had not done anything other than learn German since he had arrived in Austria. Therefore, he does not understand why he has not been given an interview appointment by now. Another minor (Majeed, 17) had already been waiting for nine months for his second interview with the Office. During these nine months, he did not receive a letter or any form of notification whatsoever from the Office. Hence, minors are kept in limbo about their stay in Austria, about their families and their future.

The long duration of asylum procedures in Austria massively and in various ways affects the best interests of unaccompanied minors. Family reunification is only possible if a minor is granted asylum by his/her 18th birthday. Since the amendment to the Act on Asylum in 2016, family members can apply to enter Austria three years after subsidiary protection has been granted at the earliest, which means that the minor cannot be older than 15 years when he/she is granted the status. Also, the new legal deadline disadvantages minors from Afghanistan additionally since they are mostly granted subsidiary protection rather than asylum (e.g. as opposed to minors from Syria).[5] Some minors we have talked to were waiting for over a year for an interview appointment from the Federal Office for Asylum and were already 17 years old or about to turn 18 (Majeed 17; Salim, 17). Only one minor, Hamed (17) from Syria, who had been in Austria for ten months at the time of our interview, was looking forward to having his parents in Austria soon within the framework of family reunification since he had been granted asylum. Unfortunately, because only minor siblings are allowed to travel with parents to the host country, Hamed's siblings, all of whom are 18 years old or older, must stay in Syria. In addition, family reunification is also delayed or precluded because minors lose track of their families or because families cannot afford the expensive DNA tests.

Both minors and experts agree that the living conditions in the overcrowded initial reception facility in Traiskirchen are not suitable for children who lack care, education and leisure activities. Facilities such as *Drehscheibe* are highly desirable both to avoid accommodation in Traiskirchen during the admission process and to carry out a clearing procedure to identify the individual degree of autonomy and care needs of minors before they are permanently accommodated in a care facility. Finally, long asylum procedures put minors under additional stress and drastically reduce the chances for family reunification for minors with subsidiary protection.

Everyday life

Once admitted to the asylum process, unaccompanied minor refugees are moved from the federal reception facilities of the *Bund* to the care facilities of the *Länder*. While most of the minors are accommodated in special care facilities for unaccompanied minors within the framework of the Basic Welfare Support for asylum seekers, only some of them, usually those who are 14 or younger, are accommodated in the care facilities of the child and youth welfare services of the *Länder*. The child and youth welfare services of the *Länder* are entrusted with the guardianship of the minors, which, according to the Austrian Civil Code, encompasses care, bringing up and education, wealth management and legal representation. The child and youth welfare services transfer the care and education to the respective care facility where the minor is accommodated for the rest of the asylum process and/or until he/she turns 18. Once unaccompanied minor refugees move from the mass accommodation facilities of initial reception centres such as Traiskirchen to the care facilities in the *Länder*, they find more favourable conditions to articulate and pursue their own interests. While asylum is foremost a bureaucratic procedure, which leaves little room for participation, the desires and needs of the minors find considerably more recognition in the care facilities (interview: Legal advisor to asylum seekers).

Accommodation

Moving from the initial reception facility into a care facility marks a huge improvement in the living conditions of minors, as Malik (18) told us. Around the same time, the child and youth welfare services of the *Land* where the minor is accommodated assumes guardianship of the minor. At the time of our interview, all minors except for two were accommodated in a care facility for unaccompanied minors within the framework of the Basic Welfare Support for asylum seekers. Two, an underage minor and his brother, were temporarily accommodated in a facility of child and youth welfare services for a clearing procedure. Three minors stayed in a single room (Hamed, 17; Majeed, 17; Salim, 17). Asif (16), Tahir (17), Karim (14) and Khalid (16) stayed in double rooms. Adam (16) and Aasiya (17) were in three-bed rooms, and Rasheed (17) shares a room with four other youngsters. Overall, the youngsters seem satisfied with their accommodation although in crowded rooms it gets difficult to enjoy any privacy. Rasheed (17) says that he cannot ask people to leave the room when he wants to be alone. Instead, he leaves the room to take a walk. A single room would be 'awesome', Aasiya says (17).

The care facilities provide minors with most fundamental needs such as food and clothing. Asif's (16) care facility provides basic nutrition such as rice, bread and milk as well as jam and one sort of cheese. Thus, Asif still spends some of his pocket money on food to complement his diet because he does not want to eat the same cheese every day. Adam's (16) care facility provides one or two meals a day – for example, dinner and lunch – and the minors buy themselves food for breakfast. In Aasiya's (17) facility, youngsters prepare food themselves. Although she did not know how to cook previously, she has now taught herself via YouTube tutorials. Salim (17) is not keen on cooking although he does so regularly: 'I am alone; so I have to cook,' he says. Most of the time, minors take it in turns to cook in their care facility. Like Aasiya, Salim cannot afford to eat outside because it is expensive. Hamed (17) is a good cook and cooks different Syrian dishes for himself and his Syrian friends, whom he calls 'my brothers' (see Kohli, Connolly and Warman 2010). In fact, when Hamed moved to his current care facility after staying in Traiskirchen for two and a half months, he asked his 'boss' (referring to the manager of the care facility) whether he could help transfer his three friends from Syria, whom Hamed had met in Traiskirchen, to his care facility. The manager agreed to Hamed's request and the three other boys have since been staying with Hamed in the same facility.

Although most of the minors we have talked to were generally satisfied with their care facilities, some minors made comparisons between care facilities which point to discrepancies between various care facilities in terms of resources. Adam (16), for example, found out through friends that the living conditions in other care facilities are much better than his, which lacks adequate resources.

Education and work

All the minors we talked to went to school in their countries of origin, some of them for a long time. Majeed (17) and Hamed (17) attended school for nine years, and Salim (17) and Aasiya (17) for ten years, for example. Although Malik

(18) attended school for ten years in Afghanistan, he had to start over in Austria due to the lack of curricular equivalency and language skills.

According to the Basic Welfare Support Agreement, unaccompanied minors are entitled to 200 hours of German classes. However, experts judge 200 hours to be highly insufficient and argue that 600 hours of German classes are necessary for a minor to acquire adequate language skills (interview: Expert from an NGO dealing with asylum). Child and youth welfare services in some *Länder* such as Burgenland and Lower Austria add on 400 extra hours from their own budgets (interview: Expert from an NGO dealing with asylum). Adam (16) and Hamed (17) are currently taking German classes and have not yet attended school. They want to study medicine and civil engineering, respectively. Others, except for two (Aasiya, 17; Majeed, 17), have attended or currently attend German classes.

Besides enhancing minors' prospects for education and a profession, German courses lend structure to the minors' everyday life. Two of our interviewees (Majeed, 17; Aasiya, 17) who did not attend any German classes seemed rather lost during the day, whereas others arranged their daily schedules (waking up, eating, sleeping, homework) according to their classes. Majeed does not attend any classes because he gets nervous during the class. Aasiya does not attend any classes because she does not wish to leave the care facility; she finds her new environment to be 'scary' – dogs and drunk people in particular. Because she has nothing else to do, she sleeps a lot of the time and watches movies to keep herself busy.

The Austrian Compulsory Schooling Act (*Bundesgesetz über die Schulpflicht, BGBl. No. 76/1985*) establishes that every child who has permanent residence in Austria must undergo compulsory education which starts at the age of six and lasts nine school years. Thus, the law applies to unaccompanied minors and, reportedly, compulsory education is an area that is relatively well organised for unaccompanied minors. At the time of our interview, only 14-year-old Karim fell under the compulsory education requirement. Some of the minors held or had pursued a secondary school diploma (*Pflichtschulabschluss*) (Rasheed, 17; Tahir, 17; Ehsan, 23) by attending either a secondary school (*Mittelschule*) or a preparation course outside school. Salim (17) was attending a preparation course at an adult education centre (*Volkshochschule*) and had classes from 8.30 a.m. to 1 p.m. or 4.30 p.m. Rasheed (17), as a late entrant, attended a secondary school for a year and acquired his diploma. Malik (18) also holds a secondary school diploma and is currently attending evening commercial secondary school (*Handelsakademie*), a vocational college. What Rasheed (17) likes most about Austria is that minors are obliged to attend school. The situation was very different back in Iran where he, as an eight-year-old boy, worked as a tailor for three years. Minors want to attend university and study a variety of subjects from medicine and engineering to accounting and history. Others wish to learn a profession. In Austria, asylum seekers who are younger than 25 years old are allowed to apply for a work permit for the duration of their apprenticeship, which has to be a profession with an apprentice shortage (Koppenberg 2014: 64–65). Those holding subsidiary protection and asylum have unrestricted access to apprenticeships and paid labour alike (ibid.: 67ff.). Paid labour is important for unaccompanied minor refugees because many of them want to save some money to support their families in their home countries, and they must also save money for when they turn 18 and have to leave the care facility. Salim (17) states that he has to support himself when the childcare benefits are cut off after he has turned 18 as well as his family in Afghanistan (see section below 'Turning 18'). His preferred combination would be to work during the day and attend high school in the evening. Rasheed (17), who holds subsidiary protection, has a regular job as a cook and works five hours a day during the week. At the time of our interview, Rasheed was planning to do an apprenticeship and become a professional cook. Tahir (17) was waiting for the outcome of his application for an apprenticeship at the Austrian national railway. Occasionally, Tahir works as a woodcutter for €5 per hour in his municipality to save some money for when he turns 18.

One expert pointed to a further benefit of education and professional training during the interview. If a minor is denied both subsidiary protection and asylum, he/she may have a better chance for a residence permit if he/she can prove that he/she is successfully embedded in Austrian society which is, according to the definition of state authorities, necessarily attached to education, professional training and social participation (e.g. in sports associations) (interviews: Legal advisor for asylum seekers; Interview care worker at care facility 1).

Pocket money and leisure-time activities

Our experts confirm that social participation such as regular leisure-time activities suffer from resource scarcity. Minors are given pocket money of €40, although this amount may vary among the care facilities. For example, Asif (16) receives €30 weekly and €10 monthly for leisure activities. Aasiya (17), too, receives €30 pocket money weekly. She spends €20 on gym and €20 on internet and saves €10 per month. Twice a year, minors are given €70 or €80 for clothing in line with the Basic Welfare Support Agreement (Article 9(14)). Unaccompanied minor refugees spend a large proportion of their pocket money on the internet to stay connected with their families and friends in their country of origin – for example, via WhatsApp (Majeed, 17). A former unaccompanied minor, Malik (18), tells us that his care facility did not have internet connection and minors could not afford individual phones, so he and his friends put some money together and got themselves a shared smartphone with unlimited access to the internet. Salim (17) gets €15 weekly and €45 monthly, which is inadequate given that Salim spends around eight hours at the preparation course and has to buy food and drink during these long hours. Buying school materials such as books and stationery is also a challenge for Salim who acknowledges that this is part of government policy (vis-à-vis unaccompanied minors) and that there is nothing he can do about it. He jokingly comforts himself that at least he does not have to spend any money on cigarettes since he is not a smoker. Majeed (17), on the other hand, is a heavy smoker and spends most of his pocket money on cigarettes. Adam (16) receives monthly pocket money of €40, plus €15 every week. He cannot afford any leisure-time activities with his pocket money, except maybe a cup of coffee or a movie twice a month with his friends. Hamed (17) receives €100 in total per month. He says €100 is not sufficient, but he still tries to put some money aside.

Due to the lack of adequate resources for leisure-time activities, minors study German, cook, watch TV, listen to music, play video games, ping-pong, card games or table soccer, take a walk (Majeed, 17; Hamed, 17) or just hang out in the parks doing nothing (interview: Activist). One care worker criticises the lack of resources for leisure-time activities for minors:

> And, yes, I have to come back to the issue of daily rates. I think it has simply to do with money how much one can do and accomplish [. . .]. Alone in the realm of leisure time [. . .] Football, it all costs money. [. . .] We have €10 monthly at our disposal [for leisure-time activities] and for €10 a month, I cannot offer much.
>
> (Care worker at care facility 1)

Medical care

All asylum seekers are provided with general health insurance within the framework of the Basic Welfare Support. Minors have very different experiences with medical care in Austria. Adam (16) has paid two visits to the doctor since his arrival. The first one was in Traiskirchen for a general check-up. The second time he went to see a doctor in Vienna because he had problems with his nose. He spoke in English to the doctor who replied that Adam had to talk in German. He did not have a translator with him because the care facility where he is accommodated has inadequate resources. Hamed (17), who stays at the same care facility as Adam, agrees that at the very beginning, when he did not have any German skills, things were difficult without a translator. Aasiya (17) went to see a doctor for general check-up and later a dentist. She communicated in English with the doctors and preferred not to have a translator although it was offered to her. Tahir (17), from Afghanistan, broke his finger while training at Taekwondo and had successful surgery. When Rasheed (17) arrived in Austria, he was told after the general check-up that he had chronic kidney failure. He has had regular medication and treatment for two years, and is very happy with his doctor who pays great attention to his health. Asif (16), in contrast to Rasheed, has not had a positive experience with health care so far. Asif's glasses were broken; however, he has not been able to afford a new pair of glasses because his health insurance does not cover the full costs and the care facility where Asif is accommodated cannot procure the amount due to their tight budget. Asif (16) is annoyed because he has no one in Austria other than the care facility who could buy him the glasses; 'in European countries, you should help the underage,' Asif complains. A first pair of glasses, in contrast, seems to be easier to get. Karim (14) realised in Afghanistan that his eyesight is poor and had asked his father whether he could get a pair of glasses. When his father told him that the family did not have any money for the glasses, Karim never asked again. Upon his arrival in Austria, he was asked whether he had any health complaints. He was immediately taken to the eye specialist and dentist.

With respect to psychological therapy, there is a widespread shortcoming both for unaccompanied minors and Austrian children taken care of by child and youth welfare services manifested in inadequate services and long waiting times. Salim (17) used to be aggressive and rather nervous, and paid a few visits to *Hemayat*, a non-profit association which offers psychotherapy to traumatised people who have survived torture. Salim was given medication for his headache and did exercises with his doctor. He was even offered the chance to change his care facility and move to another one, which Salim rejected. Aasiya (17) tells us that the care workers often ask whether a minor sleeps and eats well and whether he/she wants to see a psychologist. Aasiya personally does not wish to see one because she knows what her problem is, probably meaning separation from her family.

Turning 18

Approaching majority is burdensome for unaccompanied minor refugees who then have to leave the care facility for minors. Those who were turning 18 shortly after our interview expressed concern about the fact that they would have to move out of the care facility and make their own living. Tahir (17) holds subsidiary protection and has unrestricted access to the labour market, whereas Salim (17) was still waiting for the outcome of his application at the time of our interview and thus has restricted access to labour – for example, as a seasonal worker during the summer or winter months. Access to paid labour becomes even more crucial when minors turn 18 and care services such as guardianship and legal representation cease to be provided. Malik (18) moved out of the care facility when he turned 18 and found himself private accommodation in a flatshare. He receives €320 monthly from a charity organisation; his rent costs €120 and he has €200 left monthly to meet his other needs. Ehsan (23) told us that the municipal department of Vienna for Social Issues, Social and Public Health Law granted him €1,100 for furniture and €1,100 as a security deposit when he moved out of the care facility for unaccompanied minors. However, since in Vienna a deposit and commission in the amount of three months' rent is required from each renter, the money given by the MA 40 (*Magistratsabteilung für Soziales und Gesundheit* – municipal department for social and health affairs) is mostly inadequate. Thus, youngsters who turn 18 share small flats (around 35m^2) with three or four other youngsters; as Ehsan told us, people lack privacy and the necessary environment to study in overcrowded flats. Also, minors are additionally burdened by the expectations of their families for financial support and family reunification in Austria (interview: Officer at child and welfare services 1).

Personal contacts

Most minors come to Austria without knowing anyone. Others have extended family members living in Austria. Majeed (17) has three aunts living in Vienna and Lower Austria. He pays them regular visits although he never sleeps over. He has a cousin – he calls him 'brother' – who is also his best friend and is very supportive of him. Asif (16) and Aasiya (17) have a brother and a stepbrother in Austria, respectively. Most of the minors we have talked to have regular contact with their families and friends through the internet. Karim (14) and Khalid (16) from Afghanistan and Rasheed (17) from Iran, however, have lost contact with their parents since they left home or, in Rasheed's case, on the way to Europe. As for friendships, Aasiya (17) has contact only with one childhood friend because she does not know how to answer when people ask where she is and what she is doing: 'You don't go to school; you don't do nothing. So what do I tell?'

We observed care workers to be devoted and motivated professionals who are the immediate persons of trust for unaccompanied minor refugees. The two care workers we talked to expressed concern about the current well-being and prospects of unaccompanied minors. They wish to promote their best interests, but are structurally restrained by the scarcity of resources (interviews: Care worker at care facility 1; Care worker at care facility 2). Care facilities spend a considerable amount of time on administrative tasks and ideally need more personnel to sufficiently cover administrative *and* pedagogical tasks (interview: Manager at care facility 2). Many of the minors we have talked to have a close bond to their care workers. Salim (17) from Afghanistan says that his care worker 'does everything' for him. Yet some are more sceptical. Aasiya (17) claims that when the care workers ask a minor how she/he is feeling, they do so in order to type it down in their computer as part of their professional work. Also, Aasiya adds, they do not worry when a minor comes home late. She says she wants to feel like a family, but finds it hard to do so. Adam (16) lacks a person of trust, including the care workers at his facility. Also, he does not have any relatives in Austria. He often takes refuge in praying for comfort. Overall, he is not happy to be in Austria where everything is very different and the tasks and responsibilities awaiting him make him feel overwhelmed. When he first arrived in Austria, he did not know how to live with other people, how to talk to them and make them listen to him. He has now learned to speak up for himself.

Godparents, adults who help and support an unaccompanied minor on a voluntary basis, are also persons of trust for some minors. For example, Rasheed's (17) teacher asked him one day if she could be his godparent. At first, Rasheed did not know what godparenting was. When he found out what it was, he gladly accepted. His godparents, an Austrian couple, have since helped Rasheed out whenever they could. At weekends, Rasheed stays at his godparents' house. When asked whether his godparents have children, Rasheed replied that he had a sister and a brother now. Tahir (17) also spoke highly of his godparent. He was introduced to his current godparent through the care facility. His godparent helps him out with his pocket money, clothing and learning. At the time of our interview, Tahir was about to turn 18 and would have to leave the care facility. Fortunately, he can stay at his godparent's home until he finds permanent accommodation. Ehsan (23) does not receive any financial support from his godparents, but he can always count on them in other matters. For example, they helped him find his current flat and with his resume and job applications. He visits them once a month.

Personal development and future prospects

Most of the minors we have talked to displayed a very pronounced sense of autonomy. Not only did they fight their way to Austria under most extreme circumstances, but they have also been fighting their way through Austrian bureaucracy and society since their arrival. Despite structural discrimination against unaccompanied minor refugees compared with Austrian children without parents or guardians, unaccompanied minors learn the German language, attend schools, achieve qualifications, pursue vocational training and aspire to university degrees. Also, they look forward to earning money to support their families. At the same time, they follow the asylum procedure closely and intervene when necessary (through their lawyer and legal representative; e.g. Malik and Asif submitted complaints against the Federal Office for Asylum for failing to meet legal deadlines). They seek and find ways to make up for the absence of their families by 'adopting' Austrian adults as their godparents. Once they turn 18, they look for an apartment and a job. Tahir (17) says that he did not know much about (his) life when he arrived in Austria at the age of 14. During the time he has been in Austria, he learned to take care of everything on his own because he is alone and has become self-reliant and autonomous. Similarly, Malik (18) says that one should not expect too much from the state and should take care of things personally. To illustrate this, Malik mentions that he did not even know how to cook fried eggs back at home; now he can bake pizza as well as do cleaning, making appointments and housekeeping.

Minors' wishes and dreams for the future are shaped by a combination of longing for autonomy and the need for protection and to share responsibility with a responsible adult. This is reflected in some minors' homesickness and lack of motivation. They feel as if they do not belong in Austria although, at the same time, they understand why it is better in the long run for them and their families to be in Austria. Majeed (17) told us that he did not have any particular dream or wish for the future. Also, he seemed to be rather indifferent about the outcome of his asylum application. If it is negative, he is willing to go back to Chechenia, he tells us. Aasiya (17) feels as if she belongs in the United Arab Emirates where she grew up before moving back to Somalia and then coming to Austria. Similarly, Adam (16) would prefer to be at home in Syria than in Austria where everything is so different and he does not feel happy at all. Most significantly, minors wish to be reunited with their families.

Overall, Asif (16) and Salim (17) are satisfied with their lives in Austria although, as both agree, the future is always uncertain. Asif believes that he is going to have a 'bright future'. To him, 'bright future' means to study as hard as he can and become what he wants to be. For Salim, the idea of a happy future is also very much linked to good education. His father insisted that Salim went to Europe because he wanted his oldest son to study and learn, an opportunity Salim's father never had. Aasiya is happy as long as her family is doing fine, the internet is working and she is able to study in the future. Salim (17) wants to learn/study and work in the future; however, he does not make any particular demand of state authorities because, as 'a small man', he has no power to make it heard. Hamed (17) is happy with his life in Austria and tells us that he wants to achieve things such as education and work 'piece by piece' and on his own in life.

Also, the minors appear to have a clear understanding of their (precarious) social status as unaccompanied minor asylum seekers in Austria. In our interviews, minors reflected on racist prejudices against refugees, but also reminded the state of its legal obligation to take care of unaccompanied minors. Minors have a wide range of messages to the public authorities responsible for them at different stages of the asylum procedure and afterwards. Asif (16) wants state authorities to understand that unaccompanied minor refugees are exposed to violence in their countries of origin and that he therefore demands a chance for a good future. He adds that since these are minors, they will grow up in Austria and will finally belong in Austria where the economy, in turn, will profit from these young people. Salim (17) wants the state authorities to realise that people who are coming to Austria do so because they face serious problems in their countries of origin. Otherwise, he personally would not have decided to leave his country and his family behind. In particular, he cannot understand the aversion of the right-wing populist Freedom Party of Austria (*Freiheitliche Partei Österreichs*, FPÖ) to asylum seekers who have done nothing wrong. In contrast, Salim expresses appreciation for the Social Democratic Party of Austria (*Sozialdemokratische Partei Österreichs*, SPÖ). Malik (18) seems to be able to see through common bureaucratic practices in Austria and remarks that it is no secret that unaccompanied minors are almost never sent back to the country of origin and are at least granted subsidiary protection. Thus, restricted access to resources and the labour market is a waste of minors' time as well as a waste of great potential for Austria. When a minor learns German quickly and starts working, he/she becomes a tax payer, which is, according to Malik, a 'win-win situation'.

Conclusions

Minors take a long and dangerous journey to Europe and Austria – one that stretches over numerous countries and may last up to five months. Unaccompanied minors flee their homes due to (civil) war and related phenomena such as conscription and persecution, but also due to long-term consequences of war such as high rates of crime and poverty. Minors' reasons to escape may also be gender-specific. For example, while boys are particularly threatened by forced enlistment, girls may face threats of genital mutilation and forced marriage in their countries of origin. Our interviewees mention survival and physical integrity as primary motives to leave their countries.

However, our research shows that this is only one part of their multilayered stories which, depending on the interlocutor, are 'thinned down' or told in full by minors. This seems to depend on the stage of the asylum procedure.

During the initial police proceeding and the interview with the Federal Office for Asylum, minors tend to tell a 'thin' version of their story in order to legitimise their application for asylum in accordance with existing national and international law. Minors seem to be aware that state authorities distinguish between different asylum seekers. These stages of the asylum process are mostly characterised by concerns about national border security and labour market regulation, while at the same time minors are increasingly recognised as a vulnerable group with special needs during the proceedings.

Once admitted to the asylum process, minors are moved to a care facility in the *Länder* where they are accommodated until they turn 18. Simultaneous with the ongoing asylum proceedings, minors enter a stage of care and protection. They find a more favourable environment to articulate 'thick' versions of their stories for which qualitative in-depth interviews proved to be a particularly suitable method. Their stories went beyond the desire to escape immediate threat, but minors proactively formulated wishes, demands, complaints and long-term plans in Austria. Care facilities are eager to provide and organise schooling, German language classes, professional training, leisure-time activities and other basic needs such as food and clothing for minors. This is a real challenge both for care workers and minors given the fact that the daily rate for unaccompanied minor refugees is considerably less than the daily rate provided to Austrian children without parents and under the guardianship of the child and youth welfare services. Minor refugees view education as a central means by which to sustainably establish themselves in Austrian society in terms of autonomy, self-realisation and recognition. They pursue school qualifications and wish to learn a profession and/or attend university in the future. Also, minors reflect on structural shortcomings, such as inadequate pocket money and lack of leisure-time activities, and on institutional suspicion towards them, manifested in interviews with the Federal Office for Asylum and age assessment. A second means by which to achieve regular life in Austria entails family reunification for minors, which is mostly prevented by long asylum proceedings. Minors use a part of their monthly pocket money for their smartphones and internet access in order to stay in touch with their families unless they have already lost contact. Some minors make use of adult Austrian volunteers – that is, godparents – who help and support minors with their lessons, finding a job or offering temporary accommodation when the minor moves out of the care facility after turning 18.

The main finding of our analysis is that the Austrian asylum regime with regard to unaccompanied minors is characterised by a tension between institutional suspicion and restriction (asylum office, the police) and childcare and protection (child and youth welfare services, care workers, psychotherapists). It is the tensions between the two regimes, namely childcare and asylum under which unaccompanied minors in our sample fall as both asylum seekers *and* minors, that determine to an important degree the social position and status as well as access to resources and prospects of unaccompanied minors. However, minors are not only subjected to asylum and child protection laws; they also have agency to co-constitute the framework and conditions in which they live. Learning German, attending school, learning a profession, building and keeping friendships, contributing to the family budget through their pocket money, saving money for their 18th birthday when they have to move out of the care facility, pointing out systemic drawbacks and making recommendations for their elimination are among the manifestations of a forward-looking life under most extreme circumstances. Moreover, these activities contribute to the agency of unaccompanied minor refugees.

Notes

1 The number of asylum applications lodged in Austria dropped sharply in 2016 (as of October) compared with 2015 (Bundesministerium für Inneres 2016).
2 Traiskirchen and all other federal reception facilities in Austria are run by the private company ORS Service GmbH under the contract of the federal government.
3 UNHCR appelliert: Keine weiteren Asylsuchenden mehr nach Traiskirchen bringen (UNHCR appeals: No more asylum seekers to Traiskirchen) (2015), available online at www.unhcr.at/presse/pressemitteilungen/artikel/daa75e69c2cb7c397532a5e2b42a3e00/unhcr-appelliert-keine-weiteren-asylsuchenden-mehr-nach-traiski.html (accessed 22 February 2017).
4 Some minors spent a considerable amount of time in two countries such as Afghanistan and Pakistan. Also, when asked,'Where are you from?', minors answered based on nationality, ethnicity or family roots.
5 Newsletter der Diakonie Wohnberatung für Wohnraumspendende, Vermieter*innen und Unterstützer*innen (Newsletter of Diakonie for Housing Counselling, for Donors of Housing, Landlords and Supporters) (2016), available at www.plattform-fluechtlingshilfe-laa.at/wp-content/Newsletter-Juni-2016.pdf (accessed 22 February 2017).

Bibliography

Bundesministerium für Inneres (2015) *Aslystatistik 2015.* Available at www.bmi.gv.at/cms/BMI_Asylwesen/statistik/files/Asyl_Jahresstatistik_2015.pdf (accessed 7 March 2017).

Fronek, H. (2010) *Unbegleitete minderjährige Flüchtlinge in Österreich. Asylverfahren & Lebensverhältnisse.* Vienna: Mandelbaum.

Fronek, H. and Rothkappel, M. (2013) *Umsetzung grundlegender Standards für Obsorgeberechtigte von unbegleiteten minderjährigen Flüchtlingen.* Länderbericht Österreich. Project: Closing a Potential Gap 2.0, asylkoordination österreich, Defence for Children-ECPAT The Netherlands. Länderbericht. Available online at http://umf.asyl.at/files/DOK56GuardianshipAustriaDeutsch_web.pdf (accessed 22 February 2017).

Giner, C. (2007) 'The politics of childhood and asylum in the UK', *Children & Society*, Vol. 21, No. 4, 249–260.

Glawischnig, K. (2014) 'Kein Kind wie du und ich', *Asyl Aktuell*, Vol. 3, No. 14, 2–7.

Glawischnig, K. (2016) 'Unbegleitete minderjährige Flüchtlinge – Lebensrealität zwischen Unterstützung und Unsicherheiten', in Österreichische Liga für Kinder- und Jugendgesundheit. *Bericht zur Lage der Kinder- und Jugendgesundheit in Österreich* 2016. Available online at www.kinderjugendgesundheit.at/uploads/Liga_JB16_LAST_Web_%282%29.pdf (accessed 22 February 2017).

Heidbrink, L. (2014) *Migrant Youth, Transnational Families, and the State: Care and Contested Interests*, Philadelphia, PA: University of Pennsylvania Press.

Karakayali, S. and Tsianos, V. S. (2005) 'Mapping the order of new migration. Undokumentierte Arbeit und die Autonomie der Migration', *Peripherie*, No. 97/98, 35–64.

Kohli, R. (2009) 'Understanding Silences and Secrets When Working with Unaccompanied Asylum-Seeking Children', in N. Thomas (ed.) *Children, Politics and Communication: Participation at the Margins*, Bristol: Policy Press.

Kohli, R. K. S., Connolly, H. and Warman, A. (2010) 'Food and its meaning for asylum seeking children and young people in foster care', *Children's Geographies*, No. 3, 233–245.

Koppenberg, S. (2014) *Unbegleitete Minderjährige in Österreich – Rechtsrahmen, Praxis und Statistiken*. Vienna: Internationale Organisation für Migration, Landesbüro für Österreich.

Mezzadra, S. (2011) 'The Gaze of Autonomy. Capitalism, Migration and Social Struggles', in V. Squire (ed.) *The Contested Politics of Mobility. Borderzones and Irregularity*, London: Routledge.

Papadopoulos, D. and Tsianos, V. S. (2013) 'After citizenship: Autonomy of migration, organisational ontology and mobile commons', *Citizenship Studies*, No. 2, 178–196.

Vitus, K. and Lidén, H. (2010) 'The status of the asylum-seeking child in Norway and Denmark: Comparing discourses, politics and practices', *Journal of Refugee Studies*, Vol. 23, No. 1, 62–81.

National Legislation and Legal Documents

Civil Code (1811). Available online at www.ris.bka.gv.at/GeltendeFassung/Bundesnormen/10001622/ABGB%2c%20Fassung%20vom%2028.11.2016.pdf (accessed 22 February 2017).

Compulsory Schooling Act (1985). *Federal Law Gazette*, 21. February 1985. Available online at www.ris.bka.gv.at/GeltendeFassung/Bundesnormen/10009576/Schulpflichtgesetz%201985%2c%20Fassung%20vom%2020.11.2016.pdf (accessed 22 February 2017).

Basic Welfare Support Agreement (2004) *Federal Law Gazette*, 15. July 2004. Available online at www.ris.bka.gv.at/GeltendeFassung/Bundesnormen/20003460/Grundversorgungsvereinbarung%20-%20Art.%2015a%20B-VG%20(Bund%20-%20L%C3%A4nder)%2c%20Fassung%20vom%2028.11.2016.pdf (accessed 22 February 2017).

Federal Constitutional Act on the Rights of Children (2011) *Federal Law Gazette*, 15 February 2011. Available online at www.ris.bka.gv.at/GeltendeFassung/Bundesnormen/20007136/Rechte%20von%20Kindern%2c%20Fassung%20vom%2028.11.2016.pdf (accessed 22 February 2017).

Federal Office for Immigration and Asylum Procedures Act (2012) *Federal Law Gazette*, 16 August 2012. Available online at www.ris.bka.gv.at/GeltendeFassung/Bundesnormen/20007944/BFA-VG%2c%20Fassung%20vom%2031.03.2016.pdf?FassungVom=2016-03-31 (accessed 22 February 2017).

UNCRC (1989) United Nations Convention on the Rights of Children.

List of the interviews with experts

Activist and co-founder of pro-UAM association, 16.04.2015
Care worker at care facility 1, 21.04.2015
Care worker at care facility 2, 09.02.2015
Expert from an NGO dealing with asylum issues, 12.11.2014
Expert from the UNHCR, 01.12.2014
Godparent to an unaccompanied minor, 19.03.2015
Legal advisor and representative to asylum seekers at a joint network project, 20.01.2015
Legal advisor and representative to asylum seekers, 22.01.2015
Legal representative for unaccompanied minor asylum seekers, 23.03.2015
Manager at care facility 1, 09.02.2015
Manager at care facility 2, 04.02.2015
Manager at a non-profit organisation, 03.03.2015
National politician, 25.11.2014
Officer at Child and Youth Welfare Services 1, 16.04.2015
Officer at Child and Youth Welfare Services 2, 03.02.2015
Officer at Children's Ombudsman, 20.01.2015
Officer at the Federal Ministry of the Interior, 17.02.2015

List of interviews with (former) unaccompanied minors

Aasiya (17), 29.04.2015
Adam (16), 01.05.2015
Asif (16), 30.04.2015
Ehsan (23), 15.04.2015
Hamed (17), 07.04.2015
Karim (14), 01.04.2015
Khalid (16), 01.04.2015
Majeed (17), 07.04.2015
Malik (18), 15.04.2015
Rasheed (17), 08.04.2015
Salim (17), 01.05.2015
Tahir (17), 08.04.2015

6 'Not our children'

Unaccompanied minor asylum seekers in Slovenia

Mateja Sedmak, Blaž Lenarčič, Zorana Medarić and Tjaša Žakelj

Introduction

At first glance, the issue of unaccompanied minors in Slovenia could appear to be a marginal problem. In the political arena as well as broader society, there is widespread disinterestedness and ignorance regarding the presence of children and young people who cross Slovenian borders and travel to Western and Northern Europe in search of a safer and better life. Unaccompanied minors are neither part of public or political discussion nor do they (with some minor exceptions) benefit from the generosity of the state or civil society as in some other European countries (e.g. the UK, Scandinavian countries). Unaccompanied minors are, in fact, overlooked children.

For a better understanding of the procedures that unaccompanied minors face within the Slovene legislative and asylum system, we will first present some general features of the national social context. Slovenia is a relatively ethnically homogeneous country with more than 80 per cent of the population being made up by ethnic Slovenes.[1] Moreover, traditionally Slovenia has not been a country considered attractive for wider migration flows. From the 1960s to the 1980s, Slovenia was the most economically developed republic of former Yugoslavia and therefore was an attractive immigrant destination mostly for workers from the other republics of Yugoslavia (e.g. Bosnia, Serbia and Kosovo). Slovenia first faced the problem of forced migration and unaccompanied minors in the 1990s, during the Balkan wars, when immigrants (mostly from Bosnia) came in need of shelter. The number of migrants has significantly increased in recent years, due to armed conflict in the Middle East (especially Syria), Africa and Afghanistan. More than 309,000 migrants entered Slovenia in a period of less than two months in 2015 (from 17 October 2015 to 10 December 2015) due to the redirection of the Western–Balkan migration route[2] (Ministry of the Interior 2015a). Slovenia is mostly a transit country for those who are continuing their path to Western and Northern European countries; very rarely is it the final destination.[3] Consequently, the number of unaccompanied minors who stay in Slovenia is also relatively low,[4] and most of these are not here by choice but as a result of being apprehended by the border police.

Correspondingly, a painful lack of interest regarding better treatment for unaccompanied minors is evident. Disinterest can also be seen in the fact that the

Slovenian state does not keep statistics regarding the number of status applications, approved statuses by type of status (refugee status or subsidiary protection status) or the number of suspended proceedings and rejected applications (by age or by gender). The 2014 study *Good practices in returning and reintegration of irregular migrants* by PIC (Legal Information Centre for Non-Governmental Organisations) succinctly exposed the problematic lack of data regarding the return of aliens under the Aliens Act (PIC 2014).

Stimulated by the 2015 mass influx of immigrants and attendant events (setting up wire fences, the polarisation of public opinion regarding refugee accommodation in Slovenia, etc.), a political discussion arose regarding preparation of a new international protection law (which would also define the situation of unaccompanied minors). In Slovenia, however, the discussion took place 'behind closed doors', without professional or NGO involvement or any public discussion or transparency. In this context, the exclusion of Slovene Philanthropy (the NGO with the greatest experience of dealing with unaccompanied minors in terms of advocacy, guardianship and psychological, social and material support) was particularly problematic.[5]

How unprepared Slovenia is to accept unaccompanied minors can be discerned from the following data: on average, 38 unaccompanied minors per year applied for asylum in the period between 2002 and 2016 (2004 excluded). The highest number was in 2004 when 104 unaccompanied minors came to Slovenia. Out of the total of 679 applications in this 15-year period, status was granted in only 33 cases (Ministry of the Interior 2015b).

It is also problematic that unaccompanied minors are identified as children by the Slovenian legislative system, with special protection and rights, while everyday practice shows a rather different picture. They are frequently treated primarily as aliens instead of children and they are subjected to procedures that would never be acceptable for Slovenian children. Within the Slovenian welfare system, they are not treated as 'our' children.

Taking into account the small number of unaccompanied minors staying in Slovenia, the living conditions and the whole process of international protection could be better and more child-oriented. Why is this not the case and why is there no political will for change? A simple explanation is difficult to provide; however, the reasons could be xenophobia, political calculation and nationalism reinforced by the fear that the introduction of better living conditions and a more child-friendly approach could result in more unaccompanied minors coming to stay in Slovenia. Regardless of how strange such assumptions are, we must keep in mind that a 'banal nationalism' as defined by Billig (1995) is widespread and thus influencing the everyday reality in Slovenia. Moreover, a national state is *per se* not neutral – regardless of the international Convention on the Rights of the Child to which the Slovenian state is also committed. Indeed, it is the case that children's rights in the reality of everyday life are neither universal nor neutral. Some children (namely 'ours') benefit more from the Convention than others (Gornik 2016).

The aim of this chapter is to present the path of unaccompanied minors in search of international protection in the Republic of Slovenia and the discrepancies among the legally adopted (children's) rights and their actual implementation in daily life. In order to obtain the necessary information regarding the procedures unaccompanied minors go through during the process of applying for international protection status, we interviewed 14 experts who have either direct experience working with unaccompanied minors (such as NGO representatives, social workers, guardians, accommodation facility representatives) or whose role is to protect children's rights from within statutory bodies (representatives from ministries, the Deputy Ombudsman's office).[6] In addition, 18 in-depth interviews with unaccompanied and former unaccompanied minors living in Slovenia[7] were conducted with the generous help of a representative from Slovene Philanthropy. Our interview subjects were all boys between 17 and 23 years of age, coming mainly from Afghanistan (13), but also from Somalia (2), Sierra Leone (1), Ghana (1) and Ukraine (1). When the interview was conducted, two interviewees were 17 years old, two were 18 years old, four were 19 years old, three were 20 years old, four were 21 years old, two were 22 and one was 23 years old.[8] Interviewees had been living in Slovenia for between five months and seven years. They were all minors upon their arrival in Slovenia. All of them had legal status and were not illegal immigrants living on the streets, nor were they waiting for refugee or subsidiarity protection status. The interviews were conducted either in English or Slovenian (one in Russian) and were, with the approval of the interviewees, recorded and transcribed. In its entirety, the fieldwork took place from January to April 2015. The topics of the interviews were very broad and addressed several issues concerning arrival in the country, issues related to living conditions, treatment and basic social rights (health, education, accommodation), questions related to procedures and status seeking, and also the perception of daily life, well-being as a young person (friends, family, social life, leisure activities, identity and convictions) and aspirations regarding the future. For the purpose of this chapter, we will focus primarily on the condition and treatment of unaccompanied asylum seekers during the proceedings related to the application for international protection status. We will highlight the main steps in which the absence of a child-friendly approach is evident, with respect to the actual application of the implementation of the principle of the best interests of the child.

What follows is first the presentation of the legislative framework covering the issues of unaccompanied minors in the Republic of Slovenia and a presentation of the responsible authorities; second, the process of application for international protection is described (including border procedures, international protection procedures, the role of guardians, age assessment, accommodation, education, health care, paid work and transition at the age of 18); and, third, the analysis of the application of the principle of the best interests of the child, the discrepancies between legally guaranteed rights and their implementation, and the open issue of finding a durable solution.

Responsible authorities and national legislative framework

Although one would expect that unaccompanied migrant children would primarily be dealt with by the Ministry of Family, Work, Social Affairs and Equal

Opportunities (which is authorised to deal with the welfare of children on a general level), the Ministry of the Interior is the main government department in charge of issues regarding unaccompanied minors (UAMs). The Ministry of Family, Work, Social Affairs and Equal Opportunities plays a lesser role with regard to UAMs, being responsible for only two minor tasks: namely, the training of legal representatives for UAMs and selection of candidates for training. The third relevant institution dealing with issues regarding UAMs is the various Centres for Social Work. The role of the Centres for Social Work, which are authorised to work in a certain region (under the authority of the ministry in charge of family and social affairs), is to appoint special case guardians and legal representatives to unaccompanied minors. Special case guardians are appointed by the Centre for Social Work after apprehending a minor at the border and their subsequent accommodation in the Aliens Centre. Legal representatives are appointed to the unaccompanied minor after the application for international protection has been made and they are relocated to the Asylum Home.[9]

Only a small number of NGOs in Slovenia deal with unaccompanied minors, among which Slovene Philanthropy plays the most active role. It advocates for their rights, provides support in searching for appropriate accommodation, education and employment possibilities, and assists with health issues. Another active NGO is PIC – Legal Information Centre for Non-Governmental Organisations – which offers legal advice during the proceedings. Other associations, such as Mozaik or the Institute for African Studies, mainly organise leisure and integration activities for unaccompanied minors.

With regard to the legal framework, the Aliens Act (2011) (AA) and the International Protection Act (2016) (IPA) are the main laws which define the status, rights and responsibilities of unaccompanied minors in Slovenia. The AA, adopted in 2011 and amended several times, defines the conditions for and methods of entry into, departure from and residence of aliens[10] in Slovenia. In 2016 a new IPA was adopted (the first version was adopted in 2007 and came into force in 2008). It regulates the international protection system in Slovenia and transfers the European asylum system into national legislation.

Before unaccompanied minors ask for international protection, they are treated under the AA as alien minors. The AA does not include the best interests of the child as the guiding principle in the procedures concerning UAMs. This principle can be found only in Article 82 of the AA which defines deportation conditions:

> In cases where an alien minor, who is not accompanied by his parents or other legal representatives and resides illegally in Slovenia is deported, the police shall immediately inform a Centre for Social Work, which must immediately assign a special case guardian to the minor. The police shall then issue the alien minor with a return decision where his special case guardian, having carefully considered all circumstances, establishes that this is in the best interests of the minor.
>
> (Article 82 of the AA)

Once they apply for international protection status, unaccompanied minors are dealt with under the IPA which defines their rights and treatment. According to Article 2 of the IPA, UAMs belong to a group of vulnerable persons with special needs and are therefore entitled to specific care and attention (Article 2 of the IPA). Article 15 in particular defines the necessity to take into consideration the best interests of the child principle when dealing with minors. Additionally, Article 16 defines in detail the procedures necessary for application for international protection and the treatment of unaccompanied minors who make this application, highlighting the necessity to establish the child's identity as soon as possible and to begin the process of locating the child's parents or other relatives as well as to appoint a legal representative for the child prior to the commencement of the proceedings. According to Article 100 of the IPA, the best interests of the child principle remains the guiding principle for procedures and measures concerning unaccompanied minors who receive refugee status or subsidiary protection status.

The Marriage and Family Relations Act (MFRA) (2004) is another relevant act which partially determines procedures concerning unaccompanied minors. Generally, the Act does not focus specifically on unaccompanied minors, except for issues regarding the appointment of a guardian[11] who should act in the minor's interest: 'in all activities and procedures affecting a child, parents, other persons, state authorities and bearers of public authority must act in the child's interest' (Article 5a of MFRA). Similarly, the Civil Procedure Act (1999, Article 408) explicitly requires protection of the interests of the child in legal and parental lawsuits from the courts *ex officio*.

Within the Slovenian legislation regarding unaccompanied minors, the best interests of the child principle is integrated in the IPA to the greatest extent; however, there is a discrepancy between its determination and implementation in practice which will be elaborated on in the following section.

On the way to international protection status

The legal path towards international protection status – key points

The usual path unaccompanied minors take from the point at which they enter the territory of the Republic of Slovenia up to obtaining international protection status consists of six key steps presented in Figure 6.1.

As seen in Figure 6.1, the first contact with unaccompanied minors usually occurs at the border when the border police apprehend illegal immigrants and identify a minor as unaccompanied. If unaccompanied minors do not fulfil the preconditions for deportation, the police inform the local Centre for Social Work.

In the second phase, a special case guardian from the Centre for Social Work is appointed to the unaccompanied minor and they are transferred to the Aliens Centre. The Centre is a restricted area with no free movement, where unaccompanied minors spend several days. During this period, a special case

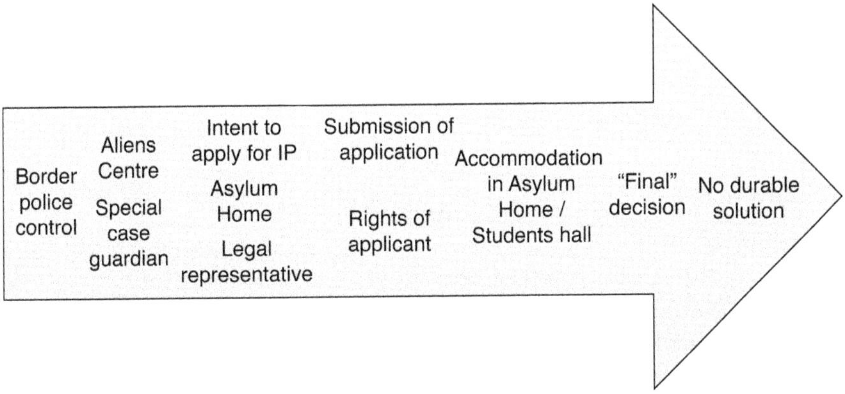

Figure 6.1 Key points in the process of obtaining international protection status in the Republic of Slovenia

guardian has one single interview with the unaccompanied minor to determine what is in his or her best interests. If this is an application for international protection, the unaccompanied minor is transferred to the Asylum Home.

At this stage, the local Centre for Social Work appoints a legal representative to the unaccompanied minor from the list of trained legal representatives. Submission of the application for international protection takes place as soon as possible.

The submission process affords the unaccompanied minors the rights granted to applicants, such as the right to schooling, health care and financial support. These rights, while clearly stated in the law, are not always implemented in practice. During this process, unaccompanied minors are accommodated in the Asylum Home or a student dormitory.

Finally, the unaccompanied minor receives a positive or negative decision regarding their status. If subsidiary protection or refugee status is granted to the unaccompanied minor, he or she obtains the right of persons with status. At this point a third person is appointed to the unaccompanied minor: a guardian whose role is to protect the unaccompanied minor's rights and work for his or her best interests. Both subsidiary protection and refugee status are often limited to a very short time period. After the expiration of subsidiary protection and/ or refugee status (when the minor turns 18 years of age) there is little possibility for an extension as status is usually based on the fact that the applicant is a minor. What follows is deportation to their home country. Finally, there is no durable solution for unaccompanied minors in the end; as they themselves expressed, they often feel they have no future.

Below is a more detailed description of all phases as seen by professionals working with UAMs and as experienced by (former) unaccompanied minors. Such subjective interpretation and critique of the existing system is vitally important because existing evaluations are always based on the assessment of various NGOs or public institutions, and very rarely are the voices of minor immigrants themselves taken into consideration. Researchers uniformly state that there is a widespread lack of research on UAMs focusing on exploring their own perspective (Wernesjö 2011). Finally, we strongly support the social constructionist point of view claiming that 'if a person perceives a situation as real, it is real in its consequences' (Thomas and Thomas 1928: 571–572).

Border procedures

Unaccompanied minors are usually apprehended while attempting to cross the border illegally or after having been left in a truck, on a road or in a forest by traffickers. What actually occurs with regard to unaccompanied minors at the borders and the role of border police in this regard is subject to critical evaluation on the part of some professionals who deal with unaccompanied minors. As observed by the Deputy Ombudsman, the prevalent approach used by the border police is:

> Let's get rid of them as soon as possible, because we will have fewer costs, less work, less liabilities. And we are really happy when they disappear and we have nothing to do with them. [. . .] I am afraid that the very first concern is to not help them, that we treat them as foreigners, who have accidentally ended up here and we as a country urgently want them to go away, because we have a lot of other problems.

There is very little information available regarding the procedures which take place at the borders and return procedures. Evidence from our fieldwork demonstrates that border police attempt to send unaccompanied minors and illegal immigrants back to either the neighbouring country or their country of origin. This is also confirmed by the representative of the Border Police Division:

> If we are not successful with refoulement, if we are not successful with the return to the neighbouring country or with the return to their country of origin, then of course a foreigner obtains authorisation to stay.

Unaccompanied minors primarily feel afraid upon being apprehended after a long and exhausting journey, whether alone or 'accompanied' by other individuals.

> Of course I was afraid. You don't know where you will go, what will happen, you don't know these people, these people can take your money and leave, you don't know. [. . .] There were more of us, some young and some women. [. . .] Police caught us and asked for documents and said if you don't have documents you go to jail. We said we were refugee, we don't want to go in jail, we didn't do anything. They said we need to ask for asylum or go to jail. And we said we want asylum [. . .] the police spoke only English,

> there were no translator. But my English . . . I cannot speak English. Some people from my group speak English.
>
> (Age 15 upon arrival)

Even though Slovenia follows a return process protocol in accordance with EU agreements, available statistical data on cases of returned persons is extremely limited and does not provide information on the actual scope of return (PIC 2014).

The border procedures as such are subjected to critical evaluation:

> I see a major problem in the procedures (at the border), which may be humiliating, intrusive, does not respect their rights. [. . .] But this culture is still present at the border, there are those that protect the border, they feel very strongly, and this influences how they behave towards minors, foreigners and especially foreigners from the third world countries.
>
> (Deputy Ombudsman)

Just how confusing an experience with border police can be is highlighted by an unaccompanied boy, now 18 years old, who was apprehended by the police four years ago and taken to the Aliens Centre in Postojna. The border police failed to give him adequate information and therefore he did not know whether or not to apply for international protection.

> I was there one month (in the Aliens Centre). Before I have not asked for asylum status. [. . .] I didn't know where I am. In which country I am. If this [to ask for asylum] is good for me or not. [. . .] there it was as if I had killed ten people. As in prison. We had 30 minutes to go out in the fresh air. Everything was closed. Thirty minutes out to play football. And then they locked us, in prison. There was nothing to do. Only TV and sleeping.
>
> (Age 16 upon arrival)

Another problem unaccompanied minors face when being questioned by the police is the lack of clear communication either with the police representative (especially if there is any doubt that the unaccompanied minor is actually underage) or with translators and interpreters. Not only can these conversations be confusing or unclear to the minor, but there has also been reported an element of verbal aggression and a lack of a child-friendly approach:

> Yes, first they took me at police station. I had translator but I didn't understand because he was speaking Persian [not the native language of the unaccompanied minor]. Just a little bit, some words, if he spoke very slowly. [. . .] I was hungry and alone. Then they brought me biscuits. I was very happy! [. . .] Then they brought me to the Aliens Centre in Postojna. I didn't know that there everything is locked. I was afraid, I was crying. I said I am not guilty of anything. They told me this is it and I said OK. After one week I went to the Asylum Home.
>
> (Age 17 upon arrival)

According to the AA, if the preconditions for return are not met, the border police should immediately contact the Centre for Social Work regarding the refugee minor. However, formal procedures in this regard are not very clearly determined. The AA is not clear on how a social worker should act upon receiving this notification and which procedures he or she should follow. It is also not clear whether the police actually inform the Centre for Social Work in all cases.

> The Aliens Act has only one article. If they come across an unaccompanied alien minor, they inform the Centre for Social Work. Now we usually get to the border for each individual case when we are notified. Well, except in some cases when the police have doubts regarding their age, it sometimes happens that we do not receive notification. And although the police should inform us about every case, I can't actually say they do.
>
> (Centre for Social Work Representative)

After that, a special case guardian is appointed to the unaccompanied minor, and from that moment on all decisions are taken by guardian and not by the police. The transfer to the Aliens Centre follows.

Accommodation at the Aliens Centre

As already indicated, unaccompanied minors perceive the Aliens Centre as an unpleasant and inappropriate place, similar to prison (locked with no possibility of free movement, where the food is neither good nor plentiful and there is nothing to do). The amount of time unaccompanied minors spend in the Aliens Centre varies from a few days to months. If the prevalent feeling of unaccompanied minors after being apprehended by the police is primarily fear, after being placed in the Aliens Centre they primarily feel alone and as though they are being treated like criminals.

> They feel awful and guilty like criminals. They do not understand that these are some formal procedures, which are purely objective, that there are some rules, they have difficulties understanding.
>
> (Representative from a Centre for Social Work)

In contrast, a social worker from the Aliens Centre describes the 'great variety' of (leisure and sports) activities which are available to the unaccompanied minors accommodated in the Centre and at the same time emphasises the limitations of their work and their role in the protection of unaccompanied minors:

> We are only social workers and we have limitations because we work in a police institution. We are bound by law and some institutionalised barriers.
>
> (Social worker from the Aliens Centre)

The beginning of the international protection procedure

After an unaccompanied minor expresses his or her intention to apply for international protection status, he or she is transferred from the Aliens Centre to the Asylum Home. A social worker from the Asylum Home explains:

> Each UAM who enters the Asylum Home is first medically checked for parasites by the nurse who is employed at the Asylum Home. Then the operative worker calls a physician who also checks the condition he/she is in. As of 2015, physicians began writing an estimation of vulnerability, meaning before the submission of the application for international protection is done, a physician fills in a form regarding how vulnerable a person is.
>
> (Asylum Home Representative)

Then the Centre for Social Work in charge of the case appoints a legal representative to the minor. According to the International Protection Act, the key role of the legal representative consists of three main tasks: looking out for the minor's best interests during the procedure to obtain status, and ensuring the health and education of the unaccompanied minor. Besides this formal dimension, there is also an informal aspect to the representative's role in the everyday life of unaccompanied minors and this depends on the level of engagement of each individual. Of all those who come in contact with UAMs, it is the legal representative who is the most important in determining the best interests of each unaccompanied minor.

> I would say the best interests of the child determination depends on the engagement of the legal representative. The legal representative is the one who is closest to the UAM. It depends how he/she accedes to the case. And from this role it also depends on how the best interests of the child and his will are recognised and taken into consideration in the procedure.
>
> (Representative of the Legal Information Centre for NGOs)

In accordance with the procedure, the application for international protection must be submitted within a very short time (usually within 24 hours of arriving at the Asylum Home); the appointment of a legal representative to the unaccompanied minor therefore takes place quickly. Prior to the official procedure, the legal representative meets the minor together with an interpreter. This meeting lasts up to an hour and its main purpose is for the legal representative to explain to the unaccompanied minor his/her role in the procedure and the procedure itself. When asked about this meeting, several experts were critical of the time pressure under which the application for the international protection must be submitted. The lack of time made it impossible to establish a confidential relationship in which unaccompanied minors could properly express their needs or expectations.

> In my opinion there is not enough time for the minor to develop a strong enough connection to the legal representative to open up and tell him what else is on his mind.
>
> (Representative of the Legal Information Centre for NGOs)

During this first interview minors feel confused, scared and without proper information about what is happening and what the possible consequences of the interview could be. It is not only the unaccompanied minors who are critical of the interview; there are also experts who point out several inadequacies regarding this procedure:

> We found this very problematic because it happens right away; this is a few hours after the arrival at the Asylum Home [. . .] and the submission of the application is of vital importance because it is the basis for decision making regarding the status of protection. [. . .] Imagine a child who might have travelled for months, who is hungry, not to mention his physical condition, traumas he may have suffered, and he is sent into a room with people who he is seeing for the first time. The first person is a legal representative who tries to explain to him that he/she is on his side, that there is a legal adviser, an interpreter and the official person. And they try to convince him to tell his story as to why he has applied for international protection status. And I find this system totally inadequate; there is no time and place to prepare a child for such an important thing as the submission of an application.
>
> (Representative from Slovene Philanthropy)

Interpreters are of vital importance; however, in some cases related by unaccompanied minors and experts, they have proven to be problematic:

> Actually no, in both the first and second interview I did not have the opportunity to express myself. The problem of the interview and the translator – he could not explain the thing I needed to say. This is a problem; everything is dependent on his interpretation. If he couldn't interpret well, that would mean that my words had no value.
>
> (Age 17 upon arrival)

Sometimes the interpreter did not even speak the mother tongue of the unaccompanied minor and consequently they could not comprehend them entirely.

> My language is Dari, the interpreter was speaking Persian. Persian–Dari is a big difference.
>
> (Age 14 upon arrival)

Throughout the administrative procedure, unaccompanied minors are not treated as children first, but merely as foreigners:

> Sometimes it seems to me, that they are treated like half criminals. And these conversations with them are not directed so much to help, but simply to tell why you don't meet the conditions for asylum and the like.
>
> (Deputy Ombudsman)

Age assessment procedure

Doubts regarding the age of the applicants sometimes arise during the procedure. In that case, the IPA (Article 44a) stipulates that within the framework of the examination of an application, the competent authority (in practice this is a medical expert) can order a review to determine the age of an unaccompanied minor. The legislation, however, does not prescribe any particular method of examination but stipulates only that the unaccompanied minor must be informed about the whole process. An NGO representative with considerable experience as a legal representative stressed that the procedures are not necessarily properly explained:

> I insisted that there needs to be a description of what the procedure involves and how it will be carried out. They really do not know what will happen [. . .] they need to know at least that it is not painful, what they may say, that they can reject an individual part of the process – this does not exist.
>
> (Representative from Slovene Philanthropy)

According to the Asylum Procedures Directives (2005/85/EC), medical examination may be used to determine age during the asylum application process; however, many European paediatricians oppose this for ethical, medical and legal reasons (Sauer, Nicholson and Neubauer 2015). Interviews demonstrate that medical examinations include various methods including a height and weight check, a conversation regarding family members (age of siblings and parents) and personal matters (e.g. how often they shave). If the physician is still in doubt regarding the age of the minor, he/she can check body hair and teeth or can even decide to do an X-ray for bone density estimation or other invasive, ethically disputed and humiliating tests. The following was reported by an NGO representative:

> This means a boy has to take off his clothes; the physician compares his testicles to balls on a chain. When it was described to me, I found it terrible, humiliating and inadmissible.
>
> (Representative from Slovene Philanthropy)

Most of the unaccompanied minors we interviewed had not experienced an age assessment process.

According to the legislation, the process of granting or denying international protection status should be completed within six months, with preferential treatment being given to the applications made by unaccompanied minors (Article 47 of the IPA). However the NGO experts stress that the process is often prolonged due to age assessment procedures, and consequently the final decision is (intentionally) delayed as an unaccompanied minor reaches the age of 18 before a decision is reached and is therefore no longer eligible for protection status based on being a minor.

> I would swear on my life and with everything I have that procedures are delayed, that they are trying to get rid of minors so that they don't have to give them status.
>
> (Representative from Slovene Philanthropy)

Accommodation in the Asylum Home

As previously mentioned, after applying for international protection status, UAMs are usually accommodated in the 'special department' of the Asylum Home.[12] This option is subject to severe criticism because this facility is primarily intended for adult asylum seekers and is therefore inappropriate for minors.

> Accommodation in the Asylum Home is problematic in itself. To my mind it is not good that minors are accommodated in the same department as single women, especially when there was a bigger crowd. There is only one shower; therefore, they shared showers. It is also true that men were bothered that women walked around only wrapped in a towel. After that, children are really unsupervised in all possible departments, there were various violations and suspicions as well as abuse, rapes, attempted rapes. So, totally inappropriate.
>
> (Representative from Slovenian Philanthropy)

The lack of appropriate (social) activities is also problematic, as stressed by the representative from the Ministry of the Interior.

> Accommodation in the Asylum Home is inappropriate. Here they are too close to adults; there is no structure, no programme, which is, in fact, what a young person needs. Because we all need 2–3 days of freedom, but sooner or later we need structure, some kind of order.
>
> (Representative from the Ministry of the Interior)

Unaccompanied minors also report the inappropriate general living conditions found in the Asylum Home: inappropriate and inadequate food, a lack of appropriate clothes, information and autonomy. One boy compares it to prison:

> Then they put us with the others. There are three places, for family, older and younger – under 18. They put us in that place in a shared room. It was

> like a jail, open jail. The room had a bed in the corner, another bed above and was like 3 × 2 metres.
>
> (Age 16 upon arrival)

Some of the unaccompanied minors who had also lived in asylum facilities in other European countries judge the conditions elsewhere as much better:

> It was the first Asylum Centre in Europe we were in. We thought it was a strange [. . .] if this is the situation in Europe [. . .] If we always have to ask people for food, for help. And then when we were in Austria and Norway. There it was not the same. Even when we were first there, we were not in prison. And we had the opportunity to leave, if we did not want something. We were not in prison. There is different.
>
> (Age 14 upon arrival)

Accommodation in student residence

After submitting the application for status, a legal representative usually starts arrangements for the unaccompanied minor's accommodation outside the Asylum Home, most often in residence halls for secondary school students. According to the interviews, this accommodation is perceived as much better. The food is more abundant and of better quality, the staff are more supportive, and these facilities are usually more centrally located and unaccompanied minors feel more integrated in the local community:

> When I moved [to the residence hall for secondary students] I was more like in society, I see more people. Even if I do not talk to them, I walk among them to places. It is refreshing, I am outside now. I got a feeling that now I am really in Slovenia. I have to do what Slovenians do. I can go to my room, do what they do. Before I could not do such things. Everything was OK when I moved to residence hall for secondary students. In the residence hall they come in the morning to check, ask you if you are OK, are you going to school, are you sick, etc. Here I share ideas, feelings. This place is far better than in asylum.
>
> (Age 16 upon arrival)

The rights of applicants

After submitting the request for international protection and while waiting for the 'final decision', unaccompanied minors obtain the rights of applicants, which are well embedded in national legislation (Articles 78 and 79 of the IPA) but rarely implemented in practice. Among others, these rights include: residence in the Republic of Slovenia, a supply of necessities in the case of accommodation in the Asylum Home or its branches (food, clothing and toiletries), financial assistance in the case of private accommodation, education, access to the labour market and pocket money.

All basic healthcare services (diagnosis, treatment and preventive care) are available to unaccompanied minors through the staff physicians at the Aliens Centre and the Asylum Home:

> As I say, they are normally included in the healthcare system, they have a personal physician. Even if they need a psychologist, psychiatrist, there is no problem to get it under the regular system.
>
> (Representative from the Ministry of the Interior)

Satisfaction with healthcare provision varies on the part of unaccompanied minors. Some are content and some are critical, especially regarding an inappropriate approach to treatment in the sense of professionalism (fast and inadequate examinations), a lack of intercultural competence and absence of basic human empathy:

> OK, they are very kind. I never had problems. I went here, it was my turn, they checked me and told me what to do.
>
> (Age 16 upon arrival)

Interviews highlighted the significant importance of mental health care since unaccompanied minors are a particularly vulnerable category of asylum seekers who have experienced not only war-related traumas but also other psychological difficulties related to their long and exhausting journey:

> We walked for weeks. Like I never did before. It was difficult to sleep in the forest without a bed, cold. I also met people going like that who also had problems. We talked and we followed in the same footsteps. We go, we walked, sometimes there were speedboats. Some could not make it, some died.
>
> (Age 16 upon arrival)

At the same time they find themselves surrounded by a different culture, different habits and different expectations which also have a significant psychological impact:

> They encounter a totally different culture, different language in a totally different environment, nobody understands them. This must be terrible. Terrible. And you are 14 years old, without parents. If we ignore what kind of trauma he has behind, what was in his homeland, why he left. Now he finds himself here. Here officials start to turn towards him and ask him, who are you, what are you, where are your papers, you don't have papers, where will you be placed?
>
> (Deputy Ombudsman)

Mental health care is undoubtedly an important topic and should be included in the comprehensive health care in the Asylum Home or the Aliens Centre. As interviewees stated, this issue is not tackled systematically:

> People with mental health issues are sent to the emergency department. They are treated as far as possible. Each time, another doctor sees them, so there is no continuous approach for these people.
>
> (Representative from Slovene Philanthropy)

Unaccompanied minors have the right to basic education and applicants should also have access to education at the vocational and secondary schools under the same criteria that apply to citizens of the Republic of Slovenia. However, it is common for UAMs to be enrolled in a special elementary school for adults and young people who did not finish elementary school (Cene Štupar Elementary School).

> In the last year, all UAMs were enrolled at the Cene Štupar Elementary School. On average they attain the 3rd or 4th grade of elementary school for adults and they take Slovene language lessons here in the Asylum Home, they receive study help. Their counsellor also offers them support so this aspect is covered pretty well.
>
> (Asylum Home Representative)

Interviewees report that in practice there are difficulties with learning Slovene. Slovene lessons do not take place on a regular basis in the Asylum Home and there is a lack of intensive courses. Unaccompanied minors usually report not being able to follow the lessons in school.

> The first day (in school) I introduced myself in English, because I didn't speak Slovenian. They didn't oblige me to finish the course or school of Slovenian language. It was hard. Then they told me to take a 300-hour Slovenian course but it was no good. The professor was talking in Slovenian and I didn't understand anything. Sometimes she was missing and I was reading alone by myself. Three hundred hours is a lot, but the system was bad. I could not learn Slovenian.
>
> (Age 17 upon arrival)

In spite of the formally prescribed access to education, one must stress that, in practice, education is not always easily accessible for unaccompanied minors as there is no systematic approach.

> The biggest problem here is the language and apart from private schools we don't have any that operate in English, so before he learns the language the year passes. In one year, the majority of them leave the country. [. . .] Those who are in secondary school could visit these schools where classes are in

> English. But here I think that is no interest on either side. Even on theirs, to stay here.
>
> (Deputy Ombudsman)

With considerable effort and the support of NGOs and other (volunteer) groups, some unaccompanied minors were able to enrol in secondary school and continue their education.

> Someone who wants to enrol in secondary school must face the fact that his knowledge is nowhere near that of his future peers or classmates. But this possibility exists. At the moment I have three or four boys who are now in different secondary schools.
>
> (Representative from Slovene Philanthropy)

Other important aspects of the everyday lives of unaccompanied minors are pocket money and access to paid work. Regarding financial issues, it is important to stress that unaccompanied minors express a constant concern over the lack of money.

> I am not even thinking about the money. I don't even know how and when I will get any money.
>
> (Age 16 upon arrival)

According to the legislation, unaccompanied minors accommodated in the Asylum Home receive pocket money to the amount of €18 per month. Additional problems arise when they want to provide financial help to their families back home.

> It is €18. What can a person do in Slovenia with €18 in one month?!
>
> (Age 16 upon arrival)

One way to increase their budgets is to obtain paid work. This option is however very rarely exploited:

> Work, here, is like this: for us in Slovenia it is considered that at 15 years old, if certain conditions are met, a child can start to work. To this it must be added the rule, which derives from the International Protection Act, that asylum seekers can start to work nine months after they applied for asylum, if in the meantime do not receive a negative decision. If we look at these combinations – these nine months and the fact that minors often leave and that there are not many jobs here, I could not tell you if any one of the minors took advantage of this and work at all in Slovenia.
>
> (Representative of the Legal Information Centre for NGOs)

If unaccompanied minors actually succeed at finding paid work, the (already very modest) financial help from the state (for those with status) is automatically reduced.

Turning 18

In many cases, unaccompanied minors are granted subsidiary protection status on the basis that they are underage and retain this only until they come of age:

> They look at when the person will turn 18 and give him status which lasts only until the person comes of age. If they will reach the age of majority in a year and two months, then they give them [the status] for a year and three months. Something like that.
>
> (Representative of Slovene Philanthropy)

As age is the key reason for the unsafe position of unaccompanied minors, they cannot reapply for international protection status. This puts them in a highly insecure position and highlights the crucial problem of finding a durable solution:

> Now we have huge problems regarding renewing subsidiary protection status. No one gets a positive decision on renewal. The decision makers write in the operative part of the decision that status is obtained on the basis of being under age. So there is no renewal of status as those two reasons no longer exist when they reach 18. Even though they believed the story of why he came and why he is endangered, they did not include it in the reason for the acquisition of status. So he can not refer to this reason.
>
> (Representative of Slovene Philanthropy)

Insecurity and the feeling of having no future are devastating:

> It is also really hard when you are getting documents for one year only. OK, you wish, you feel things starting to get better. And you are managing all your life. You are coming from the time of the Asylum Home, from that flashback, for one year, now you are in a good time. You are supporting, you are planning. Suddenly, your documents stop and you get negative. And it means again problems forgetting about this one year. This is really big problem. Because I made so many plans to have a future, make a good life. But then what happened to me.
>
> (Age 17 upon arrival)

The best interests of the child and unaccompanied minors seeking international protection in Slovenia

> I look at it this way: If Slovenia cannot extend [someone's status] or fund it, they should have stopped at the beginning and said: 'Look, we cannot give you documents here in Slovenia. We cannot finance you and you go wherever you go!' Then this person would find something for himself. But I have lived here for four years and I do not know what will happen. This is something completely different.
>
> (Age 15 upon arrival)

According to the joint UNHCR and UNICEF publication from 2014, the application of the best interests principle should be present from the very beginning – from the arrival or discovery of unaccompanied minors up to the completion of international protection procedures. It is vital that whatever the final decision in the application for international protection will be (international protection is granted, residence is granted on other grounds, no residence granted), a durable solution should always follow (UNHCR and UNICEF 2014: 23). A durable solution is needed, one that includes follow-up and monitoring – a durable solution in the form of local integration, return and reintegration or a third-country solution (ibid.).

According to Kanics (2015), the durable solution for unaccompanied minors is a solution which is sustainable, which ensures that a child is able to develop into adulthood in an environment that will meet his or her needs. It is the solution that will fulfil his or her rights as defined by the Convention on the Rights of the Child and will not put the child at risk of persecution or serious harm.

Generally, Slovenian legislation covering the rights of unaccompanied minors (especially the IPA and AA) addresses the issues appropriately; however, it is the implementation that is problematic. The professionals involved with the issues surrounding unaccompanied minors, especially those professionals who are involved in advocacy on their behalf (NGOs, Ombudsman office, guardians), state that the main obstacles to the realisation of a best interests determination are bureaucratic logic, a lack of empathy, ignorance and finally a lack of funds.

> I think that the main obstacle is that those conducting the procedure do not devote much to it. There is always a problem of time, ability, determination, resources. All of it. The question is also if they truly know what needs to be done. The easiest way is to have a regulation, to look at it and say, 'This is my responsibility, this is not.' And you are formally protected, nobody can sue you. If you step a little bit out from there, you are on thin ice. So most prefer to keep to a safe path. Moreover, most of them are counting on the fact that foreigners will not complain because they do not understand the language, do not have the power, they do not know the way, all of this.
>
> (Deputy Ombudsman)

The violation of both principles (the best interests of the child and the durable solution) can be seen from the first moment in the formal procedures as applied by the Slovene border police, during which all effort is made to return the unaccompanied children from whence they came. Such an approach is manifestly in opposition to the directives of the Convention on the Rights of the Child,[13] where the procedures regarding best interests assessment highlight that the best interests of unaccompanied children would be met in a decision to allow access to the territory in order to carry out a more thorough assessment of the child's situation (see Chapter 3 in this volume). As additionally stressed by the Deputy Ombudsman, the state should and could do more:

> The state is avoiding its responsibility. All competent authorities want them to leave as soon as possible, to not have a lot of work with them. More could

> be done. To actually find out how he/she found himself/herself in the situation where he/she is. And to actually help him/her out of this situation. To actually help, not only remove him/her from our territory and then say this is not our problem anymore. We should introduce appropriate psycho-social help, education and accommodation. Of course this is related to costs; without funds we cannot fix it.

The violation of these principles is also evident in other phases of the process. While involved in the formal hearing (which usually takes place at the Aliens Centre), unaccompanied minors feel alone and treated like criminals. They do not understand that these are formal procedures, nor do they not understand why they are being detained: *We haven't done anything, we just want a better life.* There is an obvious lack of proper, concrete and understandable information or explanations.

Criminalisation of unaccompanied minors has also been observed by the Deputy Ombudsman:

> Sometimes it seems to me that they are treated as semi-criminals. And these conversations with them are not focused so much on helping them, but simply on 'why you do not fit in the conditions for asylum'.

This is felt by unaccompanied minors as well. One boy commented: 'They treat us as if we were Talibs.'

Different rights related to accommodation, health, education and work are ignored when being put into practice, regardless of having been properly introduced into law. From the unaccompanied minor's perspective, the duration of the different legal procedures is inappropriate. The time available for the first interview is too short, and it is this interview which, to a large extent, influences their future. The first interview takes place soon after or within a day of being detained by the police or apprehended at the border, and there is no time to receive accurate information about rights, options and possibilities, or to give information (tell their story) in a clear and comprehensive manner. On the other hand, the length of time from the day the unaccompanied minor applies for international protection to the day status is approved is often too long and, above all, not clearly defined.

Finally, what seems especially problematic from the perspective of a durable solution is the fact that international protection status (which is, in essence, temporary) is obtained on the grounds of being underage. Consequently, there are no legal grounds for the extension of the received international protection status when an unaccompanied minor turns 18. Unaccompanied minors are thus living 'in between', in uncertainty, without the vision of a durable solution:

> If I had known what would happen, I would not have decided to leave. I was afraid to die or to kill someone there. Here you are not living, and you are not dying, you are in between.
>
> (Age 17 upon arrival)

BORDER PROCEDURE: best interests of the child will be met if access to the territory is allowed in order to carry out assessment of the child's situation.	• Primarily there is a tendency to return unaccompanied children to a neighbouring country or their country of origin.
STATUS: unaccompanied minors are (vulnerable) children who need special protection and treatment	• Unaccompanied minors are perceived primarily as immigrants (even criminals). • Division between 'our'/national children and 'them'.
RIGHTS: – accommodation – food	• Accommodation in the Aliens Centre (with adults, without adult supervision); not integrated into the host society; isolation. • Food: a lack of diversity, too little, culturally unadapted etc.
RIGHTS: – health care – education – paid work	• Health care: lack of systematic psychological care/support. • Education: lack of Slovene language lessons, enrolment in classes with adults. • Low amount of pocket money; cut off from financial support in the case of working.
DURATION OF PROCEEDINGS: appropriate time duration of all legal procedures.	• Too short: when preparing for the first interview, before the application of international protection. • Too long and not clearly defined while awaiting status.
DURABLE SOLUTION: living in a safe enviroment	• No durable solution envisaged. • Uncertainty. • Feeling as though they have no future.

Figure 6.2 Discrepancies between legally guaranteed rights and their implementation

Conclusion

Unaccompanied minors who seek protection in the Republic of Slovenia are often treated not primarily as children but rather as foreigners, immigrants, criminals or someone who wants to exploit the Slovenian social welfare system. They are regarded as potentially dangerous, even dirty and potential transmitters of diseases. How can we otherwise rationalise and explain the system of parasite checks during the first medical examination at the Asylum Home, or the exhausting cross-examinations in search of narrative inconsistences, the accommodation with adult immigrants, the disbelief regarding being underage and the tendency to avoid stable and long-term solutions for unaccompanied minors in the existing formal system?

Unaccompanied minors as bearers of children's rights are robbed of their basic and internationally recognised (children's) rights in Slovenia. Within the Slovenian asylum system, unaccompanied minors have a different status to national children. As already discussed, they are 'not our children', and this is, from our perspective, the explanation of the actual situation.

Unaccompanied minors are not a part of the Slovenian national body. From such a nationalistic perspective, unaccompanied minors do not have the same rights as national children. Children's rights are supposed to be applied to all children, regardless of gender, cultural background and nationality. We must bear in mind, however, that the national state is a crucial provider of (children's) rights and if unaccompanied children are perceived as a threat to the national state *per se*, how we can expect that this very state will provide their rights? The nationalistic sentiment so widely spread across the European continent in the last decade and additionally strengthened during the last mass migration of Syrian refugees is so strongly attached to the whole of public and social life that it seems as if no one is immune and it is rarely recognised and problematised (ECRI 2015). State providers of social rights and executors of law at various bureaucratic levels are a part of a national body and potentially holders of nationalistic sentiment. This is why formal legislative acts can, in reality, be overturned, thus creating an approach that is not child-friendly towards unaccompanied minors. This is further confirmed by the results of various studies from the 1960s onwards (Brezigar 2007) according to which ethnic discrimination regarding employment in public administration is still very present. Consequently, very few representatives of ethnic minorities are employed in public administration which may in turn reinforce nationalistic attitudes.

Notes

1 Slovenia is a small country with fewer than two million inhabitants (Statistical Office of the Republic of Slovenia 2016).

2 Migrants who usually arrived through Greece, Macedonia and Serbia and continued their route across Hungary in their wish to reach main destination countries in Western and Northern Europe passed through Croatia and Slovenia.

3 The reasons for this are several and most likely reflect Slovenia's weak economic position as well as the fact that it is an unrecognised, small and politically somewhat irrelevant country of the EU.

4 Data obtained by the Ministry of the Interior show that in 2014 there were 65 UAMs who applied for international protection status, in most cases coming from Afghanistan (47), but also Pakistan (5), Morocco (2), Nigeria (2), Bangladesh, Egypt, Ghana, China, Kosovo, Myanmar, Syria, Ukraine. Among them there was only one girl (Ministry of the Interior 2015b).

5 Our field research revealed that unaccompanied minors and former unaccompanied minors express the greatest satisfaction especially with the work and support of Slovene Philanthropy mostly due to the work and support they provide.

6 For a better understanding of the information we received from the experts, it is important to stress that they expressed opinions on the system and its shortcomings, but in some cases these opinions were most likely presented in a way acceptable to the institution for which they work.

7 This group represented the entire population of UAMs and former UAMs with international protection status in the Republic of Slovenia at that time.

8 Upon arrival in Slovenia, they were 14 (two), 15 (three), 16 (eight) and 17 (five) years old.

9 Each role (special case guardian/legal representative/guardian) meets the actual needs of an unaccompanied minor, but the responsibilities incumbent upon each of these roles are dealt with by various legal acts. Special case guardians are dealt with in the Aliens Act, legal representatives in the International Protection Act and guardians in the Marriage and Family Relations Act.

10 The term 'alien' is used on the basis of the official translation of the act which regulates entry of people who are not citizens of Slovenia (the Aliens Act).

11 A guardian is appointed to the unaccompanied minor after he/she is granted international protection status.

12 If the unaccompanied minors are less than 16 years old, they are usually temporarily accommodated in the crisis centres for youth where the appropriate staff and conditions for minors are present.

13 The Republic of Slovenia adopted the UN Convention on the Rights of the Child (CRC, 1989) with the Basic Constitutional Charter on the Independence and Sovereignty of the Republic of Slovenia (Official Gazette of the Republic of Slovenia, 1/91) and with the Act on Notification of Succession (Official Gazette of the Republic of Slovenia No. 35/92).

Bibliography

Aliens Act (ZTuj-2) (2011) *Official Gazette of the Republic of Slovenia*, No. 50/11.

Billig, M. (1995) *Banal Nationalism*, London, Thousand Oaks, CA, New Delhi: SAGE Publications.

Brezigar, S. (2007) 'Pojavi etnične diskriminacije v javni upravi, vojski in policiji v Republiki Sloveniji', in M. Komac (ed.) *Priseljenci/Imigrants*, Ljubljana: Inštutut za narodnostna vprašanja.

Civil Procedure Act (ZPP) (1999) *Official Gazette of the Republic of Slovenia*, No. 73/07.

ECRI – European Commission against Racism and Intolerance (2015) *Annual Report 2014*. Available online at www.coe.int/t/dghl/monitoring/ecri/library/PressReleases/197-09_07_2015_AnnualReport2014_en.asp (accessed 22 February 2017).

Gornik, B. (2016) *Človekove pravice in nacionalizem (doctoral thesis)*, Univerza na Primorskem, Koper.

International Protection Act (ZMZ-1) (2016) *Official Gazette of the Republic of Slovenia*. No. 22/2016.

Kanics, J. (2015) 'Ensuring Respect for the Best Interests of Children on the Move in Europe', *Presentation at International Conference Children and Young People on the Move: Towards a More Precise Definition of their Best Interests*, 19–20 November 2015, Portorož, Slovenia.

Marriage and Family Relations Act (ZZZDR-UPB1) (2004) *Official Gazette of the Republic of Slovenia* No. 69/04, 101/07.

Ministry of the Interior (2014) *Poročilo z delovnega področja migracij, mednarodne zaščite in vključevanja za leto 2013*. Ljubljana: Ministrstvo za notranje zadeve Republike Slovenije.

Ministry of the Interior (2015a) *Podatki o številu migrantov, ki so vstopili v Slovenijo do 10. decembra*. Available online at www.policija.si/index.php/novinarsko-sredie/index.php?option=com_content&view=article&id=82019 (accessed 22 February 2017).

Ministry of the Interior (2015b*) Poročilo z delovnega področja migracij, mednarodne zaščite in vključevanja za leto 2014*, Ljubljana: Ministrstvo za notranje zadeve Republike Slovenije.

PIC (2014) *Usmerjena študija EMM 2014: Dobre prakse vračanja in reintegracije neregularnih migrantov: Prakse držav članic pri uporabi ukrepa prepovedi vstopa in sporazumov o vračanju s tretjimi državami*. Slovenski nacionalni prispevki.

Sauer, P. J. J., Nicholson, A. and Neubauer, D. (2015) 'Age determination in asylum seekers: Physicians should not be implicated', *The European Journal of Paediatrics*. Available online at http://legeforeningen.no/Global/Fagmedisinske%20foreninger/Norsk%20barnelegeforening/Paidos/aldersbestemmelse%20EAP.pdf (accessed 22 February 2017).

Statistical Office of the Republic of Slovenia (2016). Available online at www.stat.si/StatWeb/en (accessed 7 March 2017).

Thomas, W. I. and Thomas, D. S. (eds) (1928) *The Child in America: Behavior Problems and Programs*, New York, NY: Knopf.

UNHCR and UNICEF (2014) *Safe & Sound: What States can Do to Ensure Respect for the Best Interests of Unaccompanied and Separated Children in Europe*. Available online at www.refworld.org/docid/5423da264.html (accessed 22 February 2017).

Wernesjö, U. (2011) 'Unaccompanied asylum-seeking children: Whose perspective?', *Childhood*, Vol.19, No. 4, 495–507.

7 Coping strategies of unaccompanied minors lacking protection within the French context

The key role of political and civil society mobilisation

Corentin Bailleul

Introduction

Since the early 1990s, migration of unaccompanied minors has progressively become a juridical and political concern in Europe (Senovilla Hernandez 2014: 17). In France, the first unaccompanied minors came under institutional reception programmes in the 1980s (Frigoli and Immelé 2010: 131; Debré 2010: 11). In the early 1990s, public authorities observed spontaneous arrivals of unaccompanied minor migrants in departments characterised by a long tradition of migration (Paris, Seine Saint Denis, Bouches du Rhône) (Debré 2010: 11). It took the French legislator some years to recognise unaccompanied minor migrants as 'children at risk' under article 375 of the Civil Code. From 2007 onwards, and according to article L112-3 of the Social Action and Family Code, 'the aim of child protection is also to prevent and avoid difficulties that could face minors who find themselves in a temporary or permanent situation of lack of protection from their parents and to ensure that they are cared for'.[1]

In April 2013, according to the Ministry of Justice, there were around 9,000 unaccompanied minor migrants in France (Direction de la Protection Judiciaire de la Jeunesse 2014). It should be noted that this estimate does not include around 3,000 unaccompanied minors living in the French overseas department of Mayotte. In 2013, a total of 113,772 children at risk were in the care of the Child Welfare Services (Slama and Bouix 2014: 84). Therefore, unaccompanied minor migrants represent only 6 per cent of the total number of children protected. This percentage approximately corresponds with the proportion of foreigners amongst the French population which is estimated at 6.1 per cent (INSEE 2012). Most unaccompanied minor migrants are male (80 per cent) whereas the boys represent only 59 per cent of the total number of minors under care. Most of the unaccompanied minor migrants are aged between 15 and 17. They mostly originate from Sub-Saharan Africa (61 per cent) and Asia (16 per cent) and, to a lesser extent, from North Africa and the Middle East (13 per cent). Most of them were based in the following French departments: Paris (442), Nord (258), Seine-Saint-Denis (247), Val d'Oise (183) and Bouches du Rhône (176).

Recent statistics show that around 60 per cent of the young people claiming to be unaccompanied minors were excluded from institutional care because their minority or isolation from parents or relatives were contested at the initial assessment.[2] Given the low proportion of acceptance within the institutional protection system, I decided to focus in this chapter[3] on the case of young people claiming to be unaccompanied minor migrants in France who are excluded from institutional care. They are excluded following an initial assessment, made at the administrative level, disputing their age or their status as unaccompanied.

After presenting the fieldwork parameters and a brief overview of the French legal provisions relating to the right to be protected and the age assessment process, I will first discuss how those provisions are being implemented and why this leads to a high percentage of exclusion. Second, I will describe the conditions under which unaccompanied minor migrants are notified of the decision of non-admission to protection. A large majority of the young people who have been rejected continue to claim to be unaccompanied minors, and we will therefore describe their ability to appeal the administrative decision when their age and identity have been rejected, and their access to the Children's Judge[4] who will confirm or not the initial assessment. Third, I will expose the strategies and the agentic actions employed by these young migrants in order to gain different forms of protection . I will focus on their day-to-day survival strategies in the public space to fulfil basic needs, to find accommodation or food. Next, I will underline the essential role of NGOs whose support may lead young migrants to regain institutional protection or to benefit from ad-hoc protection measures. I will further describe the individual strategies used by young migrants met in the field who were trying to find protection elsewhere by modifying their migratory aim (in another part of France or another country) and I will describe how the institutions deal with this issue. Finally, I will describe how, by politicising their cause and participating in collective actions, young migrants lacking protection can struggle for their rights and how this might result in better protection.

Methods of data collection and fieldwork parameters

Protection of unaccompanied minor migrants in France is delegated to the Child Welfare Services (Aide Sociale à l'Enfance), which are the responsibility of the French departments. Traditionally, practices of identification and admission into care have been very different from one department to another. For this reason, our field research took place in departments where large numbers of unaccompanied children arrive every year: Paris and its surroundings (Seine-Saint-Denis and Val de Marne), the city of Marseille (department of Bouches du Rhône) and the town of Calais (department of Pas de Calais). Complementary field actions were conducted in the town of Poitiers (a smaller town with no tradition of receiving unaccompanied migrant children until recently) and in the town of Bordeaux (where we had the opportunity to meet young adults who were former unaccompanied minors). Field research was undertaken during an eight-month period between November 2014 and June 2015.

With the aim of analysing the perception of professionals working directly or indirectly with unaccompanied children on the implementation of the Convention on the Rights of the Child (CRC), we carried out 13 interviews with 19 key informants. The aim was to collect their opinions on the different aspects and challenges concerning the French model of reception. We interviewed managers and frontline workers from different NGOs working in this field, both those supporting unaccompanied minors and those acting as delegates of public institutions during the reception process and implementation of the administration's policy. Other interviews were conducted with adult informants committed to working with unaccompanied minor migrants, including staff working for the Ombudsman Institution,[5] psychologists and a public school teacher. Interviews with adult informants both facilitated the access of child informants and had the purpose of getting a preliminary validation of our research objectives (Hopkins 2008: 39).

We followed a field strategy already implemented in previous research actions (Senovilla Hernandez 2013: 37–38), which consisted of being repeatedly present in several strategic public spaces within the city of Paris. Three members of the field research team were regularly present for three months at the 10th and 19th districts of Paris near the Permanence d'Accueil et d'Orientation des Mineurs Isolés Etrangers (PAOMIE) office, which was in charge of processing new arrivals, assessing age and identification of unaccompanied minor migrants.[6] This strategy allowed us to get progressively in touch with children and young people, spending time with them in order to gain their trust and help them understand our role, talking and playing games. In our view, regular informal talks with unaccompanied children constitute a valuable information-gathering tool, most likely with fewer pitfalls and inaccuracies than more traditional tools such as formal interviews. Most of the children who participated in the research came from West African countries (Mali, Senegal, Guinea, Ivory Coast, Gambia, Ghana, Sierra Leone, Cameroon and Angola), North Africa (Algeria), East Africa (Egypt, Sudan and Eritrea), Europe (Romania) and Asia (Afghanistan, Pakistan and Bangladesh). A large majority of them were boys and the average declared age was between 15 and 17 years old.

Conscious that formal interviews with children can be a biased method, we created and used a new tool involving groups of 6–15 unaccompanied children and young people whom we met over 3–4 consecutive days. We organised six series of collective workshops (21 in total) involving around 70 unaccompanied migrant children and young people. The workshops, named 'collective workshops of awareness and talking', aimed to actively involve the participants in different forms of participation and play activities (role-plays, games, debates) and to share simultaneously information about various legal and social matters relevant to their situation. The discussions in the sessions touched upon topics such as the notion of 'unaccompanied child', the rights of the child, the reception and protection provisions, durable solutions and transition to adulthood. In most cases, we succeeded in creating a favourable atmosphere for young people to talk freely about their migration experiences. The workshops were inspired by the methods of 'focus interviews' developed by Merton and Kendall (1946). In implementing this method, we expected the 'group effect' to encourage uninhibited child participation. We considered that the participation of some young people (more inclined to join the debates) could encourage the timid ones to take the floor to contradict or corroborate (Duchesne and Haegel 2004: 13). We also expected the group to exercise a function of reciprocal control regarding misappropriated discourses.

Both the observation periods and the collective workshops facilitated access and consent for individual interviews with unaccompanied migrant children and young adults. Eleven formal individual interviews were conducted, nine with self-declared unaccompanied migrant children (several of them disputed cases) and two interviews with young adults. Most of the interviewees were going through the first stages of the reception process (children in the phase of identification and assessment, age-disputed cases, children living in hotels or ad-hoc shelters, children at initial reception facilities). A number of them were also living on the street or were in a very precarious situation at the time of the interview. All interviewees were informed about the aims and objectives of the research and the guarantees (particularly ensuring full confidentiality), and they were asked to give their consent prior to the interview. Interview settings varied and depended on the situation of the informant. For instance, interviews with children living on the street were mainly conducted in public spaces such as coffee shops or parks.

The analysis of the data allowed us to observe how the best interests principle is implemented in relation to the legal treatment and status of unaccompanied migrant children, including access to protection, age assessment procedures, access to care and safeguards in place once children reach the age of majority. We had also the opportunity to analyse the care provisions in light of the principles included in the CRC, in particular access to accommodation, physical and mental health care, education, paid work, formal and informal support and leisure. After a brief overview of the French legal framework regarding the assessment procedure, I will focus on our results regarding the consequences of the identity assessment process.

The French legal framework regarding the right to be protected and the assessment procedure

Unaccompanied minors in France should be considered as 'children at risk' under the Civil Code (article 375), which involves the implementation of the Social Action and Family Code (CASF) with no restriction concerning nationality. Although in most European countries unaccompanied children's access to institutional care is concomitant with their condition as asylum seekers (the so-called 'undocumented migrant children' usually do not 'exist' in juridical terms as they do not register an asylum application), it is very important to point out that France represents an exception to that prevailing model (as is also the case in Italy and Spain, and to a lesser extent in Belgium). In contrast with other European countries, most unaccompanied children arriving in France do not seek asylum but claim for state protection as children in need. The Child Welfare Services have to provide them with the same assistance as they do with national children, including material support and educational and psychological assistance.

According to article 375 of the Civil Code and to article 221-1 of the CASF, a child is considered at risk when 'his or her health, security or his morality [. . .] is in danger, if the conditions of his or her education, his or her physical, emotional, intellectual or social development are seriously compromised'.[7] The isolation criterion matches with this Civil Code definition of danger and is also taken into consideration in article L112-3 of the CASF which states that 'the aim of child protection is also to prevent and avoid difficulties that could face minors who find themselves in a temporary or permanent situation of lack of protection from their parents and to ensure that they are cared for'.[8]

Nevertheless, these provisions only concern unaccompanied minors recognised as such following an assessment of their age and their status as being 'unaccompanied'. The assessment is carried out both by administrative authorities (the Child Welfare Services as a first step) and by judicial authorities (the Children's Judge and the state prosecutor). According the Circular of 31 May 2013,[9] every young migrant claiming to be an unaccompanied child is or should be identified and assessed during an initial five-day period after they are registered by the administrative authority. This assessment may address three main aspects: status as a minor, the fact of being unaccompanied and territorial responsibility. Despite the fact that there are significant differences between territories regarding age assessment practices, it can be said that three main tools are used.

First, 'social assessments' consist of one or several interviews with the young person, in most cases conducted by staff of Child Welfare Services or a subcontracted NGO. During the social assessment interviews, the young migrant is asked to describe his or her situation, to show his or her documents and explain how he got them, to talk about the living conditions in his or her home country and the links with his or her family. Furthermore, he or she has to accurately outline his or her migration path from departure to arrival in France, including dates of arrival and departure from transit points and means of transportation. A first initial assessment is undertaken at this stage, taking into account the child's declarations, identification documents (if any), the child's physical appearance and any other information relevant to his or her identification as an unaccompanied minor.

Second, the administration investigates the identity documents. Article 47 of the French Civil Code establishes a presumption of validity of foreign identity documents. Only if the administration has a solid doubt about validity may it order an experts' examination of these documents (carried out by border police services), at the request of the prosecutor.

Third, medical assessment has to be made at the request of the state prosecutor. The most frequently used methods in the French context are an assessment of bone development (wrist or clavicle) and of dental maturity (specifically the scale of development of third molars). In all cases, scholars state that these methods are highly uninformative and only allow an approximate estimation of the age with a significant margin of error (around 18 months or more). Some of the methods, in particular the frequently used X-ray of the wrist bones, appear to be particularly inadequate and inaccurate in estimating the age of children older than 14 years. Abundant literature refutes the validity and accuracy of medical methods to estimate a young person's age. French medical authorities refute the validity of those methods (Haut Conseil de Santé Publique 2014; Académie Nationale de Médecine 2007; Comité Consultatif National d'Ethique 2005), as well as Institutions controlling the fundamental rights' implementation (Commission Nationale Consultative des Droits de l'Homme 2014; Défenseur des Droits 2012). At the international level, UN institutions and NGOs object to the use of medical assessment (Committee on the Rights of the Child 2005, 2009; Separated Children in Europe Programme 2012).

Conditions of age assessment

We have noticed that in practice a significant number of initial age assessment decisions (made at the administrative level) are based only on 'social assessment'. Many decisions do not comply with the presumption of the validity of identity documents and children are rejected from institutional care based only on subjective criteria (e.g. physical appearance, clothes, coherence of discourse). Even in cases where the young person provides authentic documents, the Child Welfare Services (or the organisation authorised by the public authority) may dispute the credibility of the document owner. In particular, as many young people only possess a birth certificate without photographic identification, authorities may argue that there is no evidence that the young person is the real holder of the document presented. Medical assessment is rarely ordered by administrative authorities during the initial assessment but is most often ordered by judicial authorities at a later stage.

Recent statistics show that around 60 per cent of the young people claiming to be unaccompanied migrant minors were excluded from institutional care as their minority or isolation were contested at this initial assessment.[10] Given the low level of acceptance within the institutional protection system, our survey has prioritised aspects related to the procedures of social assessment. Many of the young people highlighted a number of failings at this stage that hamper their rights as children and which are obviously contrary to the best interests principle.

First, it should be noted that the accommodation conditions offered to unaccompanied minor migrants who are in the process of identification assessment are often not adequate and do not ensure implementation of an assessment in a holistic and child-friendly way; young migrants are accommodated in provisional shelter facilities if there are available places. In many departments, administrative authorities state that there is a lack of available places in the initial reception facilities, and therefore some young people are still included in the age assessment process but are not benefiting from any accommodation provisions. As a consequence, many young people are forced to live on the street; others are provided with accommodation informally by relatives or friends. A large majority of the young people in the process of identification assessment whom we have met were accommodated in hotels. However, this solution is also inadequate for children's development, especially because these hotels are often unsuitable in terms of hygiene and safety. In Paris, those who couldn't be accommodated in hotels were placed in ad-hoc shelter accommodation. A gymnasium was also used to provide shelter for unaccompanied children arriving in Paris. Officially, there was a selection process every day at the PAOMIE office to choose those young people allowed to spend a night at the gymnasium, giving priority to 'the most vulnerable' according to PAOMIE representatives. The luckiest were accommodated in initial reception centres providing night shelter and educational activities.[11] For those accommodated in hotels or gymnasiums in Paris, educational support is very limited or non-existent. Our findings also show that often unaccompanied minor migrants are not properly informed about their administrative and legal situation.

Our findings show that social assessment interviews are too short to properly understand the complexity of the young people's migratory journey. In Paris, interviews at the PAOMIE service last between 15 and 90 minutes. The young people evoked their incapacity to talk freely in a climate where they feel unwelcome. Besides interview length, it is the relationship between the evaluator and the young person that is of great importance. According to most of the unaccompanied minors we met, the interviews are not adjusted to take into account the young person's age and vulnerability. Therefore, being aware of the importance of this first assessment in order to be qualified as an unaccompanied child and to be admitted into care, young people undergo the interviews with a high degree of anxiety and fear. Physical appearance, clean new clothes and the use of electronic devices, particularly mobile phones, may also lead the authorities to dispute the young person's credibility. During our workshops, the participants expressed how they were invited to stand up while the interviewers carefully examined them.

Another important aspect relates to the content of the social assessment interview. As mentioned above, the analysis of different assessment decisions indicated that the social assessment of the young person's identity dealt with a number of factual issues, which are initially not relevant for qualifying the person as an 'unaccompanied migrant child'. Specifically, there is a continuous request from the interviewers to provide exact dates and the names of the transit points where the young person has been in order to trace the migratory journey. A number of questions relate also to family matters and living conditions in the country of origin. In a number of cases, refusals do not really refer either to the minority or the status of being 'unaccompanied'. During our fieldwork we have become aware of a significant number of negative assessment decisions reproducing a similar argument based on the incoherence of and the inconsistencies in migrants' narratives; their credibility seems to be systematically disputed at this stage. The decisions following the initial assessment confirm this practice and include arguments such as: 'Your statement lacks precision and presents several incoherencies. You do not provide any evidence of the minority alleged.' Or: 'Your statement presents several improbabilities. You do not provide any element allowing us to conclude the minority and the fact of being unaccompanied alleged.'

The above-described tools for assessing the identity and age of the young people claiming to be unaccompanied minors present a number of gaps in terms of procedural guarantees, which can have a negative impact on the unaccompanied minors' best interests and particularly undermine their development by exposing them to further vulnerability and marginalisation. Implementing the best interests principle would suggest admitting into care all young persons declaring to be minors in similar conditions to French children in need. Additionally, the assessment should be undertaken by independent professionals over a sufficient period of time and include a holistic and child-friendly approach. I will now describe the conditions under the young people are informed of the decision.

Announcement of the decision: misunderstanding and lack of an effective mechanism of appeal

Considering the lack of an objective basis in decisions of rejection, the 'dismissed plaintiffs' struggle to understand the reasons for refusal. The young people interviewed often felt aggrieved and considered the decision to be a form of prejudice. A large majority of the young people still claimed to be unaccompanied minors. In response, they tried to explain the refusal as 'random chance', arbitrariness or financial reasons. Some of them pointed out the lack of consideration of cultural dimensions or of the impact of their migratory path on their level of maturity. We observed feelings of discrimination and of unequal treatment among the group of young Africans. Many of them judged that young people from Arabic countries are more likely to be taken into care. The following quotations confirm these statements:

> What hurts me is the suspicion at the PAOMIE. If they like your face they take you, otherwise they kick you out
>
> (Amadou, 17, Paris)

> I think the problem is that they [Child Welfare Services] don't have enough money for us
>
> (Ousmane, 17, Paris)

The young people's misunderstanding seems legitimate when considering the weakness of the objective basis of the decision making. The young people's confusion is also reinforced by the inadequate conditions under which they receive notification of the decision. In Paris, the administrative authorities do not provide the decision directly to the young people concerned but send it to the PAOMIE service. Then the head of the service is responsible for notifying the decision to the young person who has been rejected. Therefore, the young people are informed of the decision for refusal by a person who has no responsibility for that decision. As a consequence, the young people interviewed struggled to identify which institution was responsible for the decision. The following quotations confirm this:

> How can the Child Welfare Services reject you without even meeting you?
> (Souleymane, 15, Paris)

> First, they told me that the Judge would make an assessment of my age, but then, when I got the results, they told me it came from the Welfare Services.
> (Mamadou, 16, Paris)

Decisions contain a statement that refers to the possibility of appealing the decision before the Administrative Court. However, the French Administrative Court declared that it had no jurisdiction in this matter given that minors are recognised as incompetent by the court. This case law was confirmed by the Council of State on 1 July 2015.[12]

The only way forward for young migrants who are rejected at the initial assessment of age and identity and who continue to claim to be unaccompanied minor migrants is to request a Children's Judge hearing in compliance with article 375-5 of the Civil Code. The Children's Judge then either confirms or refuses the initial assessment and may order a medical assessment and an investigation of the validity of the identity documents that the young person possesses. Depending on the region, the waiting period for such a hearing can be 3–8 months (in Paris it is 5–6 months). During this waiting period, children may be placed provisionally at a shelter until the date of the hearing, but this decision is at the discretion of the Children's Judge. In Paris, the number of placements pending hearing has been dropping consistently during the last few years (71 per cent in 2013, 54 per cent in 2014 and around 20 per cent during the first months of 2015 according to recent internal statistics provided by an NGO).[13] As a consequence, most unaccompanied minor migrants have to fend for themselves until the Judge's hearing. A significant number of them are recognised as unaccompanied minors following the Judge's decision, which essentially means that leaving an individual without child protection before a definite decision is made undermines their best interests. Implementing the best interests principle would suggest that the administrative authority should provide reasoned decisions in facts and law. The best interests principle would also suggest the need for the incorporation of an effective mechanism of appeal with suspensive effect. We will now describe the strategies and the agentic actions employed by these young migrants in order to regain different forms of protection.

Experiencing street life

It has to be underlined that the situation described above should not occur. However, if the administrative authorities dispute the identity of a young person and if this person does not continue to claim to be an unaccompanied migrant minor, the authorities should ensure their access to existing protection measures available for young adults. Indeed, French child welfare regulations provide the possibility of granting care provisions from 18 until 21 years of age according to article L112-3 of the Social Work and Family Code. This provision applies to all young adults – national or foreign – allowing them a gradual transition to adulthood and autonomy. The so-called 'young adult contract' between the young adult and the administration may provide them financial support, accommodation, legal, educational and psychological support. Failing that, the administration should effectively guide the young adults towards existing accommodations for young adults in need (hostels for young workers or immigrants, integrated area-based services for the reception and orientation of people facing homelessness, emergency centres and accommodation centres). When the fact of being 'unaccompanied' has been contested, but not the age, the administration, in collaboration with judicial authorities, should assess the links between the minor and the person who may take care of him or her, and, when appropriate, take all measures necessary for guaranteeing his or her protection. Last but not least, if the young person continues to claim to be an unaccompanied minor, an effective and suspensive mechanism of appeal should be incorporated, in compliance with the principle of presumption of minority as recommended by international and national agencies (Committee on the Rights of the Child 2005; UNHCR 2007; Commission Nationale Consultative des Droits de l'Homme 2014; Défenseur des Droits 2012). According to this principle, the young person should continue to benefit from childcare provisions until the judicial decision about the initial assessment is taken.

However, in practice the authorities do not apply the principle of presumption of minority. The young people who receive a negative decision are no longer allowed to benefit from childcare provisions. Moreover, they face difficulties in accessing accommodation centres for adults. On one hand, reception centres are not legally obliged to receive underage persons and therefore deny them access on the basis of their birth certificate. On the other hand, those who pretend to be adults, in order to be accommodated in reception centres, face a lack of available places. In this regard, the General Inspectorate of Social Affairs (Inspection Générale des Affaires Sociales, IGAS) underlined the overcrowdedness of reception and accommodation centres in 2012 (Inspection Générale des Affaires Sociales 2012: 19). Despite this, when young people manage to obtain temporary accommodation in facilities for adults, they often face danger from people living in precarious situations.

Due to this unfavourable situation, many young people are forced to live on the street. They adopt different ways and means for their survival; some shelter in Metro stations, in parking lots, in the waiting room of the emergency department at hospitals, or at places of worship, while others are informally accommodated by relatives or friends. Some also stay at migrant workers' hostels or community houses either free of charge or for a low sum:

> If you've got two euros, you are allowed to eat at the Malian community house. It works like a family: if they know you, they provide you accommodation; if not, they don't.
>
> (Amadou, 16, Paris)

> I've stayed one week in the community house, sleeping in the kitchen.
>
> (Balla, 15, Paris)

Young people living on the street face several difficulties when trying to fulfil their basic needs. In day-to-day life they struggle to get food, to find clothes, to access health care and to get around the city. Additionally, living on the street compromises their security and safety; many reported the presence of people who were potentially violent or who would prey on their vulnerability, as shown in the following quotations:

> It's cold, we can't take shower, it's dangerous, there's no food and we can't go to school.
>
> (Mamadou, 16, Marseille)

> My life is not good at all [. . .] Nobody likes to live on the street, especially when you are underage. At the moment, my top priorities are: getting shoes, clothes, food and going to school.
>
> (Souleymane, 15, Paris)

Children living on the street usually have to use soup kitchen services and public baths for the homeless. It is difficult for many of them to be relegated to homeless services and the young migrants interviewed often expressed feelings of uneasiness. As the following quotation describes, they often confessed to feeling hurt by other people's looks and attitudes regarding their social marginalisation:

> When you are carrying plastic bags, people look at you in the Metro and will even hold their nose. People's reaction hurts.
>
> (Amadou, 16, Paris)

When their health condition requires medical intervention, young migrants lacking protection usually go to medical services or hospitals. However, doctors often deny medical care to persons claiming to be unaccompanied minors. Many doctors consider that medical treatment is potentially intrusive and demand the authorisation of the young person's legal representative. The responsibility thus lies with the physician who decides to treat children without the consent of their parents. Article R4127 and section 1111-5 of the Code of Public Health allows doctors to override parental authority if treatment or an operation is vital to safeguard the health of the child. We interviewed young people claiming to be unaccompanied minors for whom care has been refused because physicians argued they did not have the right to treat children without the agreement of their legal representatives:

> I have a problem with my teeth. When I go to the hospital, the doctor tells me, 'You are a minor, I cannot pull out your teeth.' He puts me a plaster and I cannot sleep.
>
> (Amadou, 16, Paris)

As part of the fieldwork, we have regularly asked the children and young people about their dreams, objectives and ambitions for the future. However, most of them expressed no particular expectations about their future plans and did not think constructively about their life in the future; all of their efforts were put into struggling with everyday challenges and day-to-day survival.

> I have quite lost hope here. I don't think I'll be able to achieve my dreams.
> (Souleyman, 15, Paris)

> In our current living conditions we cannot accomplish our dreams.
> (Sikou, 16, Paris)

Many unaccompanied minors are forced to live on the street for three or four months until they get a definitive decision regarding their status. More than 50 per cent of them are finally recognised as unaccompanied minors after the Children's Judge hearing. This situation wouldn't occur if an effective mechanism of appeal with suspensive effect could be implemented.

The support of organised civil society: a way to regain institutional protection

O'Higgins defined young migrants' 'agency' as their 'ability to participate meaningfully in the construction of their daily lives, including their capacity to cope, their ability to adapt, and their resilience' (O'Higgins 2012: 81). Young migrants use individual as well as collective strategies and agentic actions when coping with difficulties in their everyday lives. As I will show in this section, NGOs and support organisations from civil society constitute an important source of support for this purpose.

During the fieldwork we had the opportunity to observe the involvement of several organisations acting on behalf of unaccompanied minor migrants such as Accompagnement et Défense des Jeunes Isolés Etrangers (ADJIE), Réseau Education Sans Frontières (RESF) and Médecins du Monde (MDM). These organisations provided legal support for access to education and access to health for minors who have been excluded from care following the initial assessment. In many cases, with their support the young migrants regained institutional protection (after their status as unaccompanied minors was finally recognised) or benefited from ad-hoc protection measures.

For the young people rejected at the initial assessment, it is very important to get legal support; many of them do not have the personal resources and know-how to deal with legal issues on their own. In Paris, a group of associations and NGOs has created a platform (called ADJIE), where they provide legal counselling and support to all young persons, especially when there is a need to file individual complaints and to request a hearing with the Children's Judge. According to the volunteers from the ADJIE platform, more than 50 per cent of the young people excluded following the initial assessment and appointing the Children's

Judge, regain institutional protection with their support and their status as unaccompanied minors is finally recognised.

The platform represents a valuable service for coping with the difficulties linked to the precarious administrative and legal situation of unaccompanied minors: it provides information on their rights, letters of support, assistance during the hearings and support to appeal negative decisions. At the same time, the platform's members are furthering the law, developing rights advocacy and raising awareness among the public and policy makers. By implementing both individual support and collective action, the organisation promotes the best interests of each particular child on an individual level (determining the concrete interests of each child supported) and as a general principle on the administrative and legislative level. These goals are sometimes contradictory; for instance, lengthy contentious proceedings may be in favour of best interests as a general principle by shaping the law, but may compromise the best interest of the child, as he or she lacks protection during the long proceedings and could have sought protection elsewhere in the meantime.

In addition to the need for essential legal support, young migrants lacking protection are also supported by NGOs when ensuring their right to health and education. Unaccompanied minors have specific health-related needs for several reasons: they often come from countries where TB and HIV are endemic and where access to care is deficient. In addition, they are in a vulnerable situation after an exhausting migratory journey; they may have travelled in hostile and precarious conditions, and if they were ill in their country of origin, they often interrupted their treatment during the journey. Their precarious situation in the host country often reinforces their psychological troubles; as discovered during our research, young people often experience deep unease: they mull over their problems, and have headaches, sleeping problems and nightmares.

Therefore, their needs in terms of mental and physical care should be attentively and conscientiously fulfilled. But when unaccompanied children's status is contested, they face several obstacles in regard to accessing healthcare services. They are entitled to the same basic healthcare provisions as any other undocumented migrant,[14] but they have to provide proof of their current residence in France (which might be impossible given their situation). This may become an insurmountable bureaucratic obstacle for young people living on the streets or at provisional shelters. For this reason some support organisations in Paris register unaccompanied children at their headquarters address in order to facilitate their access to healthcare provisions. The organisation Médecins du Monde, a group of physicians, psychologists, specialised doctors and social workers, assists young migrants, offers consultation and provides administrative support in order to help them to realise their right to health care and social security.

For unaccompanied minor migrants, especially young Africans, access to education was also highlighted as a major challenge. They have a high regard for the French public school system, as many of them were not able to attend school in their home countries; for this reason especially, they put schooling and getting instruction at the top of their migration priorities. French law ensures the right to education with no restriction on nationality and regardless of migratory status. However, during fieldwork we have noticed obstacles hindering unaccompanied children's effective access to this fundamental right.

When unaccompanied minor migrants are still in the process of identification assessment, they face extensive difficulties in becoming integrated in school. In Paris, some organisations promoting the unconditionality of the right to education assist them with integratation into public schools. For instance, during our fieldwork from November 2014 to June 2015 we observed two different practices in Paris. Before December 2014, the public institution CASNAV,[15] in charge of assessing school level and assigning pupils to an education establishment, integrated eight unaccompanied children lacking protection per week into school. Consequently, many young people living on the street in a precarious situation were attending school. Unfortunately, in January 2015 CASNAV decided to continue to assess the school level of young migrants lacking protection but to delay integrating them into school until they are in institutional care. This new practice was a source of disappointment and concern for the young people, as shown in the following quotation:

> Why do they allow us to pass the level exam? They should tell to us straight away that we are not allowed to go to school.
>
> (Mamoudou, 16, Paris)

Our fieldwork research has shown that minor migrants who attend classes are highly motivated and committed to doing well in school; all the staff from the educational institutions we consulted confirmed this trend. For migrants, school is not only about getting education, but it is also a very important space of integration; it is usually the place where migrants are able to meet and become friends with French people of their own age. In addition, school enrolment may increase exponentially the sources of support available to the young people: class teachers, head teachers, as well as the members of networks promoting education for all (Réseau Education sans frontiers – RESF) or school student unions sometimes provide individual support and organise collective action for young migrants attending school. As a result of this mobilisation, young migrants obtain protection in two different ways: on one hand, some of them obtain access to ad-hoc protection measures (such as accommodation in hotels, boarding school or even in the school's gymnasium), while, on the other hand, integration into school strengthens their chance to get beneficial judicial treatment as the judges consider school as a guarantee of their social integration.

Individual and collective strategies for coping with the lack of protection

When young people are excluded from care following the initial assessment, they often feel pessimistic about their future. To cope with the lack of opportunities in the region where they have been rejected, some redefine their migratory plans, considering that they would be luckier in another part of France or another country. It has to be noted that information about migration procedures and their outcomes circulates between the young migrants and their peer groups. For peers living in the same city or town, the network of friends serves as a source of information and support, and improves knowledge about migration. Social and migratory networks provide a range of strategic resources such as information and knowledge on constraints and opportunities through the migration's plan (Duvivier 2008: 206). Those resources allow young migrants to adapt their migratory plans towards another French department or another country. However, the exchange of information remains incomplete and the young people often make mistakes when comparing their situation with another. The following quotation illustrates this:

> All my friends are telling me that they are going to leave Paris, I think they are right. When you go to the PAOMIE service, they don't even investigate your identity documents; they just look at it and say 'it's fake'. In other French departments, they are making a real investigation and you can be admitted into care. Many people told me that they don't accept young migrants in Paris. I think the best for me is to go elsewhere, I actually thought about leaving France, about going to another country. I don't have money but trains will always be free for us.
>
> (Amadou, 16, Paris)

Social workers, employees of initial reception centres and NGOs may advise the unaccompanied minor migrants on redefining their migratory plans.

> If they don't have enough patience, courage or enough friends and sources of support, it will be complicated. In this case, we are inviting them to seek better opportunities elsewhere. It's an open dialogue, we talk freely about that.
>
> (Social worker, Marseille)

We were not able to assess the effectiveness of the information sharing between the different departments regarding applications for protection of unaccompanied minor migrants, but according to the interviewees, the information sharing between them is generally improving. Questioned about the strategy of seeking protection in another country, members of the service in charge of the age assessment described the young people as 'child-protection tourists'. By analogy, they refer to the concept of 'asylum shopping' used by EU institutions to describe the practice of seeking asylum in a particular state after transiting other states due to the Dublin regulation restrictions (Commission of the European Communities 2007: 10).

Strategies for coping with the lack of protection are sometimes also developed in a collective way, especially when the network of peers works as a source of support and solidarity. For instance, while we were spending time with a group of West Africans based at the street camps of Boulevard de la Villette and Place de la République in Paris, we observed how the newly arrived received advice from those already in place (including tips about where to wash your clothes for free, where to go for legal support and where to obtain food). The network of peers or adult migrants from the same ethnic or linguistic community also appears to be of key importance for day-to-day survival. This was especially evident during our fieldwork in Marseille, where we have been regularly in touch with two young Ghanaians who were allowed to spend the night in an African restaurant after closing time. This informal community network is vital for unaccompanied children to organise their survival until they are identified and admitted into care or until an alternative solution is found for them. However, in Paris, we were also in touch with another young person who decided to stay on his own and keep his distance from his group of peers. In the end he struggled to find opportunities and ended up moving to another region. Nevertheless, we observed that strong relations between peers raise the young people's awareness about their situation as unaccompanied minors and may lead to the politicisation of their cause. We observed that they are progressively gaining indignation and political culture and were even able to identify the policy makers and institution responsible for Child Welfare Services:

> If I could talk to the president of France I would say: don't let the foreign children sleep on the street! French and foreign people have the same rights!
>
> (Amadou, 16, Paris)

> I'm not the only one saying that, I know whose fault it is: a policy maker called X.
>
> (Amadou, 16, Paris)

Traditionally, young migrants lacking protection are supported by associations and migrant support organisations. The latter encourage young migrants to mobilise politically to claim their rights. However, during the fieldwork in Paris, there was a new association supporting homeless people (115 du Particulier) which was also supporting a group of migrant children and young people living on the streets. During winter 2014, they organised a daily soup-kitchen service in front of the PAOMIE office in the 10th district of Paris. In this way, they were in constant contact with the young migrants; they talked with them and gained their trust. The soup kitchen was exclusively intended for minors, and the members of the association refused to serve food to those they believed to be adults.

A few weeks later, the NGO decided to create an informal camp for 25–50 children and young people in front of the office. They provided tents, sleeping bags and other camping gear, and also encouraged the group to mobilise to claim their rights. Simultaneously, the children, supported by the NGO, were regularly demonstrating and organising political action. On the 26 February 2015, young people illegally occupied the PAOMIE office. The police evacuated by force around 50 young migrants. One of the young people interviewed participated in the occupation:

> I have met friends who had the same problems as me. The day after I arrived, they occupied the PAOMIE office. French people were there, it gave me courage! Security staff couldn't do anything, the manager either. The police came, there were many of them. We stayed there until dark. The police entered the building and began the evacuation. It didn't hurt but they evacuated us by force.
>
> (Ousmane, 17, Paris)

On 31 March 2015, the NGO transferred the camp to Place de la République, a central square in Paris. The aim was to gain visibility and create public awareness about the migrants' problems and at the same time to join the struggle of families who were expelled from their homes and emergency reception centres by the authorities. On 23 April, after a two-month mobilisation period, a list was transmitted to the state authority, and the Prefecture de Paris (a department of the Ministry of Interior) provided 43 unaccompanied minor migrants with accommodation. They have been accommodated in a reception centre for young adults until the Judge's hearing and the final decision on their status. Paradoxically, these young Africans were claiming protection as unaccompanied minors, but in the end they have been supported by institutions (Prefecture de Paris) with no competence in child protection. Questioned about their political mobilisation, the young people affirmed that they were the ones who were taking the important decisions:

> We were going to every demonstration, with other people living on the street. When we have seen that under-housed and homeless people were there (Place de la République), we thought we should go there to be more visible. We are the ones who decided.
>
> (Amadou, 16, Paris)

> There is no leader, we decide all together.
>
> (Ousmane, 17, Paris)

We can underline two observations regarding the outcomes obtained following this mobilisation. On one hand, the benefits for young migrants were limited; those who were not actively involved in the demonstration were not registered on the list and were not entitled to any ad-hoc provisions. On the other hand, the competence of the institution that implemented these measures did not match with the underage status claimed by migrants. The latter were considered to be adults until the definitive decision on their status was taken. Nevertheless, as seen from the case described, this kind of collective strategy and action constitutes powerful levers, ensures greater cohesion between the young people involved and encourages mutual support. This enables some young people to benefit from ad-hoc measures of protection and others to finally gain institutional protection.

This section shows that young people, far from being passive, use survival strategies and often resort to their networks and informal sources of support in order to overcome the obstacles they are facing. The fieldwork observations confirmed that personal networks are among the more important sources of support for unaccompanied children together with the support of the NGOs.

Conclusion

This chapter has described the ambiguous nature of the administrative treatment of unaccompanied minor migrants who are excluded from institutional care following initial assessment. Their status is not approached consistently as they are considered to be adults by some institutions (e.g. CASNAV and Child Welfare Services) and to be minors by others (emergency centres and accommodation centres for adults, healthcare providers). Consequently, they are forced to survive in an 'in-between' situation which undoubtedly increases their vulnerability and compromises their development. Their fundamental rights are often infringed until their age is formally determined. The presumption of minority that is recommended by international and national bodies is systematically ignored during this process. It is worth recalling that the Committee on the Rights of the Child recommends that age assessments

> must be conducted in a scientific, safe, child and gender-sensitive and fair manner, avoiding any risk of violation of the physical integrity of the child, giving due respect to human dignity and, in the event of remaining uncertainty, should accord the individual the benefit of the doubt such that if there is a possibility that the individual is a child, she or he should be treated as such.
>
> (UNCRC 2005: 11)

In France it seems that when there is doubt about the migrant's age, administrative and judicial instances tend to apply a presumption of majority. In any case, it is necessary to rethink and amend the age assessment procedure in order to guarantee a number of procedural safeguards that are now completely ignored. All young people claiming to be unaccompanied minors should have access to an independent legal counsellor during the whole process, and the administrative authority should provide reasoned decisions in facts and law. Additionally, mechanisms of suspensive and effective appeal should be incorporated in the assessment procedure (these safeguards are guaranteed by article 13 of the European Convention on Human Rights and article 47 of the Charter of Fundamental Rights of the EU). Thankfully, through the involvement of civil society, young migrants still manage to gain their rights (to health and education), to benefit from ad-hoc protection or even to retrieve institutional care. However, civil society's ability to take action at the local level varies greatly from one department to another. Furthermore, the increase in the number of stakeholders around young migrants at the same time increases the number of interests at stake. This may lead to the creation of new conflicts of interest in addition to those introduced by public action.

Notes

1 Article L112-3 of the Social Action and Family Code: 'La protection de l'enfance a également pour but de prévenir les difficultés que peuvent rencontrer les mineurs privés temporairement ou définitivement de la protection de leur famille et d'assurer leur prise en charge.'
2 According to more recent information publicly provided by a representative of the Ministry of Justice 19,000 young people claiming to be unaccompanied minors were assessed between 1 June 2013 and 31 December 2014. Only around 40 per cent of them (7,600) were identified as such. See minutes of InfoMIE's editorial board, 16 April 2015.
3 This chapter presents part of the findings collected in the French context within the framework of the European project MINAS 'In whose best interest? Exploring Unaccompanied Minors' Rights through the Lens of Migration and Asylum Procedures' – a research project carried out in four European countries (Slovenia, Austria, France and the United Kingdom) in the period from June 2014 to December 2015. The European Commission financed the project and its main aim was to identify and recommend better procedures and protection measures for unaccompanied minors (UAM).
4 Every child at risk is under the jurisdiction of the Children's Judge (Juge des enfants) who is in charge of monitoring the child's care provisions. The Children's Judge also makes decisions about unaccompanied children's access to care. Unaccompanied minor migrants may also be under the jurisdiction of the Guardianship Judge (Juge des tutelles) in order to appoint a legal guardian, but guardians are rarely appointed in practice.
5 The Ombudsman Institution (Défenseur des Droits) is an independent administrative authority. It was enshrined in the Constitution on 23 July 2008 and established by the Organic and Ordinary Laws of 29 March 2011. The institution's aim is to oversee the protection of natural or legal persons' rights and freedoms, to promote equality and to ensure greater access to rights.
6 The PAOMIE (Permanence d'Accueil et Orientation des Mineurs Isolés Etrangers), run by France Terre d'Asile, was a subcontracted clearing service in charge of unaccompanied children's identification and age assessment in the city of Paris. This service closed in January 2016 and was replaced with the DEMIE (Dispositif d'Evaluation des Mineurs Isolés Etrangers), run by the French Red Cross.
7 Article 375 of the Civil Code: 'Si la santé, la sécurité ou la moralité d'un mineur non émancipé sont en danger, ou si les conditions de son éducation ou de son développement physique, affectif, intellectuel et social sont gravement compromises.'
8 L112-3 of the Social Work and Family Code: 'La protection de l'enfance a également pour but de prévenir les difficultés que peuvent rencontrer les mineurs privés temporairement ou définitivement de la protection de leur famille et d'assurer leur prise en charge.'
9 Ministry Circular concerning UAMs reception procedures: sheltering, assessment and orientation for UAMs, 31 May 2013. Most of the provisions included in the circular and concerning the age assessment have been confirmed by a new circular: (Interministerial Circular of 25 January 2016) and later in the Child Welfare Act on 14 March 2016.

10 According to more recent information publicly provided by a representative of the Ministry of Justice, 19,000 young people claiming to be unaccompanied minors were assessed between 1 June 2013 and 31 December 2014. Only around 40 per cent of them (7,600) were identified as such. See minutes of InfoMIE's editorial board, 16 April 2015.

11 Initial reception centres providing night shelter and some educational activities seem to be one of the better solutions observed during fieldwork. We had the opportunity to be in touch with a group of children accommodated at a Red Cross specialised reception centre in the Val de Marne department (inside the Paris conurbation). In contrast with those we met on the streets, these children seemed to be thriving and, most importantly, safe. The group was living together in harmony and they were attending regular language classes and other recreational and educational activities (sports, cultural visits, etc.). A good indicator of the quality of the reception centre was that during our visits we noticed that other children or young people who had previously been accommodated at this centre came by to spend some time with their peers, to talk to the social workers, etc. However, we also saw that children could remain for excessive lengths of time at this kind of facility before their permanent placement.

12 Conseil d'Etat décision du 1er juillet 2015, n° 386769.

13 Internal statistics provided by the ADJIE (Accompagnement et défense des jeunes isolés étrangers).

14 Article L. 115-6 Code de la Sécurité Sociale.

15 Centre académique pour la Scolarisation des enfants allophones Nouvellement Arrivés et des enfants issus de familles itinérantes et de Voyageurs.

Bibliography

Académie Nationale de Médecine (2007) *Rapport sur la fiabilité des examens médicaux visant à déterminer l'âge à des fins judiciaires et la possibilité d'amélioration en la matière pour les mineurs étrangers isolés*, 16 January 2007.

Comité Consultatif National d'Ethique (2005) *Avis n° 88 sur les méthodes de détermination de l'âge à des fins juridiques*, 23 June 2005.

Commission Nationale Consultative des Droits de l'Homme (2014) *Avis sur la situation des mineurs isolés étrangers présents sur le territoire national*, 26 June 2014.

Commission of the European Communities (2007) *Report from the commission to the European Parliament and the Council on the evaluation of the Dublin system*, 6 June 2007.

Committee on the Rights of the Child (2005) *General Comment No. 6 on the treatment of unaccompanied and separated children outside their country of origin*, September 2005.

Committee on the Rights of the Child (2009) *Concluding observations: France*, 12 June 2009.

Debré I. (2010) Sénateur des Hauts-de-Seine, parlementaire en mission auprès du Garde des Sceaux, Ministre de la Justice et des Libertés, *Les mineurs isolés étrangers en France*, 11 May 2010.

Défenseur des Droits (2012) *Décision n° MDE/2012-179*, 21 December 2012.

Direction de la Protection Judiciaire de la Jeunesse (2014) *Rapport d'activité du dispositif national de mise à l'abri, d'évaluation et d'orientation des mineurs isolés étrangers*, 1 June 2013 to 31 May 2014.

Duchesne, S. and Haegel, F. (2004) *L'enquête et ses méthodes: les entretiens collectifs*, Paris: Nathan Université.

Duvivier, E. (2008) 'Du "Temps du déplacement" au "Temps de l'institution" : analyse des trajectoires migratoires d'un groupe de mineurs isolés pris en charge dans un foyer socio-éducatif de la métropole lilloise', *Revue E-MIGRINTER*, No. 2, 196–207.

Frigoli G. and Immelé C. (2010) 'Les protéger et s'en protéger: les mineurs isolés étrangers en débat au Parlement français', *Migrations et Société: Mineur isolé étranger: une nouvelle figure de l'altérité?*, Vol. 22, No. 129–130.

Haut Conseil de la Santé Publique (2014) *Avis relatif à l'évaluation de la minorité d'un jeune étranger isolé*, 23 January 2014.

Hopkins P. (2008) 'Ethical issues in research with unaccompanied asylum-seeking children', *Children's Geographies*, Vol. 6. No. 1, 37–48.

Inspection Générale des Affaires Sociales (2012) *Bilan de la mise en œuvre des services intégrés d'accueil et d'orientation (SIAO)*, February 2012.

INSEE (2012) Recensement de la population, population étrangère et immigrée par sexe et âge en 2012.

Merton, R. K. and Kendall, P. L. (1946) 'The focused interview', *American Journal of Sociology*, Vol. 51, No. 6, 541–557.

O'Higgins A. (2012) 'Vulnerability and Agency: Beyond an Irreconcilable Dichotomy for Social Services Providers Working with Young Refugees in the UK', in A. Orgocka and C. Clark-Zakak (eds) *Independent Child Migration – Insights into Agency, Vulnerability, and Structure*, New Directions for Child and Adolescent Development No. 136.

Senovilla Hernandez D. (2013) *Unaccompanied Children Lacking Protection in Europe: Final Comparative Report*, PUCAFREU – Promoting unaccompanied children's access to fundamental rights in the European Union, 2013.

Senovilla Hernandez D. (2014) 'Analyse d'une catégorie juridique récente: le mineur étranger non accompagné, séparé ou isolé', *Revue Européenne des Migrations Internationales: Mineurs en migration: enjeux juridiques, politiques et sociaux*, Vol. 30, No. 1, 17–34.

Separated Children in Europe Programme (2012) *Position Paper on Age Assessment in the Context of Separated Children in Europe*, May 2012.

Slama S. and Bouix A. (2014) 'Mineurs isolés étrangers: la fabrique d'un infra-droit d'exclusion', *Actualité Juridique Famille* 2/2014, 84–89.

UNHCR (2007), *Conclusion on children at risk*, no.107 (LVIII)-2007, Executive Committee 56th session, contained in United Nations General Assembly document A/AC. 96/1048.

8 Surely not!

Procedurally lawful age assessments in the UK[1]

Marie-Bénédicte Dembour

Introduction

Every day young people arrive in Europe who cannot prove their age. Their birth may never have been registered in their country of origin.[2] It may also be that at some stage documentation existed which indicated their age, but it has been lost, or the authorities do not believe it is genuine. This creates a problem for the authorities who must now decide how to treat the person in front of them. If this person is a child,[3] they are entitled to more rights and must be given far greater protection than if they are adults. The younger they are, the more support they must be offered.

J, as he is referred to by the High Court in a judgment of November 2011, arrived in the UK in October 2009.[4] He said he was 14 and a half years old but the authorities did not believe him. An age assessment procedure was performed by a social worker on the very day of his arrival. She felt J looked older than the age he claimed to be. Her notes record that he was 'gently spoken' and 'presented as very considered in his responses'. The form she completed concluded: 'Based on the assessment, the client's age is: 18.' The Home Office subsequently relied upon this for refusing J asylum. So did the (then called) Asylum and Immigration Tribunal (AIT)[5] for dismissing the appeal against the asylum refusal. Having been found to be an adult and being considered a failed asylum seeker, J was detained on 1 March 2010, with his removal planned for eight days later.

The removal did not happen. From the time J had arrived in the UK, he had said and repeated he had an older brother called Zaky (who, unlike J, is named in the judgment). Indeed, the social worker's assessment mentions Zaky, adding in reference to him: 'whereabouts unknown'. At some undefined stage, Zaky had also made it to the UK, and the two brothers were reunited. When this happened, the authorities had already accepted that Zaky was 16 and had granted him the status of Unaccompanied Asylum Seeking Child (UASC). Throughout the proceedings Zaky had gone through, he had consistently mentioned having become separated from his younger brother J.

This provided J's solicitor with a basis for making a fresh claim for asylum. The UK Border Agency rejected the claim one week later, with the refusal letter, dated 1 March 2010, stating:

> Despite the outcome to Zaky's case this has no bearing on that of your client who has been through the appeal system and has been found to be someone who is over 18 years of age and who is not in need of international protection. He has never been dependant on his brother's claim or vice versa.
>
> (Para 24 of the judgment)

J's lawyer did not give up and made an emergency application for judicial review before the High Court. J was immediately released as the High Court judge accepted J had been about 14 and a half at the time of the initial age assessment.

In light of national law and policy, J's initial age assessment was seriously flawed. To use the legal expression, which will be explained below, it failed to be 'Merton-compliant'. As such, it should never have been given the weight it was given by the Home Office and by the AIT, as another High Court judge subsequently pointed out in proceedings that took place in 2011 for damages for unlawful detention.

J should have been believed, or at least given the benefit of the doubt, when he said he was 14 and a half years old. Because age goes to the heart of an individual's identity, having one's age disputed is an extremely distressing experience, with potentially serious mental health implications (Crawley 2007: 102, 181). Other drastically negative consequences ensue. As is immediately clear, J failed to receive the support and education to which he was entitled as a 14-year-old. Furthermore, he was treated in a way that was completely inappropriate for his age. He spent four days in a building constructed on the model of a Category B prison, surrounded by adults (some of whom were hostile), having not yet recovered from the physical exhaustion and psychological distress of a perilous journey, and full of angst about his future. This is a deleterious experience for anybody, however mature they are (Smith 2016; Nethery and Silverman 2015; Stevens 2013); a young teenager should not have to go through it at all.

From a child rights perspective, there is no excuse for the way J was treated. Under international and national law, J's 'best interests' (the international law's vocabulary) or 'safeguarding' and 'welfare' (the UK law's vocabulary) should have been the primary concern for the British authorities from the time they entered into contact with him. Clearly, these considerations did not dominate the way J was treated. The following questions arise: Is J an isolated case or is it common for an unaccompanied minor to have their age inflated by the authorities? What are the factors that fail to prevent and perhaps positively encourage incorrect age assessments? When age assessments are procedurally flawed or factually wrong, what are the chances of these mistakes being rectified?

In the absence of documentation such as a birth certificate, passport or school attendance record, it is *impossible* for scientists, doctors or any other expert to determine age from any body measurement, scan or X-ray with certainty, as will be explained below. Defenders of children and refugee rights believe this produces a context in which age is overestimated on a regular basis. Those at the opposite end of the spectrum fear that migrants are prone to tell stories that are not true, including about their age, in order to access benefits to which they are not entitled, or simply feel their country has no moral obligation to open its doors to refugees. Local authorities, which are the bodies tasked under UK law with age assessment, find themselves between a rock and a hard place.

This chapter has two aims. The first is to show that it seems incontrovertible that age is frequently overestimated. This is despite a legal framework that insists on giving the young person the benefit of the doubt as to their claimed age. The second aim is to open up a window on to how an age assessment is actually conducted and to identify various ways in which the process can fail to respect guidance and best practice. Five elements are identified. First, the age assessment interviews too often take place in forbidding venues (police stations or immigration detention centres). Second, youngsters may be inappropriately accompanied. Third, the interview is far from always prevented from turning into an adversarial process – for example, because of intimidating lines of questioning. Fourth, the proceedings are dominated by an absurd quest to prove that which cannot be proven. Fifth, the focus on this quest has the effect of discouraging the application of the supposedly central principle of the benefit of the doubt. This chapter reviews each of these factors in turn. First, however, it briefly presents the legal framework, some statistics and the concept of Merton compliance, and gives an account of an age assessment procedure as told by an 'accompanied adult'.

The UK legal framework: the centrality of the principle of the benefit of the doubt

In 1989, the United Nations adopted the Convention on the Rights of the Child (CRC). Described as 'the most complete statement of children's rights ever produced',[6] the CRC proved popular with states, and quickly achieved the distinction of being the most widely ratified international human rights treaty. The UK ratified it in 2001, but not without making a reservation that would allow the government to avoid bestowing foreign children all the rights provided in the 54 articles of the Convention.[7] Seven years later, under pressure from different quarters, the UK government retracted this reservation, thus theoretically putting on an equal footing the rights of national and foreign children. In national law, this translated in Section 55 of the Borders, Citizenship and Immigration Act 2009, which makes it a statutory duty for authorities, when carrying out immigration, asylum and nationality functions, to 'safeguard' and 'promote the welfare' of children who are in the United Kingdom. 'Every child matters', even if they are subject to immigration controls, proclaims the guidance issued in pursuance of Section 55.[8]

When a child arrives in the UK and claims asylum, if they do not have documents proving their age, an initial age assessment is conducted by a screening officer. At this stage, the young person can only be treated as an adult 'if their physical appearance/demeanour very strongly suggest that they are *significantly* over 18 years of age', with the policy issued by the government emphasising the word 'significantly'. Two officers, one of whom should be fairly highly graded, must reach this assessment independently from each other.[9] Official guidance is clear that everyone else should be afforded the benefit of the doubt and treated as a child until a careful assessment of their age has been completed. Even though the guidance uses the conditional tense, lawyers agree that this amounts to a legal obligation. The persons concerned, the guidance continues, should be referred to the local authority (i.e. the body to whom the law gives the responsibility of supporting any child who requires support, whether British or foreign). Local authorities should come and collect the unaccompanied child, with the most pressing duty usually being to arrange accommodation. The local authority is then responsible for making an assessment of their age, so as to be able to assess their needs. On completion of the age assessment, they communicate their finding to the relevant department of the Home Office, at which time a final decision about age is made.[10]

The reason why an unaccompanied asylum-seeking child is referred to the local authority is to ensure that this child's needs, including regarding support, accommodation and education, are met. Which provision should be granted in order to meet these needs in great part depends on the child's age. For example, a 14-year-old will be placed in foster care, whereas a 16-year-old will usually live semi-independently. Similarly, the type of education the local authority offers the unaccompanied child typically depends upon the age the child is assessed to be. From the local authority's perspective, the paramount reason for performing an age assessment should be to help to determine the child's needs.

Age assessment is obviously not necessary when the person's age is reliably known. Such certainty, however, depends on the existence of documentation that is accepted to be conclusive. In the absence of such documentation, the 'Guidance to assist social workers and their managers in undertaking age assessments in England', issued by the Association of Directors of Children's Services (ADCS) in October 2015, is clear that the young people must be given the benefit of the doubt as to their claimed age. To quote:

> Age assessments cannot be concluded with absolute certainty as there is not any current method that can determine age with 100% accuracy. The only exception to that is if there is definitive documentary evidence, such as a clear history of birth, school records, or other documentation which you [social workers] accept as valid and authentic. Where definitive evidence is not available, the benefit of the doubt should be granted to children and young people presenting as such.
>
> (ADCS 2015: 23)

This message is repeated throughout the 33 pages of the ADCS guidance, whose closing words read:

> In many cases it will not be possible to know definitively the age of the child or young person with whom you are working. Where there is doubt about whether or not the young person is a child, the dangers inherent in treating a child as an adult are in almost all cases far greater than the dangers of taking a young adult into your care.
>
> (Ibid.: 33)

The practice in numbers: what the available statistics suggest

It is difficult to ascertain exactly how far this guidance is respected or violated. However, in a report recently published by its European Union Committee, the House of Lords (2016) cited a variety of evidence to conclude that the guidance, which dates from 2015, is not uniformly followed. One need go no further than the government's own documentation to be convinced of this. The latest national statistics devoted to age disputes read:

> Some asylum applicants claim to be children but there may be doubts as to whether this is in fact the case. In the year ending June 2016, 1,060 asylum applicants had their age disputed and 933 were recorded as having an age assessment. Of those who completed age assessments in the year ending March 2016, 68% were assessed to be over 18, despite claiming to be a child when the age dispute was raised.[11]

The tone in which this statement is phrased is hardly one that seems to accept that giving the benefit of the doubt is important and the proper response whenever doubts arise and subsist.

National statistics have used the exact terms quoted in the above paragraph since 2013, allowing a table to be drawn. Before discussing Table 8.1, it is worth clarifying that an age-disputed case is defined as one where the person claims to be a child and their physical appearance/demeanour does not strongly suggest they are *significantly* over 18 (taken to mean 25 by some local authorities) and they have not been the subject of a Merton-compliant age assessment which has found them to be over 18. Age can be disputed by the Home Office or by a local authority. In reply to a freedom of information request (FoI), the Council of the London Borough of Croydon reported that their age-disputed cases were always initiated by the Home Office. This appears to be an exceptional situation, which must be linked to the fact that the asylum screening unit, where adult asylum seekers are accommodated prior to dispersal, is based in Croydon. The other contacted local authorities were generally those that were disputing the claimed age.[12]

Table 8.1 demonstrates that giving youngsters who claim to be under 18 the benefit of the doubt can hardly be described as a thoroughly general practice. From July 2015 to June 2016, although more than two-thirds of youngsters were believed by the authorities when they said they were under 18, almost one-third

Table 8.1 National statistics related to age disputes

Year	*UASC applications*	*Age-disputed cases*	*Proportion*	*Age assessed*	*Assessed to be over 18*	*Assessed to be under 18 (not necessarily claimed age)*
July 2015–June 2016	3,472	1,060	30%	933	68% [634]	32% [299]
2015	3,043	766	25%	700	68%	32%
2014	1,861	310	16%	449	54%	46%
2013	1,174	324	27%	404	65%	35%

Source: Statistics available at www.gov.uk/government/publications/immigration-statistics-april-to-june-2016/asylum#age-disputes.com, published 25 August 2016 and accessed 1 October 2016; the proportions appearing in the fourth and last columns are my own calculations.

had their age disputed. Of these, only one-third managed to convince the authorities they were actually under 18 (without necessarily having been found to be as young as the age they claimed to be). Ultimately, more than one in five youngsters[13] ended up neither being believed nor given the benefit of the doubt. This was a proportion broadly similar to 2013 but higher than in 2015 and especially 2014.

FoI replies indicate variations in local practice (as well as in recording data as they all replied in different ways, with many saying they did not hold some or most of the information requested). Table 8.2 presents the information provided by Croydon Council, the local authority with the second highest intake of unaccompanied minors in the country. With its steadily increasing proportion of disputed cases since 2013 and 2014, the Croydon figures can be said to be closely aligned with the national trend captured in Table 8.1. It should nonetheless be noted that the number of new UASC cases in Croydon over the last three years has intriguingly remained similar, despite the near doubling, from 2014 to 2015, of the number of unaccompanied young people nationally (as recorded in Table 8.1). Croydon did not provide information about the outcome of the disputed cases.

Table 8.2 UASC cases dealt with by Croydon Council

Year	*New UASC cases in Croydon*	*Age-disputed cases*	*Proportion of disputed cases*	*Proportion of accepted cases*
2015–2016	212	72	34%	66%
2014–2015	195	58	30%	70%
2013–2014	218	32	15%	85%

Source: FoI F/CRT/10006208 dated 10 August 2016; the proportions appearing in the fourth and fifth columns are my own calculations.

The situation in Kent, where the port of Dover is located and where the majority of refugees not travelling by air are arriving, is worth reviewing next, as the council with the highest number of UASC in the country. Kent County Council (KCC) provided age assessment figures for 2015 and the first six months of 2016, as outlined in Table 8.3. In 2015, KCC reported having accepted the age claimed in 217 cases. Over the same period, it completed an age assessment procedure in 246 cases. As was explained to me by an independent expert in the field, prior to 2015, KCC conducted age assessments in every UASC case. As the number of arrivals increased, this produced a significant backlog, which led KCC to employ two social workers specifically to deal with it. In the first six months of 2016, the number of age-accepted cases climbed to 305, while the number of performed age assessments declined to 120. KCC did not provide any further figures or explanations. Assuming it might make sense to add the figures provided (which it may not if the backlog continued in 2016), the proportion of age-assessed cases – between a quarter and a third – would be broadly in line with national trends as captured in Table 8.1. Still, subjecting more than a quarter of youngsters to an age assessment procedure hardly seems in keeping with the ADCS advice to give the benefit of the doubt.

For the purpose of this chapter, information was collected from nine local authorities.[14] Table 8.4 computes the information received from Cambridgeshire County Council (CCC). From July 2013 to July 2016, CCC accepted the age claimed by the youngsters in 18 cases. My FoI asked whether the local authority had performed age assessment due to youngsters not knowing their age. CCC is the only local authority to have responded positively to this question (24 cases in the last three years). Astoundingly, in view of the replies received from the other contacted local authorities, CCC had disputed age and performed an assessment in five times more cases than they had accepted (96 cases). The young person was determined to have been over 18 in a somewhat paltry 16 cases, suggesting that 104 cases found the youngster to be a minor – though not necessarily the age they claimed to be.[15]

The question arises as to why CCC performs so many assessments. The explanation seems to emerge from their reply to another question included in the FoI, about how the local authority finds 'appropriate adults'.[16] CCC's

Table 8.3 UASC cases dealt with by Kent County Council

Year	*Age-accepted cases*	*Age assessments performed*	*[Total]*
January–June 2016	305	120	[425]
2015	217	246	[463]

Source: FoI/16/1183 dated 19 August 2016; the totals indicated in the last column are my own calculations. The brackets indicate the possibility that there may have been additional age-disputed cases in the period considered.

Table 8.4 UASC cases dealt with by Cambridgeshire County Council

Period	*Cases where claimed age is accepted*	*Age assessments performed because youngsters say they do not know their age*	*Age assessments performed because claimed age is disputed by local authority*	*Total of age assessments performed*	*Age assessments concluding youngster is over 18*	*Age assessment concluding youngster is under 18*
July 2013–July 2016	18	24	96	120	16	104
July 2011–July 2013	0	0	20	20	10	10

Source: FoI 6837 dated 23 August 2016; under-18 determinations appearing in the last column are my own calculations.

reply indicates that their point of departure is not the benefit of the doubt. To quote:

> Appropriate adults are always used during full Merton compliant age assessments. Appropriate adults are not used during initial visual assessments due to time constraints. If at initial visual, there are concerns that the young person *could* be over 18 years of age, they are accommodated without prejudice until such time as a full Merton compliant age assessment can be undertaken. [my emphasis]

Assessing a youngster simply because they might be over their claimed age is a recipe for over-assessing. The practice is unfortunate in that it involves a resource-hungry process (two social workers, an appropriate adult and often an interpreter), which moreover rarely produces an unequivocal result, as the evidence it is able to gather tends by its nature to be inconclusive, as will be explained below. Needless to say, the process is also stressful for the youngster who would greatly benefit from having the benefit of the doubt directly applied to them.

Merton compliance

How are social workers supposed to determine the age of the person in front of them? Given the difficulty, indeed impossibility, of fulfilling this task with accuracy, it may come as no surprise that local authorities have not been prescribed any specific way in which they must carry out age assessments. Courts have nonetheless provided guidance as to the minimum standards that should be respected. The leading case in this respect was handed down by the High Court in 2003, in a case involving the London Borough of Merton,[17] hence the expression 'Merton-compliant' age assessments. Further judicial guidance followed, elaborating on these criteria.[18]

It is now accepted that an age assessment should be conducted – some case law adds 'if practicable' – by two social workers with appropriate training and experience for this task and in the presence of an 'appropriate adult'. The assessors should pay attention to the level of tiredness, trauma, bewilderment and anxiety of the child. Their assessment should be 'holistic', meaning it cannot be limited to physical appearance and behaviour. The assessors must take a history from the child, including regarding family composition and education. Ethnicity, culture and customs should be a key focus. The interpreter's skills in both the child's language and dialect and interpreting experience in the kind of situation created by the age assessment process should be checked before proceeding. The purpose of the process must be explained to the child. The interview should be conducted in a structured, fair, non-adversarial, non-stressful and informal manner. Before a conclusive finding is reached, the child must be given an opportunity to answer any potentially adverse findings, including regarding inconsistencies in answers that they have given.[19]

Some age assessments are so lacking in Merton compliance that they are plainly unlawful. This was the case of J's assessment recounted in the introduction of this chapter. The High Court judge found it to have been marred by such 'obvious deficiencies' that these made J's detention, which would not have taken place if he had not been found to be over 18, unlawful. The judgment identifies four major deficiencies: (1) the assessment had been carried out just by one social worker; (2) J had been given no opportunity to have an appropriate adult present during the process; (3) the social worker had not explained why she thought J was three and a half years older than he claimed to be; (4) her assessment seemed to have been based solely on his appearance.[20] The judge concluded: 'It is difficult not to agree with J's legal representative that this was, in many ways, a vivid illustration of how *not* to conduct an age assessment.'[21]

Other age assessments do not so plainly fail to comply with *Merton*, even though they fall short of exhibiting the features highlighted by the ADCS guidance of 2015. It is the purpose of the rest of this article to explain how this comes to pass.

Stefanie's account of an age assessment procedure

Before doing this, it may be useful to give a concrete example of how age assessments take place. This is particularly important since age assessments conducted by social workers leave very little public trace, the more so since data protection issues are involved. In order to form a better idea of the practice, I asked three people who had acted as appropriate adults to recount in specific detail an assessment in which they had participated. This section summarises the account 'Stefanie' (not her real name) gave of the assessment interview of 'Mustapha' (not his real name).[22]

Stefanie has been a regular visitor for detainees at an immigration centre in England. When the group through which she does this asked her whether she would be willing to undertake the role of appropriate adult in age-assessing proceedings, she accepted. By the time she was asked in early 2015 to participate in Mustapha's age assessment, she had received about five hours of training.

She arrived at the immigration centre at the prescribed time on the given morning. However, there was a long wait before the process properly began. During this time she chatted with the interpreter. By the time the interview started, perhaps one hour and a half beyond schedule, she could not help being a bit worried that Mustapha might not be in the best possible condition to undertake the process – was he hungry, for example?

Stefanie was given a chair to sit on, away from the desk where everybody else – namely the two social workers, Mustapha and the interpreter – was sitting. With the exception of Stefanie's chair, the seats were bolted to the floor. The room was entirely bare. It was located in the area reserved for legal matters, behind the immigration centre's visiting area with which Stefanie was familiar. She asked that Mustapha be told through the interpreter that she was there to support him, which was done. Despite his downcast eyes, she felt he understood this.

The social workers started to go through a set of pre-set questions designed to make him talk about his early life and schooling, his arrival in the UK, his background and home life. They did this professionally and in a friendly way. The interpreter proved excellent. Originally from Mustapha's country, he was able to ask appropriate questions and to relay answers that made sense – for example, of the schooling system in his country of origin – and which would otherwise have been confusing to English ears.

Mustapha explained how he had got involved in protesting and participated in demonstrations at home, how his family became increasingly concerned for his safety and decided he needed to be removed from the country. It was clear he came from a well-to-do family. They told him he must go to England and paid smugglers to organise and take him through his journey, which turned out to be difficult. As Mustapha was travelling, he often did not know where he was. However, when he heard he was in London, he recognised the name and decided to come out, having made the last leg of his journey hidden under the axle of a lorry.

He was taken to a café owned by a couple originating from his country. The police were called. As the social workers were now assessing his age, they were keen to probe what Mustapha had said then, and why. Following the conversation developing in the detention centre, Stefanie formed the impression that Mustapha had been poorly treated by the police. In her view, he must have been disorientated and given them confusing answers, not to mention that the conversation had been taking place through an interpreter who was on the phone rather than present. Now, however, four days later, Mustapha spoke confidently and his answers were straightforward.

The social workers moved the interview to questions about his family. There, in this emotional territory, Mustapha was getting really upset. Stefanie wondered whether to intervene. As she was about to do this, the social workers themselves interrupted the interview. They left the room with the interpreter. Stefanie saw Mustapha put his head down on the table in a manner that struck her as very childlike.

She could only communicate with him through body language. Although she had only just encountered him, she could not help feeling for him, looking so young, fragile and distressed in this bare room. She was also thinking of Mustapha's parents who had believed they were sending him to safety, instead of which, there he was, in hostile surroundings, interrogated and deprived of his liberty.

After a while, the social workers came back, in an atmosphere that had completely changed. They had talked over the phone with a relative of Mustapha's (through the interpreter). They were now persuaded to believe that what Mustapha had told them was true. They were accepting he was 16. Arrangements were being made to get him out of the immigration centre as soon as possible. Even though it was already early evening, he would not spend the night there.

Stefanie gave me this account from memory. She had understood from the training she had received that she was not allowed to take any notes during the proceedings. On the positive side, Stefanie had noted the professionalism of the social workers. Most importantly, the outcome was a good one for Mustapha in that his age was accepted. Nonetheless, the proceedings cannot be said to have been unproblematic. The next five sections of this chapter review ways in which actual age assessment proceedings can fall short of respecting official guidance.

Forbidding venues that are not strictly forbidden

Detention Services Order 14/2012, issued by the Home Office in 2012, states:

> An individual who is defined as an age dispute case will not remain in detention pending a Merton compliant age assessment. He/she will be released and the Merton compliant age assessment will be conducted in the community. He/she must be released into the care of the local authority because of the possibility that he/she is under 18 years of age.[23]

Order 14/2012 ends on a note that suggests that if the local authority does not provide suitable accommodation, it may be lawful for the age assessment to be conducted in the detention centre.[24] This, however, is surely meant as a last resort rather than a circumstance that can generally be relied upon.

The ADCS guidance stresses the importance of finding an appropriate venue for the age assessment interview – or interviews if more than one is necessary:

> The venue [. . .] needs to be conducive to helping the child or young person feel safe, comfortable and able to participate to the best of their ability in their interview(s). [. . .] Facilities such as police stations would not be considered appropriate for conducting age assessments, and every effort should be made to take a child or young person out of a police station in order to conduct a lawful assessment.
>
> (ADCS 2015: 18)

The ADCS guidance does not say anything about (not) holding the interview(s) in a detention centre. It nonetheless warns about the deleterious effects immigration detention has, especially on children (ibid.: 51).

Anecdotal evidence suggests that age assessment in police stations (as happened to J) or detention centres (as happened to Mustapha) is a fairly general practice. Such an intimidating environment should not be considered acceptable. It obviously goes unreprimanded in quite a large number of cases.

Inappropriate appropriate adults?

The legal concept of the appropriate adult was introduced in England and Wales in 1984 through the Police and Criminal Evidence Act. This was in order to ensure that a vulnerable person, including any juvenile, would not be alone when facing criminal proceedings. The law makes the presence of an appropriate adult mandatory in a number of circumstances, including police questioning of a vulnerable person. In the criminal justice context, the appropriate adult's role is not just to support but also to advise and assist the vulnerable person.

In the age assessment context, the role of the appropriate adult is more limited. Once the appropriate adult has ensured that the young person understands the purpose of the interview (age assessment) and their own role (supporting them), the appropriate adult is not supposed to intervene again as the social workers proceed with the interview. Exceptions to this rule are if the appropriate adult feels the social workers are acting improperly – for example, because their line of questioning is repetitive and harassing or unsuitable in helping to determine age – or it appears that the young person is tired or hungry and needs a break. However, if things are proceeding in a manner that is not inappropriate, the role of the appropriate adult is 'just' to offer emotional support, through being present (which may be why some actors have renamed the role 'accompanying adult'[25]). To this must be added that the appropriate adult can take notes of the questions asked and answers given. Some organisations that train appropriate adults advise this, so as to put the young person in a better position to mount a legal challenge, if necessary. Other organisations prefer for the appropriate adults not to be distracted from their support role by taking notes. It is to be regretted that the authorities to do not take verbatim notes of the interviews, let alone record them.

For the purpose of writing this chapter, I have interviewed three people who have acted as appropriate adults (each time in a detention centre). What struck me at the end of these interviews was how downcast my interlocutors seemed to be after having shared their experience with me.

Like Stefanie, 'Mat' was an immigration detainees' visitor. He accompanied 'Ashraf' in March 2014. Ashraf was facing removal on the basis of a previous age assessment, undertaken in another locality about 18 months before, which deemed him now to have turned 18. Recently put in detention with a view to removal, Ashraf was now contesting the age he had been determined to be. In order to do this, he had presented a document which acts as an identity card in his country of origin. The assessing social workers had to decide whether this new evidence could be accepted. Proceedings started in the morning. In contrast to Stefanie's report of Mustapha, Mat thought it took a while before Ashraf understood he was there to support him.

Mat described the social workers as nice people, who came across as compassionate, competent and professional. At the same time, he also said he wanted to intervene all the time to stop their questioning. Ashraf was asked for an hour about the exact circumstances in which he and his father had gone to a town to obtain the document. He could not recall exactly how that morning had unfolded. He nonetheless kept being asked about this, which made him increasingly frustrated and agitated. The social workers then started to ask him about his 14th birthday, which would have happened shortly after this. Again, he said he could not remember what his family had done that day. He explained birthdays were not important occasions in his country. The social workers said they could not believe he would not remember this event, which could not but have stood out. (As I write this, I do not remember how I celebrated my birthday last year, even though I know I did and I am sitting peacefully in my study.) Ashraf's answers, or lack of answers, to other questions put to him continued to increase the suspicion of the social workers. At one stage, he was led to explain that the document had been sitting in the deserted family house for a few years. The social workers said they could not believe that it would not have been stolen. Ashraf retorted that people in his country were not interested in identity documents and that his cousin had gone to fetch it when Ashraf had recently contacted him from England. This again was found unconvincing. Eventually, furious at not being believed, Ashraf slammed down pen and paper and stormed out of the room. This was a horrifying moment, Mat tells me. From then on, Ashraf's credibility had completely gone. At some point in the afternoon, the two social workers left the room to phone their colleagues who had age-assessed Ashraf upon his arrival in the UK. During this interval, Ashraf was full of agonised questions to Mat and the interpreter about what was going to happen to him. They had to explain to him that if he was not believed, he would be kept in detention and then removed. When the social workers returned, they said they saw no reason to change their colleagues' original assessment. Mat reflected to me: '[Ashraf] could have been 19, he could have been 17. There was no way of knowing.'

Mat expressed regret at not having received more training before he accompanied Ashraf and not having had the confidence to intervene. It is possible, however, that no other appropriate adult, however well trained, would have been able to persuade the social workers to change their final determination, even if they had been asked to modify their questioning and had done so. I doubt that, in this case, Mat did not appropriately fulfil the role the policy assigns to appropriate adults, the more so since he had complemented the basic training he had received with his own online research. It must nonetheless be a concern that so-called appropriate adults may be entirely inappropriate.

Anybody over 18 can fulfil the function. 'Claire' is a solicitor who specialises in immigration and asylum and who has trained social workers in age assessment proceedings. As I interviewed her, she explained that she has been asked to act as an appropriate adult for social services who could not find anybody else. She refuses to do this on principle, feeling this would prevent her from being in a position to legally represent the child in judicial review proceedings, were such proceedings considered later. Claire regrets that interpreters, accommodation staff and foster carers are asked to act as appropriate adults. In her view, they lack the required detachment from the situation.

The question arises as to where local authorities can turn to find appropriate adults available at short notice and ready to devote a whole day at a time to proceedings they are likely to find emotionally difficult. One response is that some non-governmental organisations make it one of their services to provide trained volunteers to act as appropriate adults in age assessment proceedings.[26] One council said in their FoI replies that they were 'spot purchasing' from a range of organisations.[27] The local authority with by far the highest number of unaccompanied children's arrivals in the country, Kent County Council, has formal contractual arrangements in place.[28]

Although these arrangements seem promising, it would be important to research the training and performance of those who act as appropriate adults. In the criminal justice context, it has been noted that some problems arise that need attention and solving (Pierpoint 2006, 2011; Hollingsworth 2014). This is bound to be so in the age assessment context too, where the circumstances of the 'unaccompanied' young person are particularly isolating and traumatic. Another concern is that contracts for specific organisations to provide appropriate adults are rumoured to encompass informal gagging clauses, to the effect that appropriate adults cannot talk about their experience to journalists or academic researchers. If this is the case, this is a worrying development, particularly since there exists no public record concerning the way age assessments are performed in practice.

In J's case, the High Court considered the absence of an appropriate adult a 'substantive failing', finding it 'axiomatic' that J, who was just 14 and a half, should have been offered such assistance.[29] This perspective must be approved. However, the three research interviews I have conducted suggest that acting as an appropriate adult in the asylum process is not an easy or straightforward process. Quotations included in the ADCS guidance also indicate that youngsters often do not understand what is going on, with one young person, for example, having observed that 'Refugee Council' was a new word for him and he had no idea that the person from this organisation was participating in the proceedings in order to support him (ADCS 2015: 20).

Most importantly, it must be borne in mind that the assistance offered by an appropriate adult will always be inappropriate if the very logic of the proceedings in which they are asked to participate is defective. Could any appropriate adult have pointed out to the social workers who were assessing Ashraf that it was unreasonable for them to expect Ashraf to recollect the details of the morning when he and his father went to obtain his identity document and what they did for his 14th birthday? Would it be their role to remind the social workers of their obligation to give him the benefit of the doubt? Perhaps some appropriate adults would have the necessary skills and diplomacy to be able to do this. However, fulfilling an advocacy role is not deemed a requirement for the role.

The purpose of the interview in the midst of a refugee culture of disbelief

Where memory is concerned, we make mistakes all the time. This is because memory constantly reconstructs the past rather than storing it intact in our brains. In turn, this is because the biological function of memory is to help us live in the present – not in the past. Psychologists have long been aware of this and warned against thinking that the purpose of memory is to deliver an objectively accurate record of past events (Hunter 1964). Most often, when we remember things wrongly, it does not matter. Either we are not aware of this as we are not corrected and just carry on with our lives, or there is external evidence available which puts the record straight.

Youngsters who are subjected to an age assessment procedure are being asked a multitude of questions about their family, their education, their journey, their life. They often produce an account which immediately appears chronologically impossible to the assessors. This is not helped by differences in language and cultural conceptualisation, which may confuse further the account received by the assessors. Resulting inconsistencies may create the impression that the person who is being age-assessed is fabricating their account rather than sticking to the truth. The impression of being told a lie can be further exacerbated by reluctance on the part of the youngster to talk about sensitive issues, not to mention memory gaps and slips due to the way the brain deals with trauma. The obstacles the youngster faces in delivering a convincing account and appearing credible can be overwhelming.

The excellent ADCS guidance recognises this difficulty. It states:

> While forming your decision, you should [. . .] talk to the child or young person in an inquisitorial, not adversarial, manner. You need to bear in mind developmental stages, the memory process, as well as the impact of trauma. Gaps, inconsistencies or lack of information do not always mean that a child or young person is not being truthful, and this should not be the starting point. Inquisitiveness about finding the right age is better for the child or young person than trying to catch someone in a 'lie'.
>
> (ADCS 2015: 25)[30]

Unfortunately, the very pitfalls the guidance seeks to avoid are described by those who work in the asylum field, including lawyers and civil society organisations, as common practice. As Mat told me, 'Everything in Ashraf's line of questioning was set up to try to trick him. All that he said was being weighted not towards assessing his age but towards seeing whether he could be tripped up.'

Almost inevitably, this attitude produces adversarial proceedings, whether this is the atmosphere the social workers wish to create or not. This was the experience of Stefanie, who saw a striking change of atmosphere once the social workers were convinced that Mustapha was telling the truth. It is also indirectly recognised by the ADCS guidance, which acknowledges:

> Children and young people have often said that even when they have been assessed to be a child, at their claimed age or at a different age, they found the process very difficult and upsetting and it had left them with feelings of distrust.
>
> (ADCS 2015: 30)

In theory, the aim of the procedure is to assess age. However, the reality does not always conform to this ideal (Cemlyn and Nye 2012). The feedback Claire receives from the social workers she trains is that they do not consider age assessment to be a necessary procedure, performed in order to help them assess a young person's needs for accommodation or education. Claire tells me she reminds them that 'they are not there to do the job of the Home Office'.

Claire concurs with other practitioners in the field to say that age assessment too often becomes wrapped up in asylum (see e.g. Crawley's testimony to the House of Lords for its 2016 report). In this context, there is nothing to stop the regrettable culture of disbelief that notoriously pervades asylum determination (Souter 2011; Jubany 2011) from spilling over to age assessment.[31] This may be all the more so since doing this is in local authorities' interests. The finding by a local authority that someone is an unaccompanied child has direct financial implications for that local authority. If the person is found to be a child, services will have to be provided. This will not arise if the person is found to be an adult as they will then be the responsibility of the Home Office. The younger the child, the greater the cost to the local authority; more services will have to be provided, with no adequate funding from central government.[32] There is therefore a financial incentive to find someone who claims to be 14 to be 16, or someone who claims to be 16 to be 17.[33]

Pressure to overestimate age can be pretty direct. A former social worker told Jo Wilding that managers would come in just before an age assessment interview was due to take place and say, 'Oh that kid's definitely over 17' (House of Lords 2016). Not giving the young person the benefit of the doubt regarding their age in the absence of compelling evidence that they are older is against guidance. This does not mean it does not happen.

Evidence-based exercise or pure guesswork?

Given that social workers are tasked with assessing age, what reliable tools are available to assist them in this task? The short answer is: hardly any.

Non-scientists are often under the impression that resort could be had to scientific methods, such as X-rays, for determining age. This is a mistaken view: age cannot be specifically determined by physical examination. The reason for this is simple: people do not physically develop at the same rate within one population, let alone across ethnic groups. A multitude of factors such as genetic inheritance, nutritional intake, environment, health and illnesses influence individual development. Neither skeletal X-rays of the hand and wrist, nor dental X-rays, nor bone development imaging, nor height or testicular volume for men, or measurement of any other part of the body, can specifically answer the question 'How old is this person?' Teenagers grow, acquire bone and tooth maturity, and develop sexually at hugely different rates. What can be known is the range of ages compatible with a given measurement – but not the age of a person who presents certain measurements. Within a given population, 5 per cent of normal boys aged 14 have heights above the average adult height. Some 15-year-olds have wisdom teeth showing, even though these generally appear later. Once it is determined that an individual is physically mature because four (for boys) or five (for girls) indicators are all satisfied, this still does not mean the individual is over 18; they might be as young as 15 (Aynsley-Green *et al.* 2012). Examples such as these could be multiplied to demonstrate that physical examinations, however precise, are not a dependable age indicator (Noll 2016; Crawley 2007: 28–36).

In the UK, Sir Al Aynsley-Green, former Children's Commissioner and President of the British Medical Association, has ceaselessly highlighted the danger of ascribing adult age to individuals on the basis of their developmental maturity. Medical professional bodies in the UK are in agreement that it is not possible to determine age with certainty on the basis of body measurements. In contrast to what is happening in many other countries (Sedmak *et al.* 2015), their vocal opposition has successfully thwarted government proposals in 2009 and 2012 to introduce X-rays for the age determination process. This opposition was based not only on medical and statistical grounds but also on ethical considerations. Medical ethics give prominence to the principles of respect for autonomy and beneficence. In this case, not only is it difficult to think the young person would be in a position to give informed consent to the procedure, but X-rays would be used purely for government's administrative convenience, without therapeutic benefit and indeed with potential harm such as an increased risk of brain tumour (Aynsley-Green *et al.* 2012).

For many years now, it has been accepted in the UK that it would be wrong to assess age solely on the basis of physical appearance.[34] The result is that social workers are told they must perform a 'holistic' assessment, which combines observations of physical appearance and social development with the taking of a family and educational history, and whatever else might be considered relevant. However, even such a holistic assessment is bound to remain a hit-and-miss process, since none of its constitutive elements, taken alone, can generally be considered fit to produce solid evidence. It is a serious fault of logic to expect that the sum of these unreliable elements could secure a dependable outcome.

In order to substantiate this statement, it is necessary to discuss in turn each of the elements regularly considered in a holistic assessment. The first is physical appearance. The wide margin of error inherent in this method of assessment has already been noted. Physical appearance is a factor that should not be relied upon, except in very stark cases: a man over 25 is not a child; an infant is not a teenager.

The question arises as to why physical appearance has not been left out of the conceptualisation of Merton compliance altogether. Presumably, this is because it appears unfeasible not to rely on it, even though we know it is unreliable.

When we wish to guess how old a person is, appearance is generally our first port of call. This works well in order to recognise that a young child is not a mature adult. The problem with the visual assessment method – to borrow the vocabulary used in Cambridgeshire – is that it is not helpful in reliably distinguishing a 14-year-old from a15-year-old from a 16-year-old from a 17-year-old and even from an adult (as J's case demonstrates). A feeling that the young person does not look the age they say they are is nonetheless what presumably triggers the age assessment process in the first place.[35] So, in the absence of data indicating age with certainty, how could visual assessments, on which we rely all the time even if we know from experience they are not reliable for precisely determining age, not be part of the age-assessing process? This, I think, must be why physical appearance is not ruled out, even though science tells us that logically it gives us no clue as to what we are seeking to determine.

Admittedly, UK law requires visual assessments to be integrated in a holistic assessment. To achieve this holism, social workers are advised, or possibly simply allowed, to take into consideration the demeanour of the young person – either during the assessing interview(s) or through observations conducted in the place where they are accommodated. This is another wild card, however. What conclusion regarding their exact age can be derived from someone who has just crossed the world alone and encountered scary situations appearing more mature than home teenagers – or, on the contrary, timid and withdrawn? I was told of an age assessment where the young person was assessed to be over 18 on the grounds that he was seen befriending people who were over 18. The logic of this reasoning is not unassailable – far from it.[36]

The young person's history will generally form a crucial element in the holistic assessment. This may work well when the young person is able to produce a consistent account, and particularly when it can be independently confirmed (as in Mustapha's case, when the social workers phoned a relative in his country of origin). It can be useless when the young person cannot answer specific questions put to them because they do not know or they are not believed when they provide an answer, as in Ashraf's case. Moreover, as noted in the previous section, expecting someone to deliver an accurately dated account of their past, based solely on their memory, and therefore becoming convinced that they are lying if their account contains inconsistencies, is highly problematic.

Admittedly, social workers are in a difficult position. They are not detectives and they do not have the resources to examine and resolve every possible discrepancy that arises in an interview. They are moreover expected to come to their conclusion reasonably fast. Even if their assessment can be extended over the course of a series of interviews, and even if they can include observations of the young person in daily life, their investigations cannot take months, let alone years. They simply are not in a position to retrace exactly how the life of the young person in front of them has chronologically unfolded. The result, however, is that, in the majority of cases, age assessment cannot be anything but guesswork.

When social workers come to the conclusion, which they genuinely hold, that a person is older than their claimed age, there is a risk they do so on the basis of a misplaced confidence in their own judgment. There is a legal requirement that their assessment must be justified. However, reasons given do not always stand up to scrutiny. Worst examples include: coming from a country where everybody is friendly but not displaying that same friendliness (sexual abuse notwithstanding); making intense eye contact (despite the applicant having specifically warned the assessors he had a squint which made it difficult for him to see); wearing a shiny Gucci watch (for young children apparently do not like shiny watches); having been observed selecting the most expensive brand of hair gel in a shop.

Age upgrading, or a shrinking place for the benefit of the doubt

Let us return to asking why Ashraf was not given the benefit of the doubt, for the question is important. The assessing social workers may have genuinely believed he could not be under 19, however much evidence to this effect appeared to Mat to be lacking. Perhaps they did not want to go against the opinion of the social workers who had performed the initial assessment 18 months before. They may also have internalised an unspoken but real political pressure not to believe and accept everyone who claims to be a refugee. Whatever the case, in view of ADCS guidance (which admittedly postdates Ashraf's assessment), it is troubling that Ashraf was found to be 19. To quote the guidance again:

> Everyone involved in this process would like children assessed to be children and adults assessed to be adults. However, there will be times when, even after assessment, you have some doubt about the age of the person you are assessing; you cannot be expected to know the age of everyone you assess. In these circumstances you are advised to give the benefit of the doubt, and this is partly because of the different implications for children and adults in getting the decision wrong. Children in the UK are afforded extra levels of protection compared to adults both in terms of how they are cared for and in terms of how they are treated in the immigration system, and it is vitally important that children are able to access this protection.
>
> (ADCS 2015: 32)

From July 2015 to June 2016, 634 young people claiming to be children were assessed to be over 18, as shown in Table 8.1. How does one reconcile this number with the guidance which makes giving the benefit of the doubt a central, if not *the* central, principle of age assessment in the UK? This is not necessarily difficult, for the guidance does not say 'you must give the benefit of the doubt'. Instead, it advocates less categorically, 'you are advised to give the benefit of the doubt'. This phrasing leaves the door open for an age determination which rests on weak evidence to be lawful. In other words, the governing framework suffers from double speak.

Table 8.1 indicates that the proportion of young people who are being age-assessed has been increasing over the years, from one-sixth in 2014, to a quarter in 2015, to almost one-third in 2016.[37] The number of young people who are assessed to be under 18, but determined to be one or two years older than they claim, is not known. However, experts comment that this is a common situation. Age upgrading, if we can call the phenomenon so, blatantly disregards the principle of the benefit of the doubt which is supposed to be central to the legal framework. How can the assessing social workers be sure of their conclusion that, for example, the teenager in front of them is really 17 rather than 16 as they claim?

One should not need to repeat that any additional year wrongly attributed to a young person will have enormous consequences for the care they will – or rather will not – receive. Needless to say, it will also serve to slightly relieve pressure on local authorities. This is especially so for those whose geographical position puts them on the frontline of the responsibility to support unaccompanied minors.

Let us imagine for a moment that one could magically find the real age of all the young people who are age-assessed just after their assessment has concluded. Let us further imagine that the social workers were systematically sanctioned every time they had got it wrong by overestimating age. By contrast, they would attract absolutely no opprobrium, however slight, if they simply gave the benefit of the doubt, as they are supposed to. In such a scenario, it is not difficult to believe that the statistics presented above would look rather different. The high number of age assessments performed and young people found to be over 18, not to mention those found to be under 18 but over their claimed age, might be expected to drop drastically.

How supposedly 'Merton-compliant' age assessments that are actually not Merton-compliant are allowed to stand

A number of guarantees are in place in order to ensure the fairness of the age determination process. In a context where a determination detrimental to the young person made on the basis of guesswork is not ruled out, these guarantees nonetheless lose much of their effectiveness. For example, the two social workers must be trained and experienced. However, long service as a social worker in the children's services or asylum unit of a local authority is in itself no guarantee that the philosophy of the ADCS guidance is understood and will be applied. Some staff may even have learnt over their professional career that determining a young person to be one or two years over their claimed age, because this makes sense to them even though their feeling is not backed by robust evidence, is what is expected of them.

Similarly, the case law is very clear that a Merton-compliant assessment must give the young person the opportunity to elucidate discrepancies and contest negative findings which the assessors are contemplating. This is important, and no doubt this proviso can be instrumental in dissipating misunderstandings and convincing assessors of the truthfulness of the young person's claim.[38] However, there will also be many cases where assessors will have formed the impression that the person in front of them is not credible (which the very fact that they are being age-assessed may be taken to suggest), making it virtually impossible to dislodge this view.[39] In J's case, even the appearance of his older brother did not convince the authorities to proceed swiftly to accept his age.

Although five years old, the case of J remains instructive. Particularly significant for the argument developed in this chapter is that J's age assessment was described and treated as Merton-compliant throughout all the stages of the asylum and judicial proceedings, up to the moment when the High Court judge agreed with J's legal representatives that the assessment had been an excellent illustration of how *not* to assess age. J's asylum refusal letter noted that a Merton-compliant age assessment had been completed by Wiltshire Social Services. In the proceedings for damages for unlawful detention, the High Court judge noted that after the Wiltshire age assessment was described as Merton-compliant in the asylum refusal letter, this assertion had been 'picked up and repeated, mantra-like, in all of the later documents'.[40] In other words, although the deficiencies may well have been 'obvious',[41] they nonetheless went unnoticed until the proceedings before the High Court. Had it not been for the rather unlikely event of J's reunion with his older brother, the Wiltshire age assessment would have continued to be treated as Merton-compliant and reliable rather than fundamentally flawed.

Any asylum lawyer will tell you that few age assessments are successfully contested in the UK. Figures are not readily available for the number of judicial review proceedings concerning age assessment (see, however, Thomas 2015), but it is clear they are few and far between, as borne out by one of the responses of Kent County Council to my FoI. It stated that in the two years since August 2014, KCC had had 26 judicial review proceedings issued against it concerning age assessment. Of these, only three were due to go through the full judicial process; the 23 others had either been refused permission to proceed or had been withdrawn, settled or struck out.[42] To recall, in the 18 months between January 2015 and June 2016, KCC performed 366 age assessments.

The statistics of three judicial review proceedings (which may or may not ultimately find the KCC's assessment in need of revision) is the most startling since KCC is not only the local authority which age-assesses the most, but also the local authority which takes care of the largest number of unaccompanied minors in the country. In 2015, it started to run out of foster families and school places. Understandably, it called for a system that would see the responsibility for unaccompanied minors in the UK shared between local councils (Wilding, forthcoming). If there is one authority that one might expect to be inclined to sometimes overestimate age, this must be it. In this county, the paltry number of three judicial reviews confirms, if need be, that the gap that so easily emerges between theory and practice, as highlighted in this chapter, is rarely identified, denounced and corrected in judicial proceedings. A number of factors contribute to explain this absence of reaction.

First, a legal representative contracted to do public law would need to take up the case. That the young person could find such a lawyer is not certain. Legal aid cuts have had the effect of reducing the number of lawyers willing to provide judicial review services in general, including on age assessment. In some parts of the UK, what has been termed 'advice deserts' have emerged: there is not one legal aid lawyer available to challenge some issues. Due to the most recent changes to funding for judicial review, lawyers must now put in many hours of work before having it confirmed they will be paid for this work, as no payment will ensue if permission to proceed to full court proceedings is not ultimately granted. Unsurprisingly, given this context, it is anecdotally reported that lawyers have become more reluctant to start judicial review claims.

Second, even if the young person has access to a lawyer willing to pursue the case, the case is no longer proceeding from a blank slate once an age assessment that is described as Merton-compliant has been performed. There needs to be either new evidence submitted that demonstrates that the initial age assessment was unlawfully conducted (which is difficult to prove in the absence of a verbatim record of interviews and given the interpretative leeway the assessing social workers enjoy in practice) or new evidence proving that the first determination is factually wrong.

Third, even if evidence to this effect exists, the young person's legal representative still needs to weigh the pros and cons of starting judicial proceedings. Lawyers may make the judgment call that it would be uncaring for them to pursue the case of their client, even if they think they would be in a strong position to win it. This is because the proceedings may prove psychologically damaging for the young person and bring them only a relatively small gain. As Claire told me, if High Court proceedings go all the way, the youngster will have to face hostile cross-examination by a barrister acting for the local authority or the Home Office. Even if the judge eventually determines that the young person is the age they claim to be, months will have passed by the time this happens. There is also the problem that during the protracted age dispute, the young person may find themselves in additional turmoil, without any service provider and local authority clearly taking responsibility for them (Crawley 2007: 127).

Fourth, if a lawyer decides the case is worth pursuing and takes the first step towards this by sending a letter before action, the authorities may decide to withdraw the initial age assessment and effect another one. In this case, the young person may benefit. However, there is no guarantee that the local authority will be persuaded to draw general lessons and transform its practice – or even change the eventual conclusion in that case.

Fifth, and perhaps most disappointingly, if the proceedings go through, the young person may face a judge who displays a baffling disregard for the law and its underlying premises and logic. This is no better exemplified than by a recent judgment of the Court of Appeal, which sided with the London Borough of Croydon in insisting that dental examination form part of a new age assessment to be conducted in view of the legal challenge to a previously performed age assessment, which had been based exclusively on physical appearance.[43] More generally, there is a conspicuous tendency in the case law for the judiciary to discount the potential value of a paediatrician's report submitted to support a challenge to age assessment (a position that appears logical to me), but then proceed to elevate the social workers' assessment as a reliable piece of documentation because there is no evidence proving it is not (which makes no sense).[44]

This discussion would be worth taking further, but this cannot be done in the context of this chapter. For our present purposes, the point is that the legal system allows age assessments which should never be conceptualised as Merton-compliant to stand.

Recommendations and conclusion

The aim of this chapter was not so much to think about the opportunities (or lack of) for challenging age assessments that are not Merton-compliant as to reflect upon what makes an age assessment Merton-compliant in the first place, thereby averting the need for legal challenge. In this respect, official guidance insists on the centrality of the principle of the benefit of the doubt, recognising that the damage done to a child who is not believed, and as a result is treated as an adult or substantially older than they are, is too great to be acceptable. Indeed, the only position from a human rights and child rights perspective is to recognise the obligation to treat the youngster as a person of the age they claim to be – in the absence of incontrovertible evidence showing they are a different age. From this, the following recommendations emerge:

1 Performing age assessment procedures should be avoided altogether. The default reaction of the authorities should be to accept the age a young person says they are (except if there are compelling reasons not to believe them).
2 Assessing social workers should constantly bear in mind that the procedure is there to determine needs. Age assessment interviews should be conducted in congenial venues and in a child-friendly manner. Ideally, regional age assessment centres should be created, which would be funded independently of the local authorities that take responsibility for children.
3 There should be further thinking about the role that the appropriate adult should fulfil and guidelines produced and followed as to how they should be recruited and trained.

This chapter has made use of the available national statistics and information collected directly from local authorities in reply to FoIs in order to show that many unaccompanied minors in the UK are not believed to be the age they say they are, with disastrous consequences for them. However, we should not forget that these statistics also demonstrate that the majority of young people, currently two-thirds, are believed outright or given the benefit of the doubt. There has never been any suggestion of age-assessing them. This, for example, happened to 'Hussein', interviewed by Jo Wilding in the course of the MinAs research conducted for writing the UK report. When Jo asked Hussein about the reaction of the authorities when he told them he was 13, his response was: 'It was my age so they had to accept it.' It had never even occurred to him that he could have been doubted. This is how things should be.

However, despite the benefit of the doubt being given theoretical prominence, it is far from always applied in practice. In a context where a limited number of local authorities must care for the majority of young refugees, this is not surprising; it is crucial that an effective and positive responsibility-sharing scheme be put in place (Wilding, forthcoming). However, it is important also to recognise that the development of a gap between theory and practice is also encouraged by particular practices – for example, interviewing the young person in a forbidding place such as an immigration detention centre; not taking the time to introduce them to the appropriate adult who is there to support them and ensuring the appropriate adult is trained and encouraged to play an effective role; not bothering to record the interviews, thus making it impossible to check the exact sequence of questions and answers; failing to insist that the benefit of the doubt must stand in the absence of incontrovertible evidence proving the young person is older than they say they are; failing to sanction social workers and local authorities who do not abide by this rule.[45]

Ultimately, the real reason why the benefit of the doubt is not always given the upper hand is that a fundamental contradiction mars law and policy in the UK as elsewhere (Hastie and Crépeau 2014; Goodwin-Gill 2012). On the one hand stands the legal principle that children must be protected, which is difficult for anyone to oppose directly. On the other hand, the British government has made very clear its policy goal of keeping the number of refugees down. The result is an age determination procedure which looks excellent on paper but does not consistently live up to its ideals in practice. It is incumbent on all of us to try to get this practice improved.

Notes

1 My thanks go to Jo Wilding for sharing her knowledge and insights, the experts and young people Jo interviewed in 2015 as part of the MinAs research project, as well as two lawyers and three appropriate adults I interviewed in June–July 2016. People directly involved in age assessment proceedings kindly commented on a draft of this chapter in September and October 2016. They prefer to remain anonymous.

2 Lack of birth registration affects one in three children worldwide. This situation is especially prevalent in South Asia and Sub-Saharan Africa (UNICEF 2013).

3 Under the Convention on the Rights of the Child, a child is any person under 18; this is how this chapter will use this word, even though this usage is not unproblematic.

4 *J, R (on the application of) v Secretary of State for the Home Department* [2011] EWHC 3073 (Admin) (24 November 2011), referred to simply as J below.

5 This is now the First-Tier Tribunal (Immigration Asylum Chamber).

6 UNICEF, How we Protect Children's Rights with the UN Convention on the Rights of the Child, available online at www.unicef.org.uk/UNICEFs-Work/UN-Convention (accessed 21 February 2017).

7 As had long been predicted. See Newell 1991, who also records the practice of age assessment of unaccompanied minors at the time.

8 'Every child matters' policy presented to Parliament in September 2003, bearing reference Cm 5860.

9 This had not happened in the age assessment at the heart of *AA v Secretary of State for the Home Department and Wolverhampton City Council* [2016] EWHC 1453 (Admin), judgment of 20 June 2016. AA's detention as an adult was therefore found unlawful.
10 For more details, see ADCS 2015.
11 National statistics concerning asylum, available at www.gov.uk/government/publications/immigration-statistics-april-to-june-2016/asylum#age-disputes (accessed 21 February 2017).
12 The exception was Hillingdon, where Heathrow Airport is based. There the local authority had disputed age in five cases and the Home Office in seven cases in the last 12 months. For the same period, the age claimed was accepted in 33 cases. FoI reply dated 16 September 2016. All the FoIs mentioned in this section were sent by me.
13 634 out of 3,472, to which must be added an unknown number of youngsters accepted to be under 18 but not their claimed age.
14 There seemed little point in doing this in relation to the authorities which Jo Wilding's previous research had indicated had few or no UASC in their care (respectively, 109 authorities and 30 authorities). Wilding had moreover warned me that the information I would obtain from different councils was unlikely to be directly comparable, each council having their own way of recording UASC-related data. I decided to direct my FoIs to the local authorities with the largest UASC intakes, namely, Kent, Croydon, Hillingdon, Surrey, Essex and Northamptonshire. I was also interested in getting information from the two local authorities that had been involved in the case of J with which I opened this chapter, namely Wiltshire in England and Cardiff in Wales. I finally contacted Cambridgeshire as they had intriguingly referred to visual assessments in reply to Wilding's earlier FoI. Neither Wilding nor I had come across this phrasing.
15 In the previous two years, CCC had had fewer dealings with UASC, but these indicated an even lower rate of acceptance. The figures for July 2011 to July 2013 are as follows: no cases of age readily accepted, 20 disputed cases, ten over-18 assessments. The 18–25 Service had performed the assessments in the 2011–2013 period. Thereafter they were being done by FREDt.
16 The notion of the 'appropriate adult' is borrowed from criminal law. It is used in contexts where it is recognised that a vulnerable person should not face certain difficult proceedings alone but must be accompanied by an 'appropriate adult'.
17 *B v London Borough of Merton* [2003] EWHC 1689 (Admin), judgment of 14 July 2003.
18 See e.g. *FZ v Croydon*; *R (AS) v London Borough of Croydon* [2011] EWHC 2091 (Admin).
19 The above paragraph is adapted from: *IG v London Borough of Croydon* [2015] EWHC 649 (Admin), judgment of 13 March 2015, para 7.
20 J, paras 13–16.
21 J, para 18, emphasis in the original.
22 Whenever I put a name in inverted commas below, this indicates that I have changed the name of my interlocutor. I do this only at first usage, so as not to overburden the text.
23 The order's original implementation date was 28 September 2012. It was last reviewed in March 2015, with a so-called 'rebranded' outcome, and its next review is due in March 2017.
24 'In the event that the local authority placement is delayed by the local authority, the removal centre will make immediate arrangements to safeguard the individual within the centre whilst awaiting the local authority response.'
25 FoI reply of Kent County Council. See also Young Lives Foundation, Volunteering with the Young Lives Foundation, available at http://ylf.org.uk/wordpress/

wp-content/uploads/Volunteer-AccAdult-Info-Pack.pdf (accessed 17 February 2017).

26 CORAM is an example. See www.coramvoice.org.uk/professional-zone/appropriate-adults-age-assessments (accessed 17 February 2017).

27 FoI reply FR6639 by Northamptonshire County Council dated 12 August 2016. Northamptonshire spot purchases from a range of organisations including the National Youth Advocacy Service, Leicester Inter Faith Forum and Northamptonshire Children's Rights Service.

28 Whilst KCC used to rely on Barnardos and the Refugee Council, it has now commissioned the Young Lives Foundation to provide an accompanying adult service for all UASC who require an age assessment. My FoI request to see the contract was refused on the grounds that disclosure would be an advantage to competitors. It would certainly be worthwhile to study the history of these public authority–voluntary sector relationships.

29 J, para 14.

30 The guidance continues: 'Consider also that many children and young people have been told by their families, smugglers or traffickers to tell particular stories about their life in order to protect others, which are not necessarily reliable indicators of their age. Children and young people being age assessed will also often not know yet who to trust, so may not reveal their entire situation at the assessment stage. Note that this is not dissimilar to other young people who are coming into care and may not be clear who to trust.'

31 It is worth adding that in fact, as Farbey (2014) notes, the benefit of the doubt should also be central to asylum determination.

32 For exact figures, see Wilding and Dembour (2015).

33 Due to the resulting conflict of interests, a key recommendation of Heaven Crawley's comprehensive study on the process of age assessment in the UK (2007) was the establishment of regional age assessment, funded independently of the local authorities taking responsibility for children. Unfortunately, this central recommendation has not been acted upon.

34 This is only acceptable if the individual is *significantly* over 18 and there is absolutely no doubt they are an adult. For this to be the case, they would have to have wrinkles, a lawyer jokingly told me. More seriously, in Kent, this has been taken to mean that the person must distinctly look to be over 25.

35 I have heard it said that in one place age assessments sometimes appeared to be used as punishment for perceived bad behaviour on the part of the youngster. This allegation was strongly disputed by the local authority which was implicated. It is nonetheless concerning that this was reported by more than one person, independently of each other.

36 I was also told by another person of a case in which two young children (eventually determined to be 10 and 11) had actually said they were 16 in order to avoid separation from the teenagers whom they had befriended. Yet again showing the limits of the records kept by local authorities or their willingness to be open on the subject of age assessment, my FoI question asking whether the local authority had come across cases of age assessment due to the claimed age appearing too high attracted no positive response.

37 In 2013, the proportion was over a quarter, making it possible that 2014 represented a dip. In the absence of figures prior to 2013, it is impossible to tell whether it is 2013 or 2014 that appears out of line.

38 As a result, best practice is now understood to consist of at least two interviews, one for the assessing social workers to come to (preliminary) conclusions, and another for the young person to explain why these conclusions are mistaken.

39 One person who had participated in many age assessments as an appropriate adult told me that they had been 'surprised and pleased' when social workers had

changed their mind at the second interview, after having put their findings to the young person who then challenged them. I asked how often this would happen. Pushed to give me a number, the appropriate adult eventually responded: 'Perhaps one in twenty.' On the lack of standards to assess credibility in the asylum determination field, see Byrne 2007. On the negative impact of a finding of non-credibility regarding the age claimed on the asylum determination procedure, see Warren and York 2014.

40 J, para 30.

41 Idem.

42 To give another statistic, Northampton replied to my FoI that they had received 12 letters before action in respect of applications seeking to judicially review age assessment in the last year. Of these, nine cases were withdrawn and three had yet to be resolved.

43 *London Borough of Croydon v Y* [2016] EWCA Civ 398 [2016] WLR(D) 211.

44 *A v London Borough of Croydon & SSHD; WK v SSHD & Kent County Council* [2009] EWHC 939; *R v London Borough of Croydon* [2011] EWHC 1473, cited approvingly in section 6.5 of the Home Office Guidance about 'Assessing age', updated in June 2015.

45 A more comprehensive research project would need to look at further elements, including the role played by interpreters.

Bibliography

ADCS (2015) 'Age assessment guidance: Guidance to assist social workers and their managers in undertaking age assessment in England'. Available online at http://adcs.org.uk/assets/documentation/Age_Assessment_Guidance_2015_Final.pdf (accessed 7 March 2017).

Aynsley-Green, A., Cole, T. J., Crawley, H., Lessof, N., Boag, L.R. and Wallace, R. M. M. (2012) 'Medical, statistical, ethical and human rights considerations in the assessment of age in children and young people subject to immigration control', *British Medical Bulletin* Vol. 102, 17–42.

Byrne, R. (2007) 'Assessing testimonial evidence in asylum proceedings: Guiding standards from the International Criminal Tribunals', *International Journal of Refugee Law*, Vol. 19, No. 4, 609–638.

Cemlyn, S. J. and Nye, M. (2012) 'Asylum seeker young people: Social work value conflicts in negotiating age assessment in the UK', *International Social Work*, Vol. 55, 675–688.

Crawley, H. (2007) 'When is a child not a child? Asylum, age disputes and the process of age assessment', ILPA research report. Available online at www.ilpa.org.uk/data/resources/13266/ILPA-Age-Dispute-Report.pdf (accessed 7 March 2017).

Farbey, J., Q.C. (2014) 'A legal analysis of child-sensitive asylum procedures', *Journal of Immigration, Asylum and Nationality Law*, Vol. 28, No. 3, 254–264.

Goodwin-Gill, G. (2012) 'Expert roundtable discussion on "The United Nations Convention on the Rights of the Child and its application to child refugee status determination and asylum processes" – Introduction', *Journal of Immigration, Asylum and Nationality Law*, Vol. 26, No. 3, 226–231.

Hastie, B. and Crépeau, F. (2014) 'Criminalising irregular migration: The failure of the deterrence model and the need for a human rights-based framework', *Journal of Immigration, Asylum and Nationality Law*, Vol. 28, No. 3, 213–236.

Hollingsworth, K. (2014) 'Bright lines and best interests: Children, age and rights in police detention: *R (HC) v. Secretary of State for the Home Department*', *Child and Family Law Quarterly*, Vol, 26, No. 1, 78–98.

House of Lords (2016) 'Children in Crisis: Unaccompanied Migrant Children in the EU' (European Union Select Committee report). Available online at www.publications.parliament.uk/pa/ld201617/ldselect/ldeucom/34/34.pdf (accessed 7 March 2017).

Hunter, I. M. (1964) *Memory: Facts and Fallacies*, Harmondsworth: Pelican Books.

Jubany, O. (2011) 'Constructing truths in a culture of disbelief: Understanding asylum screening from within', *International Sociology*, Vol. 26, No. 1, 74–94.

Nethery, A. and Silverman, S. J. (eds) (2015) *Immigration Detention: The Migration of a Policy and its Human Impact*, London: Routledge.

Newell, P. (1991) *The UN Convention and Children's Rights in the UK*, London: National Children's Bureau.

Noll, G. (2016) 'Junk science? Four arguments against the radiological age assessment of unaccompanied minors seeking asylum', *International Journal of Refugee Law*, Vol. 29, No. 2, 234–250.

Pierpoint, H. (2006) 'Reconstructing the role of the appropriate adult in England and Wales', *Criminology and Criminal Justice*, Vol. 6, No. 2, 219–237.

Pierpoint, H. (2011) 'Extending and professionalising the role of the appropriate adult', *Journal of Social Welfare and Family Law*, Vol. 33, No. 2, 139–155.

Robjant, K., Hassan, R. and Katona, C. (2009) 'Mental health implications of detaining asylum seekers: Systematic review', *British Journal of Psychiatry*, Vol. 194, 306–312.

Sedmak, M., Lenarcic, B., Medaric, Z. and Zakelj, T. (2015) *A Journey to the Unknown. The Rights of Unaccompanied Migrant Children: Between Theory and Practice*, Koper: Univerzitetna založba Annales.

Smith, A. (2016) 'The Detainee's Tale', in D. Herd and A. Pincus (eds) *Refugee Tales*, Manchester: Comma Press, 49–62.

Souter, J. (2011) 'A culture of disbelief or denial? Critiquing refugee status determination in the United Kingdom', *Oxford Monitor of Forced Migration*, Vol. 1, 48–59.

Stevens, D. (2013) 'Asylum Seekers, Detention and the Law: Morality in Abeyance?', in S. S. Juss (ed.) *The Ashgate Research Companion to Migration Law, Theory and Policy*, Farnham: Ashgate.

Thomas, Robert (2015) 'Mapping immigration judicial review litigation: An empirical legal analysis', *Public Law*, Vol. 4, 652–678.

Warren, R. and York, S. (2014) 'How children become failed asylum seekers', *Journal of Immigration, Asylum and Nationality Law*, Vol. 28, No. 2, 123–145.

Wilding, J. (forthcoming) 'Unaccompanied children seeking asylum in the UK: From centres of concentration to a better holding environment', *International Journal of Refugee Law.*

Wilding, J. and Dembour, M.-B. (2015) 'Whose Best Interests? Exploring Unaccompanied Minors' Rights through the Lens of Migration and Asylum Processes (MinAs). The UK National Report'. Available online at www.brighton.ac.uk/_pdf/research/crome/14-oct-15-final-minas-full-report.pdf (accessed 7 March 2017).

UNICEF (2013) 'Every Child's Birth Right: Inequities and Trends in Birth Registration'. Available online at www.un.org/ruleoflaw/files/Embargoed_11_Dec_Birth_Registration_report_low_res.pdf (accessed 7 March 2017).

Index

For Product Safety Concerns and Information please contact our EU representative GPSR@taylorandfrancis.com
Taylor & Francis Verlag GmbH, Kaufingerstraße 24, 80331 München, Germany

www.ingramcontent.com/pod-product-compliance
Ingram Content Group UK Ltd.
Pitfield, Milton Keynes, MK11 3LW, UK
UKHW011013180926
475701UK00004B/727
9780367267001